BURIED TREASURE

BURIED TREASURE

Secrets for Living from the Lord's Language

2ND EDITION

_____

Rabbi Daniel and Susan Lapin

Lifecodex Publishing Company

Published by Lifecodex Publishing, LLC.,
Mercer Island, Washington.

Library of Congress Control Number: 2012905661

ISBN: 978-0-9822018-0-0

Printed in the United States of America

A MESSAGE FROM PASTOR JOHN HAGEE

Several years ago by the providence of God, it was my pleasure and eternal blessing to meet one of the most brilliant and scholarly expositors of the Bible; Rabbi Daniel Lapin.

As I interviewed Rabbi Lapin on our national and global television network I was amazed by the treasures of truth that tumbled effortlessly out of his mouth without limit.

Rabbi Lapin presents the hidden mysteries of the Hebrew language with a vibrant, electrifying force that reveals the unknown and brings a confidence that the Bible is indeed God's blueprint to life's greatest adventure.

In "Buried Treasure" you will find hope for a better world, and a life richly blessed by the favor of God!

Let the adventure begin!

Pastor John C. Hagee
Cornerstone Church
San Antonio, Texas

Discover why everyone needs a rabbi!

CONTENTS

FOREWARD

A t age 12, as part of the preparation for my Bar Mitzvah, I committed myself to an eccentric, silly and controversial plan. Despite the disapproval of my Rabbi and my Hebrew school principal, I insisted on reading through the Bible on my own—all the Hebrew scriptures—in the all-but-impenetrable King James translation.

My teachers warned me that I'd get little from it and might be distracted from the important work of memorization and rehearsal related to the upcoming ceremony, but I stubbornly slogged forward. I read big clumps of indigestible verbiage, proudly reporting on my progress and understanding almost nothing. Meanwhile, I also attended to my main responsibilities as a Bar Mitzvah boy—using a tape recording to master a succession of Hebrew words in their traditional cantilation so I could publicly chant my assigned portions from the book of Genesis and Isaiah.

The amazing thing about this experience is that no one helped me draw the obvious connection between the minimal Hebrew reading and reciting skills my teachers emphasized, and the lengthy reading of biblical translation I was determined to complete. Because I never connected these two endeavors, I remained confused and befuddled in two

different languages—Hebrew and English. If only I had met
Rabbi Daniel Lapin twenty years before I did!

The great gift that Rabbi Lapin bestows on all his students
is a vibrant, even electrifying sense of the Hebrew language
as a key to understanding God's blueprint for the world. Until I began studying with Daniel in 1978, I remained appall-
ingly ignorant about the "buried treasure" contained within
the ancient tongue that the Almighty chose as his vehicle
for first communicating with his children. Without some
sense of this deeper significance of Hebrew, the study of
the language can seem deadly boring—as generations of Bar
Mitzvah boys can attest. And without some knowledge of the
linguistic clues, uniquely Hebraic and essential to a deeper
understanding of the biblical text, long passages of Scripture
can seem dry and confusing.

As you pick up this book and dig for buried treasure with
Rabbi Lapin, you will get some taste of the excitement and
insight that makes him one of the pre-eminent Jewish teachers of our generation. A mutual friend introduced us, believ-
ing we'd both benefit from the connection but not realizing
that he was launching more than a quarter century of warm
friendship and close collaboration. I was a 29-year-old writer
who had enjoyed my first best-seller and also a Jewish
activist and seeker. The Rabbi, passing through Southern
California, was teaching physics part-time; trying to escape
the family business (his father and two brothers were all distinguished rabbis); hoping to avoid his parents' determination to see him safely married off; and thinking about taking
his cherished sail boat on a round-the-world cruise. Instead,
Daniel Lapin began teaching classes in living rooms in my

old beachside neighborhood of Venice/Santa Monica, and within a few years he had drawn some 400 students—with study sessions so crowded that eager applicants often had to be turned away.

These classes gave rise to Pacific Jewish Center, the congregation that Rabbi Lapin led for fifteen years. It was a unique institution with a single membership requirement more demanding than financial dues: In order to join, you had to commit yourself to a regular study program. The essence of that study never featured Hebrew as an ordinary language, with tedious emphasis on mastering vocabulary, grammar, or conversational sentences like "Do you know the way to the bus station in Tel Aviv?" Instead, Rabbi Lapin always used Hebrew as a unique, precious window into the mind of God and as a necessary pathway into the mountainous accumulation of more than 3000 years of Jewish wisdom and tradition. That tradition emphasizes the joys of family, of course, along with the importance of intellectual and spiritual fulfillment.

In his classes the Rabbi acquired one particularly brilliant and challenging student from Brooklyn. Fortunately, I succeeded in persuading him to make an exception to his sensible rule that he never become socially involved with female members of the congregation. As a result of this flexibility, Susan Friedberg soon became Susan Lapin and has joined the Rabbi in raising seven remarkable (and home schooled!) children to carry on the traditions of their people and their families.

In more recent years, Rabbi Lapin has performed a priceless service in making some of this information accessible to Christians as well as Jews. I've been privileged to attend some of his wildly popular "Biblical Blueprint" lectures in Seattle—festive events that draw audiences representing every religious tradition, united only by their resolve to enrich their understanding by taking Hebrew scripture and Jewish tradition seriously.

The book you will be reading reflects the same energizing approach that has changed the lives of so many of Rabbi Lapin's students over the years. Its approach is unafraid to employ some of the author's wide-ranging secular education to elucidate and illuminate Jewish tradition. Similarly, it uses timeless religious insight, passed down from father to son for 100 generations, to measure and judge our contemporary world.

I know in the most intimate way that Rabbi Lapin can make the Hebrew language come alive in a truly life-changing manner. Some years ago, a trendy, well-established journalist was commissioned by a glossy magazine to interview the Rabbi for an article on "The Jewish Revival in California." She found herself so intrigued by his approach that she began sitting in on his classes—including one group of notoriously curmudgeonly scientists and professionals known as "The Skeptics Group." The writer became so excited by the substance the Rabbi offered, and particularly his revelations about Hebrew as God's language, that she renewed her own dormant Jewish heritage and became an active member of our congregation. Diane also became my wife in 1985, and in a real sense I owe my marriage and our three kids to the effectiveness of Rabbi Lapin's teaching. And yes, of course, he presided at our wedding.

I had reason to celebrate years ago, but now there is additional cause for rejoicing—as, with his book, Rabbi Daniel Lapin explores mysteries, reveals secrets, upholds timeless truths, and unearths buried treasure to a larger audience than ever before.

You are fortunate to now take part in the adventure!

Michael Medved
Seattle, Washington

INTRODUCTION

by Rabbi Daniel and Susan Lapin

Over the years thousands of people have asked us questions about God, about relationships, about sex, about money and about almost anything else you can imagine. Is this because they think we are more intelligent or better educated than they are? I doubt it. I suspect they come to us for another reason altogether. They turn to us in the same way as they might turn to a cardiologist for advice about heart disease or to a financial planner when they are ready to invest. They understand that years of learning, working with and applying information allow people to gain expertise in certain fields. People have brought us the questions which impact their lives because they believe that we have had exposure to a valuable branch of knowledge. We are the fortunate recipients of a three thousand year line of oral transmission that has been passed down from generation to generation. This vast body of ancient data reached my father, Rabbi A.H. Lapin, and in due course, over many years, he passed much of it on to me. Susan was blessed to learn from him as well, in the years following our marriage.

What is this data? The best way to explain it is as a general theory of the totality of all existence—a set of theorems or permanent principles that apply everywhere and in all times. The Jewish people call it the Torah. Eventually translated into many languages, the Torah, or Bible, can be studied through a competent translation, but unfortunately, in this fashion, one obtains a mere microscopic morsel of the available wisdom. This is because the message is bound up with the language. We tend to associate French as the language of romance, whereas Russian lends itself to brooding epics about the darker side of human nature. Hebrew, the language first spoken by Adam and in which the Torah was given, is the language of ancient wisdom.

While English, like most languages, employs grammar rules that keep changing, Hebrew's rules of grammar are fixed. In English, many antiquated usages have long been abandoned while conventions that Shakespeare would never recognize are commonplace. While modern Israeli Hebrew has made some changes, the Bible does not have an 'updated' version and is still studied and understood exactly as it was transmitted to Moses. In addition, a student of Biblical Hebrew could still understand and be understood in modern Israel. The reason for this stability is that Hebrew's grammar rules are no more than an attempt to identify the patterns of structure and syntax found in the Torah. What is even more striking is that Hebrew's syntax is not arbitrary and its word structure is not capricious. We understand and are thrilled by the logic that links the elegance of the language to the infinite wisdom of its Creator.

This book reveals some of the fundamental truths of the Torah without requiring the reader to master the Hebrew language. Like us, you may sometimes wonder whether the latest modern theories about the things that ultimately count are really reliable. Each day, experts churn out ever more radical notions about how we ought best to live our lives. Each day the media hype these notions as fail-safe guides by which to totally rearrange our priorities. Seldom does anyone mention the inconvenient fact that today's pronouncements invariably contradict yesterday's. We intend this book for readers who suspect that the more things change, the more we need to depend upon those things that never change.

Without even mentioning the diet fad of the month, we can cite trends of past decades where young couples have been told that they should have no children or at most one and also that at least two children are needed for optimum emotional health. Day care has been invoked as the surest way to raise well-adjusted children. A little while later it is blamed for physical and psychological damage. Remaining committed to one spouse and one employer were each recommended and subsequently discouraged. All these contradictory pieces of advice were uttered as if from Mount Olympus with great solemnity and assurance. When popular trends change, as they always do, the unfortunate people that followed the experts are often left feeling that they made a horrible mistake.

The treasure buried in the Hebrew language won't explicitly tell us how many children to have or whether to seek new employment. Neither will it eliminate the challenges of being human by announcing the direction each of us should take in the countless decisions we need to make each and every day. However it will expose us to the idea that there are fundamental concepts for us to employ as we make those decisions. No engineering text book will rob a designer of his freedom to design the most beautiful bridge of which he is capable. But it will provide him with knowledge about fundamental concepts such as gravity, the tensile strength of steel, and wind force, which he will use to build both a beautiful and durable bridge. In the same way, reading this book will never deprive anyone of free choice and independence but hopefully it will offer insights to enable the reader to make wise decisions using eternal wisdom found in the Hebrew language.

You may be asking how you can access wisdom from Hebrew when you aren't even familiar with the alphabet. Read on...

HOLY HEBREW!™ TOOLS

I f you don't read or understand Hebrew how are you going to follow an entire book based on Hebrew words? Actually, quite easily.

Feel free to skip this section and just read the book. This is a book featuring real-life ideas that flow from the Lord's language. But if you are interested in delving a bit deeper into the language itself, we do reference certain tools in each chapter that will help you to do so. Below, we expand on each tool. In general, the idea is to treat the Hebrew letters as if they were symbols. Can see that the following two lines look identical:

and that this line is slightly different?

Just look at the Hebrew letters in the same way and you will be able to "see" the messages coming from the Hebrew. To make things easier, on page 15 you will find a chart showing the Hebrew alphabet.

TOOLS

Tool #1: We read Hebrew from right to left.

Example:

Hebrew   *English*
←   →

שׁ ל םּ

M   L   SH

SHaLoM   Shalom

Tool #2: When looking at Hebrew words written in English letters, most vowels should be ignored.

Example:

←

M   L   SH   =   SHaLoM

Tool #3: In Hebrew, if two words are spelled the same, even though their meanings seem to be totally unrelated, they are in fact telling you different dimensions of one unified idea.

Example:

In the sentence, "She rose early in the morning," we don't spend a lot of time wondering why the word "rose" is also the name of a fragrant flower.

If that same similarity was in the Lord's language, we wouldn't understand either getting up or flowers if we didn't understand how they were linked. So, in Hebrew, the word for house, bayit, has a second meaning, 'inside.' This teaches profound lessons about privacy and about one of the main functions of a house.

Tool #4: When looking at a word in Hebrew it helps to isolate the root (main) letters of the word, since pronouns, prepositions and other parts of speech are often added before and after the root rather than being separate words as in English.

Tool #5: Some Hebrew letters have more than one appearance and more than one possible pronunciation. You can see to which letters this applies by looking at the alphabet chart.

Tool #6: Hebrew words can frequently be pulled apart to yield meaning. Certain combinations of first and last letters form patterns as do combinations of letters within words.

Tool #7: The names and shapes of the letters in the Hebrew alphabet have meaning in and of themselves. The letters also have numerical values which add an additional layer of meaning to Hebrew words.

HEBREW ALPHABET

The corresponding numerical value
of each letter appears above the Hebrew letter.

Some letters have more than one sound and shape.
To know the alternate pronunciation,
refer to the tinted English letters beneath.

9	8	7	6	5	4	3	2	1
tet	chet	zayin	vav	hay	dalet	gimel	bet	aleph
ט	ח	ז	ו	ה	ד	ג	ב,בּ	א
T	ba<u>CH</u>*	Z	SILENT or V	H	D	<u>G</u>ood**	V,B	SILENT

90	80	70	60	50	40	30	20	10
tsadi	pay	ayin	samech	nun	mem	lamed	kaf	yud
צ,ץ	פ,ף	ע	ס	נ,ן	מ,ם	ל	כּ,כ,ך	י
TS	F,P	SILENT	S	N	M	L	ba<u>CH</u>*,K	Y

400	300	200	100
tav	shin	reish	kuf
ת	שׁ,שׂ	ר	ק
T	S,SH	R	K

*CH is pronounced as it is in the name Bach.
**G as in good; not G as in general.

PART ONE

RELATIONSHIPS AND MARRIAGE

Chapters 1–5

Be sure to check out pages 337–342
to discover helpful resources on this topic

CHAPTER 1

WINDOW INTO THE SOUL

פנים

PaNYM

Suggestion: See Holy Hebrew! Tools #1, 2 and 3 for help in understanding this chapter.

One day, an advisor to President Abraham Lincoln brought to the White House a man whom he thought Lincoln should appoint as a cabinet secretary. The President met with the man and interviewed him. After the guest left the White House, Lincoln called his advisor into the Oval Office and said, "This man won't do for the job."

"Why not?" the advisor asked.

"I don't like his face."

"B-b-but..." stammered the advisor, "that's unfair! A man can't help what his face looks like."

"You're right," the President replied, "up to age forty, he can't. After age forty, his face is him."

It's intriguing that Lincoln fastened on the age of forty, since *kabbalah*, the tradition of mysticism in Judaism, likewise identifies forty as the age before which a personality is still in formation. In other words, a person must live through four decades to reach full maturity. But more important is Lincoln's insight into an aspect of human personality that was pointed out thousands of years earlier in the grammar of the Hebrew language.

To our modern ears, the statement "I don't like his face" may indeed sound unfair. But the Hebrew word for face, PaNYM, tells us otherwise. Of course, we should endeavor to avoid judging others superficially. But when we find ourselves in a situation where we must assess someone—for instance, when we are considering a prospective spouse, employee, or even a prospective employer—the Lord's language tells us it is wise to take his or her face into consideration.

PaNYM, the countenance we turn to the outside world, also means something that might seem to mean almost the opposite. The Hebrew letters, pay-nun-yud-mem

also spell P'NYM, the word for "inside." If you visit the State of Israel and wander into a government office building, you will see signs for the Ministry of the Interior, called in Hebrew the MiSRaD Ha'P'NYM, literally the "Office of the Inside." You see, though we've all heard the old saying that "the eyes are the windows to the soul," it is closer to the truth to say that the entire face is the window into the soul.

Actions Impact Appearance

I saw this concept played out in a somewhat unusual way while I was a young rabbi-in-training. You have probably never had the occasion to visit a slaughterhouse, but as part of my training I had to make many such inspections and I can tell you that it was among the least pleasant aspects of my preparation.

While I had to visit these abattoirs in order to learn the many and complex laws of kosher meat preparation, it was also instructive for me to look at the faces of the employees there. I observed how rabbinically trained slaughterers, called *shochtim*, slaughtered the animals. Before killing a cow or other kosher animal, the *shochtim* would recite a liturgy of psalms and blessings, asking God's favor and giving Him thanks.

I used to question the need for all this praying before the simple and rather upsetting act of slaughtering an animal. It was only when I studied the faces of the non-rabbinical men employed at the slaughterhouse, those who went about their business unaccompanied by worship that I understood.

These latter individuals looked like they worked in an abattoir. Their faces were dark, heavy, somewhat crudely modeled. But the *shochtim* had quite a different appearance. Their faces were benign, refined, and serene. They were not slaughtering animals because it was an available job. They saw providing kosher meat as a way to serve God and their fellow man. The entire process was clothed in holiness and spirituality. In this way they were protected from the coarsening effects of what they were actually doing— namely, taking life. The faces of the shochtim taught me just how powerfully our actions eventually impact our appearance.

Needless to say, positive experiences affect our PaNYM

just as negative ones do. I'm reminded of the story in the book of Exodus about Moses descending from Mount Sinai. Having just concluded a close encounter of the ultimate kind—with God himself—it is not surprising that this experience changed his face. How could it not have done so? The Bible speaks of rays of light emanating from Moses. But the truth is that since we don't know exactly what happened to Moses in his dialogue with the Lord, we can't exactly picture what effect this would have had on Moses' appearance. Whatever the case, being the "most humble of men," (Numbers 12:3) Moses could probably not tolerate the fact that this exalted experience could be read so easily just by looking at him. Showing this side of himself to the world must have struck him as the opposite of humility. Yet he couldn't change his face. From then onward, anyone looking at him was able to tell that he had experienced something very special.

Men and women alike, spend countless hours and dollars trying to make their faces conform to a cultural ideal. This is going about the task backward.

In my rabbinical work I have come to know quite a few parents of handicapped children. I am fairly certain that I could now recognize such a parent in the street. Any mother or father who has lavished selfless love and devotion upon a child over a period of years will come to possess a face that shows it.

Learn to trust your ability to read people's faces. Will you

always be accurate? Of course not, but just like riding a
bicycle or making an omelet, practice will improve your
odds for doing well. When you encounter an individual with
a truly refined-looking face, enjoy the treat. You are meeting
someone special.

Treasured Wrinkles

As we get older, no matter how much we might wish we
could keep looking young, the aging of the face reflects
something very positive: the acquisition of wisdom. We speak
about an aged face being "wizened." This literally means that
its owner has *become* wise.

A biblical tradition—or *midrash*— alludes to this. Speaking
symbolically, this particular midrash tells us that before the
time of the Biblical patriarchs, faces didn't become visibly
older. People had pretty much the same face when they
entered old age that they had had as children. The message
is that until the beginning of the era of Abraham, Isaac, and
Jacob, opportunities to acquire wisdom (i.e. wisdom about
the Creator) were scarce. Human faces back then reflected
this scarcity of wisdom that matures a face. Thus, we should
treasure every one of our facial wrinkles as a certificate of
wisdom and understanding.

A deeper reality here is that our faces reflect more than just
our mood at the moment. Over the years, with a startling,
even frightening permanence, they assume features in accord with our inner selves. Maybe Lincoln was right when
he observed that this tends to happen by around age forty.
For some it may be earlier and for others later, but eventually

we end up with the faces we deserve.

Literature and popular culture are full of stories that reflect these principles. Take Oscar Wilde's insightful novel, *The Picture of Dorian Gray*. The plot concerns a dissolute young man who wishes never to grow old, and more to the point, never to see his corrupt lifestyle reflected in the appearance of his face. Dorian makes a bargain with the devil: rather than his face aging and changing in accord with his behavior, a portrait of Dorian, hidden in his home, will mutate over the years as his face ought to have done. Years later, as an old yet still young-looking man, he views the portrait and is horrified to find that the terms of his bargain have been kept exactly: The face in the painting has become that of an unspeakably ugly monster.

Men and women alike spend countless hours and dollars trying to make their faces conform to a cultural ideal. Makeup, skin cream, acne medication—you name it, we use it. This is going about the task backward. Superficially, it's obviously true that emotional and behavioral factors affect appearance as much as anything else. They can change the way we look overnight. A bad night's sleep, overindulgence in food or drink, or an upsetting night can make us wake up the next morning with a bad outbreak of acne. That bottle of ointment in the medicine cabinet can only partially correct the emotional havoc making its appearance in that form.

But a more important lesson to keep in mind, one of more permanent relevance, is that if we want to look a certain way—refined, handsome, or beautiful—we stand a better chance of doing so if we begin acting that way. We have

all had the experience of meeting people who carried themselves so royally that we never realized their features were
uneven, or their hair less than silky. Conversely, all the beauty
creams in the world can't correct the damage to our appearance caused by a nasty disposition.

Our Many Faces

In English we naturally speak of a person having one face. In
fact, the term "two-faced" is viewed as an insult. Surprisingly
however, the Hebrew language treats a singular face, PaNYM,
as if it was a plural noun. The 'YM' at the end of a Hebrew
word marks a plural word. This grammatical fact about the
Hebrew word, PaNYM, reveals another fundamental truth
about human beings: There is no word for the singular of
"face" because no person has only one face. In fact each of us
has many, many faces. We have one for dealing with the UPS
man, one for playing with our children, another for whisper-
ing sweet nothings to our spouses, and still another for dealing with subordinates at work.

Even when dealing with each of these various people, we
have many faces. Ideally, we should never get truly angry
with our children. However, it would be a mistake not to
recognize that sometimes we need to show an angry face to
them. On other occasions we need to show a face of joy—
even if, for instance, we've heard our child's riddle ten times
before. In fact, it is disconcerting to try to relate to someone
whose facial expressions never change according to circumstance.

I hope you won't think me too morbid for pointing out that
the only time our facial muscles stop changing and fully

relax is in death, when the expression flees the face entirely. As long as we are passionately alive, our enormously complex existence and personality can only be captured by a plural, not a singular. No matter how filled with integrity we may be, nobody can describe any one of us with only a one-dimensional depiction. This is what makes cartoon caricatures so funny. They work because the cartoon artist focuses on only one facet of his subject and highlights it disproportionately. This suggests, humorously, that the grotesque exaggeration is all there is to the victim. We laugh because we recognize that no human being can be depicted by only one feature.

Being a person of integrity is the challenge we know it to be, because it is so very difficult to reconcile all the various aspects of our personalities under one unifying umbrella. The face's many moods reflect how our very essence is not singular; instead, like the word PaNYM, it is plural. And this is true not only over the course of an hour or a day, but also over a lifetime. It would be weird if it were otherwise. Imagine a man whose face remained, at age sixty, what it had been when he was a boy of five. Unnerving, right?

No True Heroes

The word PaNYM tells us something else very useful about how to go about evaluating people. I refer to the idea of the "hero." From childhood on, we've all been encouraged to seek heroes we can emulate. I remember the aftermath of Israel's 1967 war with its surrounding Arab nations. The Jewish state was led to a seemingly miraculous victory by General Moshe Dayan, whom many Jewish school children came to view as the world's greatest Jewish "hero." Dayan may well have been one of the greatest military men of the century, but he was also an adulterer and possessed many other personal frailties. Not exactly an appropriate hero for a nice Jewish boy or girl.

What is a hero, exactly? In a simplistic world, it's a man or woman whom we can profitably imitate in every way, by copying every aspect of his or her personality. But if we learn anything from PaNYM, it is that human beings are far more complex than the idea of a "hero" is prepared to concede. We all have too many faces—and not all are attractive ones—ever to be a true hero.

The most famous book ever written in Hebrew, the Bible, clearly recognizes this. There are no heroes in the Bible—as indeed there is no word for "hero" in the Hebrew language. Even the Bible's noblest and most powerful characters are flawed. Consider King Saul with his terrifying temper or King David's overreaching in his relationship with Bathsheba. Even Moses was unexceptional as a husband and father; his two sons achieved no great distinction. While each of these individuals, as well as the matriarchs and patriarchs, has specific traits well worth emulating, none are perfect. Only God is perfect.

The corollary to that idea is that even those people who have a flaw that renders them worthy of our contempt will have some strengths. People are never all good or all bad. Having multiple faces, or multiple parts to our personalities, is a consequence of being human. It is also a guarantee that none of us can ever achieve perfection in every one of our

many PaNYM. Rather than causing us to be depressed by
the impossibility of attaining perfection, the ancient Hebrew
book of wisdom called *Pirke Avot* advises that a wise person
is "he who learns from every man." In other words, even the
most humble among us has at least one face from which our
friends and colleagues can learn something.

These are some of the reasons that I do not believe for a
moment that the Internet will eliminate travel. In no way will
e-mail or even video conferencing render *face-to-face* meetings unnecessary. See, I just used the key phrase: face-to-face.
Whether for business purposes or for family get-togethers,
we humans absolutely need and desire to see one another's
faces. Deep within us is the subconscious realization that
our faces really are the windows into our souls.

CHAPTER 2

LOVE'S ENDURING FOUNDATION

חבה

CHiBaH

*Suggestion: See the alphabet chart and Holy Hebrew! Tools
1, 2, 3 and 5 to get the most out of this chapter.*

"**M**y husband has just told me he doesn't love me!"
I struggled to make out what my caller was saying.
She was not only distraught—the emotional pain evident in
her voice—but she was also gasping for breath. I pictured
her and the electric breathing apparatus to which she was
hooked up most of each day. Her husband, Sam, came on the
line and urged me to hurry to their home.

During my short drive to their luxurious mansion in Santa
Monica, I had time to reflect upon their unbelievable story.

Shortly after their marriage thirty years earlier, Miriam was
stricken with polio and severely restricted in her activities
due to the mechanical devices she depended upon to keep
her breathing. Young Sam Rosen, whose management brilliance had already caused *Time* magazine to dub him a "corporate whiz-kid," was urged by his family to terminate the
ill-fated union. Well-intentioned friends also gently advised
him to divorce Miriam and place her in a care facility that

could be paid for by an annuity that Sam would fund. That way, they reasoned, he could do the decent thing for her while preventing her misfortune from wrecking two lives instead of only one.

"So why didn't you do that?" I had asked him soon after we started a Bible study together some five years before Miriam's anguished phone call. In a calm and logical voice, Sam had explained that he had not seen how he could possibly follow the advice of his family and friends. After all, he had married Miriam for better or for worse, in sickness and in health; it was a commitment. Surely I could see that, he said. Humbled and amazed, I assured him that I understood perfectly.

Now, as I pulled into their driveway, I wondered what had precipitated Miriam's frantic phone call. Sam greeted me at the door. "This is one of the biggest crises of our marriage," he said. "I've never seen her so upset."

I entered Miriam's room which always looked more like a hospital trauma center than a private bedroom.

"He doesn't look after me out of love," wailed Miriam. She pointed her finger in accusation at her husband. Sam was silent. It turned out that earlier that morning she had asked Sam why he had so selflessly and devotedly lavished such care and attention on her for so many years. He answered as directly as he knew how—that it was his obligation to do so. Upon hearing this answer, Miriam had become inconsolable and had finally called me.

"Tell me honestly, Miriam, what is your worst nightmare?"

I inquired of her once she had calmed down a little.

She answered candidly. "That Sam will tire of constantly caring for me and place me in a hospital for the rest of my life."

I explained to her how unreliable was a benefit received when the donor was simply responding to a feeling or an emotional reason such as love.

"If the feeling of love was the only reason Sam cares for you, Miriam, then indeed you have cause to fear your worst nightmare coming true," I explained. "Perhaps one day, any day now, Sam will wake up 'out of love.' He might search his heart and find it empty of all feelings for you. It could happen."

I went on to explain that if his care was the result of his feelings, if those feelings should ever vanish it would be fully consistent for him to stop caring for her. I explained how fortunate she really was. Sam had only been trying to tell her that he cared for her because of an obligation that could never change, instead of a fickle feeling that could fade away and condemn her to a lonely hospital bed forever. Indeed, she had nothing to worry about.

And so for thirty-five years until the day she died, Sam cared for Miriam. He built a house in which she could move everywhere by motorized wheel chair. He had a car engineered to accommodate her wheelchair and would tenderly carry her in and out of the car as he took her with him on short business and social engagements. He revealed through his actions that he knew what the foundation of love really was.

What Is Love Anyway?

What Sam understood intuitively is that love is as much a decision as it is a feeling.

One Hebrew word for love and affection is CHiBaH, based on the word for "obligation," which is CHoVaH.

In Hebrew, the consonant sounds B and V are made by the same letter. They are both the second letter of the Hebrew alphabet. How do you tell the difference? If the letter is written with a dot inside it— בּ —it sounds like a B and is called a 'bet'. Without the dot— ב —it is read as a V and called a 'vet'. Secondly, vowels are less important—roots of words depend only on the consonants. So for our purposes, you may safely ignore the vowels.

Thus, CHiBaH is identical to CHoVaH—love equals obligation.

ח ב ה   ח ב ה
affection   obligation

We are exposed to this lesson by recalling the Hebrew word for "friend"—

ח ב ר
CHaVeR

In this word we clearly see the root word "obligation," or CHoVaH. Sam lived his life with the clear understanding that his love, affection, and yes, even friendship with Miriam were rooted in a simple concept: obligation.

Many a wife has been tormented by the following remorseless logic. Having originally accepted her boyfriend's marriage proposal because he once said "I love you," she is now stuck in a marriage that is viable only as long as these feelings of love are intact. What can a wife say when her husband demands a divorce saying, "I no longer feel in love with you"?

If, on the other hand, their marriage is established on the basis of not only love but also promise, commitment, covenant, and obligation, the difficult moments of their relationship can be more easily endured.

A wife can respond by saying, "Look, I really am sad that you no longer feel love for me, I really am. I will do whatever I can to try to restore the love you once felt for me. However, that wasn't the basis of our marriage. We undertook permanent obligations toward one another that simply were never meant to depend upon something as unpredictable as feelings. I hope you will once again come to love me as you once did, but meanwhile our mutual obligations continue unchanged. How we act toward one another and toward our children cannot change."

The same principle applies in the other direction as well, of course. In the timeless musical *Fiddler on the Roof*, Tevya the milkman asks his wife of twenty-five years, "Golda, do you love me?"

She replies by more or less asking him in return, "What's the difference?"

She points out how they have always lived together happily. They have shared the tasks of conducting their business and raising their family successfully. Her song shows that she has grasped one essential buried treasure from the Lord's language: Love is the consequence of accepting and discharging our obligations. Call me sentimental, but I always thought it would have been nice had Golda ended her song by confirming that she was still quite overwhelmed with love and passion for her milkman husband.

Human relationships must be built upon the foundation of obligation and commitment rather than feelings. It is for this reason that the Jewish marriage contract, called a *Ketubah*, contains only a list of obligations that the husband henceforth undertakes toward his wife. By accepting those obligations and by living up to them, love is indeed nurtured between the young couple. I am not saying that the feeling of love isn't important and wonderful. I am emphasizing the wisdom of the Lord's language, which insists that love that that is grounded in obligation endures. When obligation is grounded in love, both are doomed.

> **Obligations have the capacity to expand the envelope of your life.**

In refutation of the sentimental 1970s novel *Love Story* by Eric Segal, I would consider it dreadfully dangerous advice to declare that "Love means never having to say you're sorry." Feeling that you never owe an apology means that you never feel any obligation. When a responsible person falls down on an obligation, he apologizes profusely. No relationship exempts you from having to say you're sorry. On the contrary, failing to deliver on an obligation absolutely compels you to apologize sincerely and ask forgiveness.

An Enduring Friendship

Not only does love, CHiBaH, best endure when constructed upon the foundation of obligation, CHoVaH, but friendship, CHaVeR, does the same. Acquiring a new friend places me under new obligations. Likewise, the way to most effectively make new friends is to shoulder new obligations.

It is almost as if the Lord's language is describing a mathematical equation that can be read both forward and backward. For instance: $2 + 2 = 4$. It is just as true, even if a little obvious, that $4 = 2 + 2$. If acquiring a new friend creates new obligations for me, then it is just as true that shouldering new obligations is a way to acquire new friends. This is why, when moving to a new city, many folks immediately join volunteer groups or other civic and service-minded organizations. Assuming new obligations inevitably wins us new friends. How odd! I am actually advising you to go out of your way to identify new obligations to undertake. This may seem counterintuitive since so many people we know go through life trying to evade obligations, but assuming them is a great life strategy. Obligations are good things that have the capacity to expand the envelope of your life.

Over 2,000 years ago, ancient Jewish wisdom presented a case study in the context of a discussion of civil law. The rabbis described a hypothetical situation that gives us some excellent insight into one aspect of friendship. While I am updating both the names and the monetary unit, here is the essence of the discussion.

Tom claimed that Jerry owed him a hundred dollars, insisting that Jerry borrowed this sum from him last year, at exactly 2 P.M. on the day before the Passover holiday. Jerry denied that he ever borrowed the money from Tom.

Witnesses were found to shed light on the dispute. They said that although they cannot attest to whether Jerry ever borrowed money from Tom, they do know that he did not borrow anything from anyone at 2 p.m. on the day before the previous Passover holiday. They know this because at that precise moment, they happened to have seen Jerry relieving himself in a field far away from where Tom claims the transaction took place. The legal conclusion, obviously, is that Tom's claim is disallowed.

The real question, however, is this: Why would a handbook of morality which scrupulously avoids vulgarity, unnecessarily conjure up an image of Jerry urinating in a field? After all, the example's purpose would have been just as well served had it described Jerry plowing that same field.

Many people wrongly assume the Talmud to be thousands of pages of irrelevant rabbinic musings. They dismiss these complex discussions as having roughly the same importance as how many angels can dance on the head of a pin. Nothing could be further from the truth. In those densely packed pages that have been pored over for millennia lies a treasure trove of insights into human nature and secrets of life on this planet of ours.

In the hypothetical story about Tom and Jerry, the important data being communicated is not whether the court determines that a legal loan was made. That is quite straightforward. The really fascinating information is about the nature of human relationships and human friendship.

The Talmud divides all human relationships into two categories: those that are sexual and those that are not sexual. Clearly, sexual activity establishes a pretty profound relationship between two people. What kind of activity, asks the Talmud, creates an equally profound relationship of a non-sexual kind between two people?

The answer: creating or assuming an obligation. In other words, in our strange example of Tom and Jerry, the two opposite ends of the spectrum of non-sexual human relationships are anchored by borrowing money at one end and by going to the bathroom at the other.

Lending Money is a Kindness

What is one of the greatest acts of goodness and friendship that one person can do for another? This may surprise you, but one of the greatest acts of kindness one can do for another is to lend him money. (Needless to say, this discussion is confined to interest-free loans.) It is possibly less an act of kindness to *give* someone money, for that risks robbing the recipient of his dignity and self-respect. By contrast, a loan implies confidence that the borrower will do better in the future. Maybe he'll acquire independence by starting his own enterprise. He could repay the loan with the proceeds and stand upon his own two feet. Some people like giving money away to poor people in a form of patronage. That kind of generosity is not as great an act of kindness as is helping a person toward independence.

You will agree, I am certain, that anyone benefiting from a great act of kindness automatically incurs an obligation toward his benefactor. You may have heard the aphorisms warning against borrowing money from, or lending it to, your friends. The Talmud turns that idea on its head and suggests that you ought to make friends of those to whom you lend money.

The story is told of the great Winston Churchill who was once asked for an urgent loan by an opposing Member of Parliament. While enjoying a collegial friendship with the great statesman, the strapped politician had been a thorn in Churchill's professional side for years. Whatever Winston proposed, this Member opposed. When Churchill voted aye, this Member voted nay. When Churchill offered a reason for some national policy or another, this Member refuted Churchill's argument. But as soon as Winston loaned the funds to his colleague, all opposition ceased.

For the next two months not a peep of political protest was heard from Churchill's old antagonist. Finally, one day after lunch and on the way back into the House, in front of some mutual friends, Churchill confronted his old tormentor.

"Either pay me back my money by midnight tomorrow or resume arguing and fighting with me on the floor of the house," Churchill thundered at his bewildered opponent. The man's eyes filled with tears. He hugged Winston Churchill in silent gratitude and then took his seat across the aisle, immediately resuming his diatribes against the British lion.

What about the story of Jerry relieving himself in the field? Well, try to think of some activity you could engage in that would benefit absolutely nobody except yourself. Not easy, is it? Buying an ice cream? Sorry. You see, you pleased the proprietor of the ice cream store. If that were not true, he would hardly have rushed forward to help you the moment he saw you enter his store. You may well enjoy eating that ice cream, but in so doing you also pleased someone else.

One activity that truly does nothing for anyone else is going to the bathroom. We often refer to it as relieving oneself. That is appropriate since you are precisely the person the activity does relieve. It relieves nobody else. Thus, because going to the bathroom does nothing for anyone else, it also sets up no obligation with respect to anyone else; therefore it does very little for human relationships.

The Talmudic story of Tom and Jerry is there to teach us that almost everything we do each day falls somewhere on that spectrum between relieving oneself and lending money. One valuable secret of life is to organize our lives so that most of our activities resemble lending money rather than relieving ourselves. This is to say that we will get more out of life and we will win more friends if we always seek ways to benefit others, thereby creating obligations and friendships, rather than seeking ways to relieve ourselves.

Metaphor for Friendship

We can see that it makes sense that the Hebrew word for friend—CHaVeR, should be rooted in the Hebrew word for obligation—CHoVaH. But is CHaVeR the only word for friend? Considering that God's blueprint for humanity regards friendship as so important, it would be strange was

His language to have only one word to describe friendship. Well, there is a second word for friend and it is YeDYD.

D   Y   D   Y

That four-letter word is actually made up of two identical two-letter words placed one after the other.

D   Y

YaD spells the Hebrew word for hand. So two hands next to one another mean friendship? Of course they do. Just imagine what kind of simple clip-art image you might select to symbolize friendship. Wouldn't two hands clasping one another be near the top of your list?

Now you can clearly see the probable origin of the handshake. The original tongue, the Lord's language, declares that the word for friend is two hands touching one another. How better to announce friendly intentions than to try to "touch hands"? People who knew Hebrew, and in those days most educated people did, shook hands with one another as if to say, "hand-to-hand." Shaking hands with someone was tantamount to sign language for "Hello, friend."

Furthermore, since the Kabalistic symbolism of the hand means, "acquiring that which the world has to offer," the word for a friend, YeDYD, has an additional important meaning and lesson. Just as my hand helps me survive by moving food and drink from the table to my mouth, so the juxtaposition of two hands to mean "friend" suggests that two friends help one another to survive and prosper. They do this by each trying to move toward the other those things he thinks his friend needs or wants. In other words, each serves as an additional hand for the other. They are like two adjacent hands. What a perfect metaphor for friendship.

Having friends is a great blessing. The rabbis of old who wrote their transmissions in *Ethics of the Fathers* advise us to always be working at acquiring a new friend. Good advice it is, and not terribly difficult to do either. First, seek out obligations to undertake. Find new and unexpected ways to help other people, even if they did not ask for your help. *Especially* if they did not ask for your help!

Some would consider it manipulative to embark on a program of finding ways to do people favors knowing that this creates obligations toward you. But just imagine asking one of the recipients of your thoughtfulness how he feels. Would he rather benefit from your good turn even though he now "owes you one," or proudly spurn your assistance?

The wise person humbly and gratefully accepts any extended hand. This simple idea demonstrates the other side of the coin of friendship. In addition to seeking opportunities to benefit others and thereby create obligations, one must just as graciously accept kindness from individuals and assume obligation toward those individuals seeking to become friends. In this way, the seamless web of social connectivity grows and strengthens, allowing the blessings of friendship and love to bring happiness and prosperity to all.

CHAPTER 3

GIVE UNTIL IT STOPS HURTING

קר בן
KoRBaN

Suggestion: See the alphabet chart and Holy Hebrew! Tools 1, 2, 3 and 5 to get the most out of this chapter.

What does the word "sacrifice" mean to you? Does it not suggest a difficult action in which you yield or surrender something of value?

If that's what you think, sacrifice probably has a negative connotation for you. The Hebrew word for sacrifice, KoRBaN, suggests differently. It appears frequently in the Torah, especially throughout the book of Leviticus in the context of the Temple's sacrificial rites. The root of the word is KRB, meaning "close or related." For instance, the Hebrew word for a relative is a KaRoV.

What does sacrifice have to do with closeness? Picture the following scenario. Sarah and Kimberly are friends. They often play together and one particular summer they each want the toy that is the all the rage in their twelve year old circle. They spend hours deciding to sell lemonade and then making signs and setting up their stand. They forego bike riding, watching TV, and an occasional swim in the afternoon in order to run their business. After watching their daughter work so hard for a week, Sarah's parents decide to reward her with the desired object. Kimberly mans the stand by herself for the next three weeks until she has earned enough money to buy the toy.

At first both girls are inseparable from their new possession, but by the end of the summer, Sarah is yearning for a still newer object and her previous treasure has lost its luster. Kimberly, on the other hand, is still playing with her toy when the next summer rolls around.

I'm willing to guess that you can relate to that scenario. Don't we all appreciate something that we worked for—you could say sacrificed for—more than something that was handed to us? This turns a sacrifice into something positive not negative. We are closer, more KaRoV—to something for which we have sacrificed.

Who Needed the Temple Sacrifices?

Let's start by examining Biblical usage. Were sacrifices brought in order to please or placate a vengeful deity? Hardly. If that were true, after the Temple was destroyed about two thousand years ago, the Jews would have needed another venue in which to bring sacrifices and keep God happy. Jews didn't bring sacrifices to make God feel closer to us. Animals were slaughtered and burnt upon the altar in order to help the worshipper feel closer to God.

Was God in trouble when the Temple was destroyed? No, the Jews were. With the loss of the Temple in Jerusalem, the Jewish people lost their chief mechanism for bringing themselves closer (KaRoV) to God, namely the sacrifice or KoRBaN, which had been rendered inoperable by the Roman destruction. (An interesting aside: It is easy to see how the word for our twelfth element, carbon, got its name. Burning organic material such as an animal in a KoRBaN produces that familiar black substance we call carbon. Just say the Hebrew word for sacrifice, KoRBaN—and the English word, carbon, once or twice and you will sense the connection.)

Giving a gift to a person has a similar result. It causes us to be a little closer to that person; making a sacrifice for someone causes us to love that person a whole lot more.

Parents and Children

Let's examine the relationship between parents and children. It is rare indeed for parents to cease loving their children and reject them. Sadly, it is far more common to encounter instances of children who want little or nothing to do with their parents. I recall once stunning my radio audience when I conducted a live interview with a man who had evicted his aged parents from an apartment building he owned. "They were late with their rent money," he insisted. It would be hard to imagine the reverse situation. Just think of how many families have unmarried children in their twenties and thirties still living at home. The children are trying to save money on rent, and for the most part, parents seem happy to help.

Funnily enough, many adult children spend countless therapy sessions describing to psychologists how their parents ruined their lives. I say "funnily enough" because you would think that the nation's therapists would have waiting rooms brimming with parents eager for help with their feelings of anger toward their children. After all, after bringing children into the world, parents can no longer take vacations at will or eat out in fancy restaurants. Money spent on baby-sitting, orthodontia, athletics and piano lessons mean fewer dollars for parents to spend on themselves. It would seem that parents have a far more legitimate complaint against children than the other way around. Yet, generally speaking, we find that parents love their children more unconditionally than children love their parents.

We should now understand the reason for this. During the eighteen or so years that a child is being raised, who makes more sacrifices for whom? During those years, parents are constantly making sacrifices for their children. The result? The parents love their children more. This is the predictable effect of sacrifice.

> **The more we give to someone else, the more of ourselves we have invested in that person.**

This helps us understand the Biblical requirement to honor our parents. In addition to whatever other purposes it serves, honoring a parent helps keep a child psychologically healthy. Not only do we appreciate things or people more when we sacrifice for them, we humans have a need to be givers. There is little that stunts our souls more than constantly being a recipient. Wise people make sure that relationships they are in are reciprocal ones—sometimes one side gives while the other receives while other times the roles are reversed.

Wise parents do their children a favor when they demand help around the house and courteous manners from them. Otherwise the children are only in recipient mode, which leads to resentment and unhappiness.

Work Sacrifices

You have undoubtedly met the loyal employee who feels that he has sacrificed a lot for his employer. He has worked many overtime hours and often missed family events because he felt he was needed at the office. Perhaps I'm describing you. Yet now you may feel that your sacrifices are not appreciated.

Once you understand the concept of KoRBaN, you see that the employee who gives his company considerably more than his position demands establishes no claim to his employer's gratitude. His sacrifice does not make his employer feel any closer to him; instead it guarantees that he will feel closer to his employer. For this reason people who make what they intend to be a one-time sacrifice to their companies find that it is easier to do so again later. It becomes easier and easier to sacrifice for your work because each time you do so, you come to love your work just a little more.

In Giving, We Receive

I once heard a wife hurl this grenade at her husband:"Do you know how much I have sacrificed for you?" Oddly enough, it seemed to evoke in that husband more resentment than gratitude.

The spouse who sees herself as sacrificing herself for her

husband is mistaken if she expects gratitude for her sacrifice. Oh, sure, all wives and husbands are obliged to demonstrate constant gratitude to their spouse. However, this is not due to sacrifice, but because an essential part of marriage is to be constantly giving.

The root for the Hebrew word for giving, NaTaN,

נ ת נ

N   T   N

is a palindrome. That is to say, it reads the same forward and backward: No matter from which end you view this word, the effect is identical. This indicates that in giving, we also receive. By handing you a gift, I receive as much gratification and benefit as you do by accepting it from me. However, the motivation for giving can never be to elicit gratitude or love.

When one spouse feels like a martyr, it is a sign that the relationship is in deep trouble. While there can be no keeping count in a relationship—I did this for you today so tomorrow you must do something for me—in a healthy relationship, both sides will benefit from both the giving and the taking. If either wife or husband feels like a martyr, that is a severe warning sign.

The Why behind the What

Why does giving have the effect on us of liking the recipient of the giving more? One reason is that we all tend to like ourselves. The more we give to someone else, the more of ourselves we have invested in that person.

Another reason is that our emotions tend to fall in line with our actions. It would be nice if we could be such rational creatures that we always acted in accordance with how we feel. Unfortunately we don't do that. We usually act the way we really want to and then we bring our feelings into line. We find it painful when our feelings are violated by our actions. For instance, most people who have just bought a new car are not comfortable examining the possibility that they overpaid or that they made a poor choice. Having taken the action of purchasing a new car, their emotions fall in line to convince them that it was a good buy. Psychologists have a name for our tendency to try to avoid the pain caused by conflicting emotions or by a conflict between action and feeling. They call it *cognitive dissonance*.

Another example of this human tendency can be seen among ex-smokers. People who have given up smoking tend to become aggressively anti-smoking. In general, they seem to be far more hostile to smoking than those who have never smoked. You would have thought that ex-smokers would be most tolerant of the habit in others. Instead, having performed a significant act in overcoming their smoking habit, their emotions and feelings fall into line. They now hate smoking.

Is there a useful general rule or life-lesson to be learned here? You bet. *If you don't like the way you feel toward someone or something, start acting the way you would act if you already felt the way you wished you would feel.* Pretty soon, you will find your feelings falling into line.

For instance, suppose you had a major fight with your wife before leaving for work this morning. All day long you seethe with indignation at her attitude. All you can think about are the clever things you should have said during the morning's argument but were too angry to think of. Finally it is time to head for home, but you know the fight will resume as soon as you walk through the door. Wouldn't it be nice if the fight was resolved and your heart was filled with love and appreciation for your partner?

Remember the general rule: Act the way you would be acting if you already felt the way you wished you would feel. On the way home, stop at the florist and pick up a pretty bunch of flowers to take home. Is this hypocritical? No, it is merely acting inconsistently with your feelings. And acting differently from the way you feel is not only good, it is the basis of all civilized human intercourse. Not always telling people what you think of them is a good inconsistency. Getting up in the morning for work, although you feel like sleeping late, is another good inconsistency. And acting kindly toward your spouse and children even if you feel angry is also a good and useful inconsistency.

You are not doing this to change her or to make her forget the morning. You are doing it because it will help *you* to change *your* feelings. It will make it easier for you to overcome your anger and allow good feelings to displace any lingering hostility you still feel.

So you walk through the door clutching a bundle of flowers. Your wife greets you with one of two possible reactions. If the relationship is basically sound, she will either happily seizes upon this excuse to forget the morning's pain or she will happily accept the floral sacrifice and remind you that there are still unfinished issues from this morning's argument. Either way, you are now in a much better position to restore marital harmony than had you walked into the house while *you* were still seething with resentment.

Dealing with Unreasonable Colleagues

If you work with an unreasonable or unpleasant colleague, what are your choices? You cannot change her nature. You *can* quit your job, or try to get your co-worker fired, or change the way you feel about her. The last choice is the only practical one. This alternative will not necessarily convert her into a kind and benevolent friend, but it will cause you to feel less aggravated by her.

How do you generate warm feelings for a fellow worker about whom your only uncertainty is whether she is mad, evil, or both? The answer is KoRBaN—a sacrifice. You bring this unpleasant individual a gift. Actually, purchasing a gift for this monster probably feels more like a sacrifice than a gift. Is it inconsistent to purchase a gift for someone you detest? Of course it is, but it is also very wise if you are going to have to continue working with her. Giving her a gift accomplishes two valuable goals. First, you're going to enjoy the utter confusion she will experience upon receiving a gift from someone she knows not to be one of her biggest fans. Second, you will be depriving her of her ability to irritate you. You may never come to be truly fond of her, but you will feel closer to someone to whom you have given a gift. You will have enormously improved your work environment.

This then, is a major lesson of KoRBaN. You may not be able to change other people, but you can work on yourself to change the way you feel about them.

CHAPTER 4

WHAT DO WE KNOW?

יד ע

YaDA

*Suggestion: See the alphabet chart and Holy Hebrew! Tools
1, 2, 6 and 7 to get the most out of this chapter.*

Those hygienically edited movies that airlines provide to
anaesthetize their passengers into compliant immobili-
ty just don't do it for me.Trying to be productive by opening
a laptop computer is also out of the question.The traveler
in front of me invariably reclines his seat back so far that if
I yawn, my lower jaw will strike the top of his head and in-
flict a concussion. No wonder that on cross-country airplane
trips, many of us resort to trying to talk with our seatmates:
There is little else to do!

While earning my frequent-flier miles, I have participated in
countless high altitude conversations and overheard many
more. Invariably, it's a sort of dance to exchange information. Each person tries to elicit from the other details that
might include their fellow traveler's line of work, marital status, and/or reasons for travel.There are no nefarious motives;
getting to know a stranger involves asking certain types of
questions.

Do We Really Know?

Have you ever wanted to scream, "I know, I know," when some bore starts relating a tale you've already heard him tell three times? Or how about your child who, during an intense lecture from you about misbehavior, puts her hands over her little ears and says, "I know, Mommy, I know." Whenever we say, "I know" do we really, *really*, know? Do we even know what we mean by the phrase "knowing something" or "knowing someone"? I think not. I suspect that many of us are not even certain of how to help others to know us.

Business, personal relationships, and acquiring inanimate objects are three areas in which we need to effectively use our ability to know. In your business and professional lives, you might want to get to know an employee before hiring him. You might need to get to know someone whom you are contemplating making a preferred vendor for your business. If you are applying for a job, it would be useful to get to know the company so you could determine whether you would really like to work there. And if you felt you knew that car salesman, wouldn't you feel a little more comfortable about signing the contract?

The second area in which we could all benefit from learning how to know someone is our personal lives. If you felt confident that you really knew the man your daughter was dating, you would be in a better position to offer guidance. Making new friends and keeping old ones surely depends on your ability to get to know people. Knowing the man behind the charming smile or the girl behind those sparkling eyes

might help you decide if you really want to spend the rest
of your life with that person. Similarly, continuing to know
your parents as they change or your own children as they
develop all require that you know how to know.

Finally, the third area in which we use our ability to know is
with objects or facts. When I go shopping for a lawnmower,
I try to get to know several machines in order to choose
the one I prefer. I might study the Highway Code in order
to "know the rules." My teenage son insists that he "knows"
how to drive. I handle, try on, and examine the sweater
that caught my eye in the department store to get to know
whether it will suit me, and whether it is worth more to me
than the fifty dollars in my pocket.

Possessing the ability to accurately know people and things
in different contexts seems to be an essential part of life. Just
as in knitting a sweater, it is easiest when one knows how.
Fortunately the Lord's language provides useful insights into
this skill of knowing.

Hand and Eye

The Hebrew word for "know" or "knowledge" is YaD-A

ע ד י

ayin dalet yud

and is made up of the three letters yud, dalet, ayin. The first
two letters spell out the word for hand,

YaD.

ד י

dalet yud

The name of the last letter, ayin, means an eye. Hand and eye? What do these two words have to do with knowing?

The word "know" is a composite of the two very organs that the human being uses to know—hand and eye. Could this be why, upon meeting someone for the first time, we give the person a firm handshake and look him in the eye? Coincidence? You be the judge.

The meaning of the compound Hebrew word, *hand-eye*, offers a way to understand what knowing really means. Let's start with the word "hand."

If I were to call out the word "hand" to you, what might be the very first word to spring to your mind? Fingers? Grasp? Grab? Fingers only fold one way—toward the palm—the better to grasp and grab with. The beggar's outstretched hand silently says, "Give me." You may have responded to my little game with the word "fist." That would have been fine, too. The purpose of a fist is also to further your gains and advance your own interests just as grabbing and grasping are usually attempts to get what you want.

How might you gesture with your hand to someone who strolled into your office to offer you some jellybeans while you were on the telephone? Quite unconsciously you would hold up your free hand and mimic the gesture that traffic policemen use when they want drivers to halt their vehicles. Or you might extend your arm and point your fingers at the ceiling while showing your visitor your palm. The unspoken rule: Palm toward me and fingers pointing in my direction means "Give me" while rotating my wrist to signal the opposite gesture suggests "No, thank you."

Hebrew possesses the kind of astounding consistency one usually expects from a mathematical system rather than from a language. Perhaps that is because the Lord's language is both. As we have seen, in Hebrew,

ד   י

D   Y

means hand, or as we have seen, "Give me." However, if we rotate the word and write the Hebrew word for hand backwards like this,

י   ד

Y   D

←

we obtain the Hebrew word "enough" or "sufficient." In other words, "No, thank you, I have sufficient." So we see that YaD backwards means "No, do not give me anything, I have sufficient." YaD forward means a hand and suggests that I would like something from you.

Let's continue to probe. The hand is not the only human organ word contained in the word "know." The other, as we have seen, is eye. Is it possible that eye also suggests a similar focus on me and my own wants and desires just as hand does? Let's find out.

The Eyes Have It

Have you ever bought something that later turned out to be unnecessary? I know I have done so more than once. Whenever I have impulsively purchased something, one of my organs is more to blame than any other. The guilty part of my anatomy is usually my eyes. Think about it. Whenever your mother told you that your eyes were bigger than your tummy, she was observing the same thing. Somehow, the eyes have the capacity to powerfully influence our emotions, particularly those emotions having to do with our desires and wishes.

Marketers realize that if they want to make us act impulsively, they must appeal to our eyes. For this reason many shopping networks can be found on television. People will buy things they see on TV, more than things they hear described on the radio. Catalogs that fill our mailboxes are heavy on color photographs of the merchandise on sale. Most of us are not nearly as susceptible to auditory sales pitches—such as we might hear on the radio—as we are to the visual sales pitches of television, catalogs, computer screens and in-store displays.

Have you ever known a young man who fell in love with, and perhaps sadly even married, a completely unsuitable young woman? Often, when a man makes a stupid mistake about a woman, his eyes are chiefly to blame. Very few men abandon their wives and children to run off with women they have never seen. While on-line, phone conversations or e-mail may well be the start in such instances, full and final folly usually comes when a man allows his eyes to dictate the rules.

I have often joked with single male listeners to my radio show, warning them that they should have lengthy phone conversations with single women. No face-to-face meetings should be allowed. Men cannot be trusted with women once their eyes become part of the decision-making process. Sight unseen conversations will help them avoid being sabotaged by their eyes. Some men become infatuated with unsuitable women because their eyes mislead them, while others refuse to get to know very suitable women for the very same reason: their eyes mislead them. Eyes tend to supply self-centered emotional data.

Now we might be making some progress toward understanding the true meaning of knowing. We have discovered that the Hebrew word for knowing, YaD-A, is made up of two words, hand and eye, and that both imply self-centeredness. Hand suggests a tendency to grasp and grab while our eyes seduce us into wanting things. What does this have to do with knowing? To further illustrate, let's watch people drift around the room at an imaginary cocktail party. The dance usually looks something like this: People approach other people, talk for a while, and then move on. As they chat, their eyes often rove around the room trying to find another, more interesting, person. Conversations only get animated when two people focus on each other and stop seeking better prey.

> **Whenever we say, "I know" do we really, *really*, know?**

You may have noticed that a party at which you only spend a few minutes conversing with dozens of people can be very depressing. In contrast, if there was someone there with whom you really connected, you may return home feeling energetic and revitalized. Only when you get to "know" someone do you have a satisfying experience.

What is the difference between the two encounters? In the first type, one or both participants quickly conclude that the other has little to offer, whether sparkling conversation, prospective friendship, or possible business connection. Both drift off to get to know other guests. In other words, both parties explore their new acquaintance from the perspective of what he or she might receive from them. How awful!

And what is more, that *is* pretty much how we all get to know car salesmen, friends and lawnmowers. Oh, and it is not really that awful either. Let me explain.

The Hebrew word for "know" informs us that when we get to know someone or something, we nearly always do so from a very personal point of view. In other words, we really aren't entirely objective. After meeting someone for the first time, we may say, "That is a most wonderful person." In saying this, we are actually revealing as much about ourselves as we are about that person. The point is that we find him or her to be a wonderful person. Others may not.

But the hand-eye theme in the Hebrew "know" tells us much more than that we are subjective in judgment. It also tells us that the criterion we subconsciously use when getting to know someone or something is: "What can he, she, or it do to enhance my life?"

What Can You Do to Enhance My Life?

It is well to bear this in mind the next time you are aware that someone else is in the process of getting to know you.

In some way, the other person is evaluating what you can do to improve his life. Yes, I know that it seems as if it would be wonderful if self-centeredness played no role in human affairs, but it does. And it does have a very positive side.

For instance, the reason you can step outside your front door early each morning and reach down to pick up a container of milk, or perhaps that morning's newspaper, is not because the milkman and the newspaper carrier are filled with affection for you. You are able to enjoy these luxurious services only because the milkman and the newspaper carrier are actually rather selfish. They deliver your morning conveniences because they wish to be paid, not because they care for you. What is important is that you are able to receive what you really want. Simply ask yourself which you would prefer: having your milk and paper delivered sporadically and unreliably by people who really love you or having milk and the news delivered absolutely reliably by people who do not even know you?

You only have to ask yourself which approach best lubricates communal interaction and allows a modern society to function: measuring the emotions others harbor within their hearts, or looking at their actions. As for me, I would rather be surrounded by fellow citizens who are all doing the right thing regardless of what naughty thoughts they were thinking, than by citizens who filled their minds with thoughts of love and goodwill but failed to act accordingly. We humans are not built for consistency; if it is to be a choice between bad thoughts and good actions or good thoughts and bad actions, I would much rather we all perform good actions and keep our evil ruminations to ourselves.

It is just fine if someone comes over to talk to me even though he is secretly motivated by finding out how knowing me might help him advance socially or professionally. If I were totally honest with myself, I might have to confess that in responding to his social overtures I am doing exactly the same thing. This is perhaps one reason many of us feel flattered and exhilarated to be invited to a party thrown by a wealthy and popular host. Part of us is saying, "Oh good, those people throwing the party are richer and more socially successful than we are, and perhaps being with them will allow some of that glitter and glamour to rub off."

Every interviewer talking to an applicant for a job is asking himself only one question: How would this candidate help me, my colleagues and our company if he or she were hired? A girl deciding whether to accept an invitation for a date is likely asking herself how this guy might help her achieve her goal of being married and raising a family.

Paradoxically, by recognizing our self-interest in knowing others, we become aware of how we must behave for others to want to know us. Once we understand this principle, we ourselves become motivated to discover the ways in which we can do something for a new acquaintance. One of the important lessons adolescents learn when they enter the work force is that their prospective employer is not interested in the fact that they are saving for a car. If they want the job, they must convince the interviewer that despite their tender age they have something to offer the company. And rather than babbling on about ourselves when we meet a new person, wc should know that our new acquaintance also wants the satisfaction of speaking about himself. This is not a bad thing.

If we work hard enough, we will eventually reach the point with our spouse or other loved ones where we "know" them so well that their interests are totally intertwined with ours. Have you ever seen a mother wince when her toddler falls down and scrapes his knee? The mother literally felt the wound as if it were on her own body. A lovely story is related of a great rabbi in Jerusalem who escorted his wife to the doctor when she was experiencing a pain in her leg. As they sat down in front of the medical professional, the rabbi spoke revealingly when he said, "Doctor, our leg hurts us." Can any of us ask for more than that from a marriage?

Let's return to the passenger engaging his seatmate in conversation on a cross-country airplane flight. When he asks "and what do you do?" or "and what field are you in?" he is subconsciously (or perhaps quite consciously) trying to discover whether there is mutually beneficial business they could do together. That is why these conversations typically lead quite quickly to the well-known ritual called the business card exchange. Rather than being predatory, this desire to "get something from the other" is the first step in developing human relationships. That is the secret of YaD-A, to know. We will all be more effective once we understand and accept both our own and other people's self-centeredness in getting to know one another.

CHAPTER 5

HOW FUNNY IS THAT?

צ ח ק

TSeCHoK

Suggestion: See the alphabet chart and Holy Hebrew! Tools
1, 2 and 4 to get the most out of this chapter

As the father of seven children, I'm in a position to make observations about how people react when they meet a baby. Each time my wife Susan gave birth, I'd watch in fascination as family friends dropped by our house to pay a visit and inspect the newest Lapin. If the baby was more than a few weeks old, the visitors invariably set to work trying to make my little daughter or son laugh—clucking her on the chin, laboring to tickle him, and so on. At times, otherwise articulate people sounded quite absurd: "*Koochee-koochee-koo! Koochee-koochee-koo! A-goo! A-goo! Boo-boo-boo-boo-boo-boo! Chucka-chucka-chucka!*"

After our guests departed, Susan and I would also have a go at getting a giggle from our precious newborn. And we would try whatever it took. For a mother or father, few experiences are more satisfying than the first time you hear your child laugh.

Getting an infant to laugh can be quite a challenge, as very young babies have not yet developed the physiological mechanism necessary to produce laughter. But the desire among our visitors to win a giggle was unquenchable. It was almost as if people were reluctant to recognize the new arrival as a real person until they had heard it laugh. Or could they really be seeking validation of themselves by winning a response from the baby? Let's explore why that inaugural giggle is such a triumph for everyone concerned.? A clue is contained in the first instance in the Bible of the Hebrew word for laughter.

ק ח צ

K CH TS

←———

Contrary to what many of us learned as prepubescent Sunday school students, the Hebrew Bible is not a mere storybook or law code but rather a comprehensive instruction manual for achieving maximum human satisfaction and fulfillment. I usually think of the Torah as being the general theory of the totality of all existence. It doesn't prescribe or proscribe behavior and attitudes, but instead describes the sort of behavior and attitudes that are most conducive to lifelong happiness. Like any instruction manual, it defines its terms as it goes along.

When the Bible first presents us with the idea of laughter, it offers a definition of the term. One of the ways in which this is done is through the structure of the language itself.

"He Will Laugh"

The three-letter Hebrew root meaning "to laugh," is tsadi-chet-kuf,

צ ח ק

It first appears in the book of Genesis. There, the son of the patriarch Abraham and matriarch Sarah is born and given the name "Isaac"—in Hebrew, YiTSCHaK,

י ק ח צ

literally "he will laugh"—as a tribute to the laughter induced by Isaac's birth. As Sarah says in naming the boy, "God has made laughter for me; everyone who hears will laugh with me" (Genesis 21:6). After all, Sarah was a ninety-year-old woman when Isaac was born, and there's something deeply amusing—wildly, joyfully out of kilter with the natural order of the world—about such an elderly lady giving birth.

If you are reading a translation of the Hebrew, you won't pick up something of key importance here, but in the original language, just three verses later (21:9) the very same root appears, this time with a much darker meaning. Isaac had a half-brother, Ishmael, born to Abraham by the maidservant Hagar, and Sarah observes Ishmael doing something very naughty indeed. What did he do? The Bible is mysterious about the details. It does note that Sarah saw him being meTSaCHeK.

מ ק ח צ

Most English Bibles correctly attempt a negative connotation for the word and attempt to translate it as "to mock" or "to sport," rather than its correct meaning, "to laugh." Thus, the translation often reads, "And Sarah saw the son of Hagar the Egyptian, whom she had born to Abraham, mocking."

What exactly does this mean? Was the boy making funny

faces or giggling at inappropriate moments? Drop your eye
down just one more verse (21:10) and you will see that Sarah
reacts to this by going nuclear. She insists that her husband
expel Hagar and Ishmael into the desert, which Abraham,
encouraged by God, proceeds to do. A bit of an overreaction
on the part of Sarah, the mother of all monotheists, wouldn't
you say?

That's precisely the question the Bible wants us to ask. Fortunately, Jewish oral tradition—conveyed in the Talmud and
other rabbinic works and as old as the Bible itself—supplies
an answer. The root tsadi-chet-kuf,

$$\text{ק ח צ}$$

K CH TS

means to "to laugh" but that meaning is only a spin-off, a
secondary meaning derived from the primary one, which is
harder to translate.

Basically, when one is TS-CH-K he or she is acknowledging or
committing a rupture of the natural, customary order of the
universe. In other words, the heart of laughter is a violent
contrast with the natural and proper order of things. The
more violent the departure from the natural, the funnier it is.
In regard to the birth of Isaac, Sarah laughs in joy at the miraculous event of an old lady giving birth. There is something
here that defies the expected course of events.

Most laughter we hear each day is in response to this general
pattern. Take slapstick humor, for instance. What happens in
a *Three Stooges* film, when a dignified character like a judge
or an ambassador, slips on a banana peel and falls flat on his

posterior? It's funny, right? It is hilarious only because it is not in the nature of a dignified, pompous individual to slip on a banana peel and wind up on his fanny on the sidewalk.

But what if you see a drunken hobo slip and fall? That's not nearly as funny, partly because we feel bad for the poor fellow, but also because it is indeed in the nature of drunken hobos to stumble to the ground. Puns make us laugh because a word is used differently from how we would expect. In successful jokes, the punch line delivers something totally unexpected; a joke falls flat when we can guess the ending. Laughter is one way of responding to something that conflicts with our expectations.

When the Book of Genesis tells us that Ishmael was miT-SaCHeK, it means that he was committing evils much greater than just making fun of his little brother. He was acting in a

Laughter is a defining mark of humanity.

way that utterly violated the moral rules by which Abraham and Sarah lived. In that sense, I suppose you could say he was mocking his father and adopted mother. Without knowing this principle of laughter, we would have assumed he was merely engaging in boyish pranks and that Sarah's reaction verged on the insane or spiteful, which is unthinkable from the Bible's own viewpoint. But that is not what happened at all.

The traditional understanding of this episode, supplied by the midrash (an ancient compilation of ancient Jewish wisdom), is that Sarah had spotted Ishmael committing the three cardinal sins: idol worship, immoral sexual behavior, and murder. So antithetical are these to a mono-theistic worldview that only the strongest reaction was possible. As the first Jewish mother, Sarah realized the need to prevent her son from being exposed to the slightest indication that these crimes were normative. Any other sin might be pardoned, but not these for they stand in direct opposition to God's order for humans. Therefore Sarah had to insist upon the expulsion of Ishmael from the family home.

And this, you ask incredulously, is the Bible's idea of humor? Of course not. TS-CH-K doesn't mean "humor" precisely. Instead, as I said earlier, the meaning is better described as an outrageous rupturing of fundamental norms. Such a rupture can be outrageously good or outrageously bad. Either way, what result is TS-CH-K, typically taking the form of laughter.

Virtually all forms of laughter spring from this violation of norms. When schoolboys furtively giggle about some bodily function or a sexual innuendo, their laughter reveals that, deep down, they understand these matters are meant to remain private. If those same jokes are moved from the suburban playground to the state penitentiary, we wouldn't be surprised if nobody laughs at them. Those comparatively innocent jokes just aren't funny to human beings for whom few rules apply. They laugh, when they do laugh, about things that violate their imprisoning world—matters that most of us wouldn't even find funny. That is also why there are categories of humor that are industry-specific and occupation-specific. There are jokes that only doctors find funny, for instance. Lay folks like us are unaware of the principles that the medical joke is violating.

It's Only Humans Who Laugh

To understand why a baby's first laugh is so precious, we must make one further observation. Laughing hyenas to the contrary, human beings are the only creatures on this planet who laugh. (Hyenas don't really laugh, of course. Their bark only *sounds* like laughter.) To be sure, dogs and other pets experience pleasure while eating or being petted. But they don't laugh. How could they? Laughter is a defining mark of humanity because only humans understand that there are norms in the universe. For that reason, we humans are the source of all laughter in the world.

When a baby is born, everyone coos and oohs and aahs and tells the parents what a beauty the child is. And to its mother, every baby is indescribably beautiful. To be honest, I must say that I consider most brand-new babies to be pretty funny looking. With their disproportionately large heads and rounded features they look more like Mickey Mouse than anything else. For the most part, all they do is eat, sleep, and defecate. Just think about it. Most newborns are limited in their range of activities to animalistic functions. When a baby laughs for the first time, long before he or she ever speaks, we are overjoyed, for the child has expressed a profoundly human uniqueness.

Laughter and God's Judgment

Not for nothing is laughter, TSeCHoK, associated with the Jewish New-Year festival, *Rosh Hashanah*. On that day, God sits in judgment over the world, portioning out the rewards and punishments as will occur in the coming year. That

sounds pretty solemn, even scary, doesn't it? Actually, fear
is not at all the mood of this festival, which is also called
Yom haDin, the "Day of Judgment." On the contrary, we re-
joice on *Rosh Hashanah*, a fact underlined by the Biblical
readings for the day which include the story of Isaac's birth
with all its accompanying merriment. The holiday is also distinguished by the repeated blowing of a ram's horn, a *sho-
far*, which interestingly enough is meant to sound both like
laughter and crying.

In fact, both of these emotions serve as emotional releases,
and both may result in tears running down the face. Surely
I'm not the only parent to have dashed into the children's
bedroom upon hearing wailing, only to find out that the
noise was not crying but hysterical laughter. On the "Day of
Judgment," our highly imperfect lives are viewed in the light
of God's very demanding expectations of us. The contrast
between what we should be and what we are is so great
that *Rosh HaShanah* becomes the ultimate occasion for
TSeCHoK, or laughter.

In that contrast, however, is our very salvation. Laughter
makes us human. It affirms that we are not mere animals but
creatures of an all-knowing, all-loving Deity. We are created
by Him and thus given a supernatural, transcendent structure of normative values to guide us in life. But the Deity
who gave us these rules by which to live, also endowed us
with the humanity that causes us to stumble and fail through
the course of the year. *Rosh Hashanah* is a joyful holiday because we are aware that God, even when judging us, accepts
our human failings and is eager for us to request another
chance, another year of life in which to improve.

Without humor and laughter, it would be easy to over-
look the contrast between what is and what should be.
That would condemn us to spiritual stagnation—a terrible
prospect!

Laughter and Intimacy

It's not surprising that another function of laughter is to create among men and women a sense of commonality—of
community and intimacy. As human beings, we yearn for and
thrive upon connection with one another. Laughter binds us
in our common humanity and distinguishes us from other
creatures, most of which lack the gift of community. Just
think how you feel when sharing a great laugh with others.
Don't you feel a moment of genuine closeness?

Laughter, TSeCHoK, joins people in all manner of ways, including some unexpected ones. One of the surprising ways
in which laughter helps to bond people is actually alluded to
in the spelling of our word for laughter: tsadi-chet-kuf.

kuf chet tsadi

In Hebrew, the letter tsadi exhibits an intriguing relationship
with another letter in the Hebrew alphabet, shin.

shin   tsadi

The shin can be pronounced both like the sound "sh," or like
our English letter "s." In the latter case, the same letter is not
called "shin" but it is called "sin."

Here we need to discuss one of Hebrew's amazing properties. Certain letters in Hebrew have 'partnerships' with other letters. Frequently, replacing one of the letters with its 'partner' helps us understand both words. In this case, the idea suggested by words beginning with the letter tsadi frequently lead to, or brings about conditions designated by an almost identical word, except that the second word begins with the letter shin or sin.

Needless to say, you won't find any such relationship between letters in English, or in any other tongue besides Hebrew. It is really rather remarkable. It would be like suggesting that English words that begin with a *p* typically designate conditions that lead to other words that sound the same but start with a *b*. As if by any logic at all, "patting" would lead to "batting," or "wishing" to "fishing." Looking in other languages for complex patterns of the kind one regularly detects in Hebrew is a hopeless time waster. But in Hebrew, profound lessons emerge from the exercise, giving us great insight into laughter.

I said earlier that TSeCHoK has the ability to bond people in unexpected ways. One of the most profound ways in which people unite with one another is, of course, sexually. Sometimes Hebrew euphemistically refers to this form of bonding using the word SeCHoK, literally "playfulness" which, according to the last rule I mentioned, follows right after the word for laughter, TSeCHoK, on account of their respective first letters.

Does TSeCHoK lead to SeCHoK—"laugher" to "sex"? You bet it does. Just watch the local Don Juan attempting a

seduction. Does he corner his quarry and beguile her with
a learned discourse on the depressing thoughts of German
philosophers like Schopenhauer and Hegel? Of course not.
He intuitively knows he must make her giggle and laugh.

You see, Biblical teaching doesn't limit itself to prohibiting
incest or commanding Temple sacrifices. Actually, its counsel encompasses the whole range of human activity, including sex. And on that vital topic, we are notified that if you
want to keep sex out of the picture—or instance, if a man
happens to be dealing with a woman to whom he is not married—he'd better keep the discussion serious rather than
humorous. Humor invites intimacy. Many well-known executives and politicians would have spent less time in the news
had they recognized that playfulness with women leads to
intimacy. Many a teen-age girl has learned to her detriment
that excessive joking with male friends caused them to think
of her in less respectful, even explicitly sexual, terms.

Make Her Laugh!

On the positive side, when courting a woman, make her
laugh! I remember advising a friend who had a long-stand-
ing but off-again-on-again relationship with a young woman.
He could have married her years before, but he kept getting
cold feet. Each time his feet froze, he would terminate their
relationship. Finally, at long last, the resolution to propose
matrimony crystallized in his mind. He decided to act. It was
a long shot, for the two of them hadn't spoken in almost ten
months, but he wanted to burst into her life and sweep her
off her feet forever.

My less-than-optimistic advice to him: Rather than make
your avowal with some solemn declaration of love and devotion, do something loving but playful. In any event, engage
her emotions; make her react to you with joy and laughter!
When he reported back to me that his attempt at eliciting a
giggle or a smile from her had failed, I knew that the girl was
not going to accept him. Poor, indecisive lad. In the end, the
joke was on him. But in a postscript I can tell you that he did
eventually learn to laugh and to make others laugh. Today he
is happily married.

Laughter Also Brings Groups Together

Thus we see that TSeCHoK, in relationship to its derivative
word SeCHoK, can bring individuals together. Similarly, the
same concepts and principles can link groups together.

Few activities can as quickly enhance a group's sense of common bond as laughter. I generally don't enjoy art-house movies, especially "artistic" comedies from overseas, which to me
tend not to be very funny at all. But the art-house audiences
always intrigue me. I've sat through some painfully unfunny
French farces, stony-faced myself, while the very cosmopolitan crowd of New Yorkers or Los Angelinos on all sides of
me burst out in wild laughter every couple of minutes. If
closely listened to, the laughter, however uproarious, lacked
the subtle qualities you hear in genuine, unforced laughter. It
just didn't sound *real*. And it wasn't: The movie wasn't funny
enough to merit genuine laughter. But the crowd laughed
anyway because, through laughter, the audience affirmed its
place in a wide community: the community of people sophisticated enough to enjoy a worldly, cosmopolitan foreign-

language film at a New York art-house theater.

These big-city sophisticates would be appalled to learn that they have a lot in common with much humbler folk who enjoy TV sitcoms. For decades (though less so recently) sitcoms were punctuated by bursts of repetitive hilarity from obviously canned laugh tracks. Why didn't the producers of 1970 staples like *Happy Days* or *The Mary Tyler Moore Show* simply broadcast their shows and let home viewers supply all the laughs themselves? Because that's not the way humans operate. We prefer to laugh in a community with other people who are also laughing. Sitting in our living rooms, we actually find a sitcom *funnier* if we hear other people laughing at the jokes. And we find ourselves more drawn to the show and later feel that we enjoyed it more. We felt more joined to other people by laughing together with others, even though their laughter was contrived by the producers. Laughter is so powerful a bonding agent that the artificiality of canned laughter barely diminishes its effectiveness.

Though all this may sound rather cynical or condescending, in fact laughter joins people in other, much more noble contexts as well. Most of the greatest rabbis of the Talmud, for instance, were jovial. Before starting a *shiur* (a learned discourse on some legal or theological topic) it was a common custom first for the rabbis to make their audiences laugh. Learning is best done not in isolation from other people, but intimately bonded together with them. A good joke would get the learning off to a fine start. Great leaders like Churchill, Lincoln and Reagan all had the ability to unify an audience with them through humor—not the harmful type that hurts and pushes people away from each other and God, but the positive, self-deprecating variety that binds people together through sharing an exclusively human experience—laughing together. And unlike the makers of French art-house "comedies," these great communicators didn't have to strain for it.

As we've already observed, laughter depends on a structure of values that transcends our lives and gives them meaning. In the absence of such a structure, laughter fades and dies—which is why nihilistic, atheist regimes like that of the old Soviet Union tend to be humorless. Without God to provide a structure as to what is right and wrong, we cannot be sure whether something is a departure from the norm. What was funny yesterday may land you in jail today. In contrast, genuine holy men are often found with a smile or a laugh on their lips. Beware of a person who wants to teach you about God but is grim and humorless!

And should you ever find yourself doubting Him, that He exists and that He loves us, the best proof that your doubts are unfounded is not the complicated theoretical proof in which theologians delight. It is, instead, the smile and laughter on the face of a newborn baby, and the joy it provokes in all who see it.

PART TWO

FAMILY AND CHILDREN

Chapters 6–10

Be sure to check out pages 337–342
to discover helpful resources on this topic

CHAPTER 6

EDUCATED HANDS

יֶלֶד

YeLeD

Suggestion: See the alphabet chart and Holy Hebrew! Tools
1, 2, 3, 4, 6 and 7 to get the most out of this chapter.

"**R**abbi, my business partner has a son who is a patient in
the West Los Angeles Medical Center. Do you think you
might be able to visit him today?"

Although I don't want to sound heartless, my response to
this type of request was usually negative. Being the rabbi
of a large and busy congregation, I felt that members had
a priority claim on my time. It simply was not possible to
minister to those who were merely friends and associates
of our members and maintain an adequate level of service
to the members themselves. This I could best do by making
certain services available only to those who had "paid their
dues," as it were, by formally affiliating themselves with the
community.

But the request to visit his partner's son on that busy Friday came from someone who was not only a member of my
synagogue but also a respected and close friend. Fortunately
I realized that this was not the time to be hostage to my own
impersonal policy. Anthony was a Los Angeles investment

manager and a leader of our community. He not only knew my policies in these matters, but he had helped me formulate them several years earlier. Surely he had a good reason for his request. So I assured him I would visit young Roger Levin and headed out to my car.

As soon as Los Angeles traffic allowed, I found myself at the gleaming hospital tower and was directed to the patient's bedside. The first thing that struck me was how very thin Roger seemed. I guessed his age at about twenty and found myself charmed by his eyes. They were bright and sparkling and appeared to have a permanent smile implanted in them.

I introduced myself, and to convert what might have become a slightly awkward exchange into a conversation, I asked him whether he knew that Hebrew was the Lord's language. It turned out that he knew very little about his faith or its language, but he was inquisitive about what I meant.

"Well, to quote Sir William Bradford, second governor of the Plymouth colony, 'Hebrew is the language in which God spoke to the patriarchs of old'," I explained. "More than merely a medium of communication between man and man like most languages, Hebrew is also one of the means of transmission between God and man. It thus conceals within its structure many of the secrets that a benevolent Deity wanted us to know."

His eyes brightened still more and he asked for some examples which I provided, and which I later wrote down for this very volume. After we had grown comfortable with one another, Roger told me the reason for his hospitalization.

It turned out that he suffered from a gastric problem that diminished his ability to eat and digest food. This malady was complicated by undiagnosed psychological and stress-related factors. He asked me what the Lord's language might reveal about his disease. I shared a few Biblical insights and we spoke for many hours.

> **The cultural message that is beamed into our homes is that children must go their own way.**

Sooner than I wished, I could see the sun starting to set into the Pacific Ocean. This signaled the imminent arrival of the Sabbath, so I took my leave and rushed home.

I returned to Roger's bedside several times over the next few weeks. On each occasion we lost ourselves for hours as we meandered along the byways of the Hebrew language.

After his discharge from hospital, Roger became an active member of my congregation and experienced dramatic improvement in his medical condition. Now this in itself was not uncommon. Public health statistics tell us that people who are members of a religious group and enjoy close relationships with family and friends experience better health and more rapid recoveries. However, Roger's progress was even more exciting. He was soon completely healed and attributed most of his "miraculous cure" to something he learned from the Lord's language.

When I first met Roger he was pursuing a career in art, although his father enjoyed considerable success in the world of finance. He confessed to me that he had never felt passionate about art. He did not wake up each morning yearning to return to his creative endeavors. It became clear that despite being extremely close to his parents, he had embarked on an artistic career chiefly to make his own mark in a field different from that in which his father had achieved prominence. In this his parents had encouraged him, because they too felt that he ought to find his own area in which he could develop without being overshadowed by his father. It was then that his disease struck. The further Roger progressed in his artistic pursuits, the more debilitating his illness became.

Joining the Family Enterprise

Roger Levin's doctors finally ran out of treatments, and the only remaining medical option was serious surgery. The family consulted with me, and I recommended they try one rather radical idea before agreeing to a major operation: I suggested that Roger take a leave of absence from art school and join his father in the family finance business.

Roger's dad, Abraham Levin, was uneasy at this suggestion. He was reluctant to appear to be pushing his son into his business. He had always been disdainful of parents who try to relive their lives through their children's accomplishments and considered it a virtue for parents to encourage complete independence in their children. But in spite of his misgivings, Abraham confessed that he could really use the help of a trusted assistant and would certainly enjoy spending time with his son. I detected that he was considering the plan.

We have all seen parents who bully their sons into some preferred career or who nurture unrealistic ambitions for their
daughters. In many cases, parents err by insensitively ignoring their child's true nature. And it is true that many parents
force their children into roles that satisfy the parents' needs
but do nothing to fulfill the latent talents and ambitions of
the children. But it is equally true that many parents, fear-
ing the accusation that they are trying to relive their lives
through their children, drive their children away from a lifetime affiliation for which both parents and children really
yearn. Many a family business has ended up on the auction
block because the entrepreneur's children were unnecessarily discouraged from joining the family enterprise.

Abraham Levin agreed that there was little to lose by the
experiment and invited Roger to join his business. On the
surface, success seemed improbable. After all, what connection was there between art and business? How could a free-
spirited artist who had been trained to respect spontaneous and sometimes unfocused creativity adapt to a world of
numbers and deadlines driven by very real considerations
of profit and loss? I recommended that Abraham and Roger
view the learning process as a father-son project. Pretty soon
they started enjoying their time together at the office, and
Roger prospered as he caught on to the business. Indeed,
many of Abraham's clients preferred working with the sensitive young man with the impish sense of humor rather than
with his more driven and business-like father.

Roger never went back to art school. He and Abraham later
opened their own boutique investment company and Roger
experienced a full recovery without surgery.

What aspect of the Lord's language persuaded the Levin family to try these changes?

Even as a child, Roger was devoted to his parents. When he became an art student, it was largely because he sensed that this was what his parents wanted him to do. He was, unknowingly, acting out the meaning of the Hebrew word for child, YeLeD. This word is made up of the two letters Yud and Dalet (sounds Y and D) with the letter Lamed (sound of L) inserted between them.

ד ל י

D L Y

Now, the letters Yud and Dalet spell another Hebrew word meaning "hand." And the letter lamed, possesses its own meaning: "teach/learn."

Placing this lamed (teach/learn) inside the word for hand, explains an essence of the word "child." In one way, a child is similar to a hand that has been programmed or taught what to do.

In what way is a child like an educated hand? The hand is the organ we chiefly use to convey the things we either need or desire, from the world to our body. Whether food, drink, a book, or our paycheck, almost everything we acquire comes to us through the agency of our hands.

Many of the phrases we use in English—as well as in many other tongues—confirm our understanding of the hand as a symbol of reaching into the world around us. These phrases include "hand it to me," "it came into my hands," "I have the papers in hand," "lend me a hand," and "give him a handout."

Agents of the World's Benefits

Similarly, as our children grow, they too become agents through whom some of the benefits of our world can reach us. One of these benefits, for instance, is that our own social circles often expand as our children expand theirs. We meet their schoolteachers, we often become friendly with the parents of their playmates, and later we might encounter their workplace acquaintances. These new friends add to our lives socially and, perhaps—if we end up doing business with them—even economically.

During earlier times, nations and countries often found peace and prosperity by uniting with one another through the intermarriage of their royal families and aristocracies. Today too, many families enhance the quality of their lives by the marriages entered into by their children. Happiness can come from these enlarged and extended families. Family gatherings for religious or national holidays, or family celebrations such as birthdays and anniversaries are now large, boisterous, and joyful. When sad times strike, there are more loving family members to provide support and share the pain.

Also, in earlier times parents often depended upon their grown children for their very lives. The unspoken social compact called upon parents to raise their children, while in return, during the parents' old age, those children would care for them. Back then it was perfectly clear that children were literally their parents' hands. The adult children did all that those original hands were now too weary to accomplish for themselves.

Today it is easy to mistakenly suppose that government-provided Social Security and private investments such as Individual Retirement Accounts render this old social compact obsolete. It may appear that we no longer have need for our children to ease our later years. Nothing could be further from the truth. No government Social Security check can provide the emotional gratification of children. No investment portfolio can offer the spontaneous surge of joy that older couples enjoy when their grandchildren bounce through the front door. What is more those government checks do not come from some vast accumulation of wealth. They are paid, month by month, out of the paychecks that are earned by our children and by the children of our friends and fellow citizens.

Perhaps you have investments. What do you think might happen to the value of the underlying companies if our children suddenly ceased working for them, earning pay and purchasing their products? No, that old social compact is far from dead. It is alive and well. We still depend upon children in the twenty-first century as much as we did in the eighteenth. The next generation is most surely "our hands," helping provide our bodies and our very selves all those benefits that life offers and which we so ardently desire.

There is another way we can see the link between child and hand in addition to the Hebrew word for child, YeLeD, meaning "educated and programmed hand." A second word in the Lord's language unites one of our limbs with our offspring. The Hebrew word for "sperm" or "seed" is ZeRA. It is the word often used in the Hebrew Bible when referring to children. Interestingly, the word also means "arm" which is pronounced ZeRoA.

ז ר ע

A   R   Z

seed

ז ר ו ע

A   R   Z

arm

You can see the words for arm and hand used in the same place when the Bible tells us, "God took you (the children of Israel) from there (Egypt) with a strong hand, (YaD) and an outstretched arm (ZeRoA)" (Deut. 5:15). The three root letters, ZRA, of both arm and seed/children are identical. Once again the Lord's language clarifies that children and parents both benefit when the hand/arm metaphor is observed.

It always amazes me that many wealthy philanthropists create charitable foundations that they then staff with complete strangers. They frequently suffer aggravation while trying to educate total strangers about their values and charitable priorities. Meanwhile these complete strangers proceed to disburse their employer's wealth with which they were entrusted, often to causes hostile to the philanthropist's true beliefs. Appoint your own children, I urge them. Who is better equipped to intuitively know what you would think of a particular cause than a child whom you yourself raised?

Your Arms and Your Hands

See your children as your arms and your hands. I recognize that this is not good advice for every parent and for every child. But it is worth at least considering. The cultural message that is beamed into our homes is that children must go their own way. Many will do just that, but many children will thrive if that cultural message is overturned. Many families will bloom if children are invited to become real hands and raised in a way that prepares them for that role.

While growing children certainly want their parents to recognize them as independent people, they also enjoy being considered as "hands." Just watch how that little girl dresses herself in imitation of her mother's sense of fashion. See her beg to be allowed to help bake that cake. She wants to be seen as a member of the team. She wants to be linked to her mother. That is why she imitates her mom and loves to help her. Dads, if you are handy around the home, try giving your young son his own toolbox. Or better yet, earnestly enlist his assistance on some home maintenance project. Even though his help will undoubtedly complicate what may have been a simple task, invite him to participate with you. Be sure to ask for his help in a way that conveys your genuine need for "another hand." Do it right, and he will leap forward with unrestrained enthusiasm.

Should you be fortunate enough to own a family business, go ahead and feel free to invite your son or your daughter to join that business. Don't worry; if they don't wish to do so, they will decline. When inviting a child to become part of your enterprise, avoid sounding like a monarch bestowing a favor on a lucky serf. Nobody feels uplifted by receiving charity. Invite him into your business in the way someone with a paralyzed arm might beseech his limb back into service: "I need your help" is the magic phrase. That is exactly how Abraham Levin invited his son Roger into his business.

With the sun plunging toward the Pacific Ocean that Friday afternoon, I raced homeward to change for the Sabbath and to walk down to my synagogue on the Venice beachfront. During the evening service I noticed an elegant gentleman accompanied by an attractive woman whom I had never before seen in synagogue. All of a sudden it dawned on me. Roger must have told his parents of our encounter in his hospital ward. They might have decided to attend Sabbath services in my synagogue in order to see just who their son had befriended. Following the conclusion of the worship service, I walked over to the striking-looking couple and took a chance: "Good evening, Mr. and Mrs. Levin and *Shabbat shalom* to you both."

"Good evening, Rabbi Lapin. Thank you for visiting our son today," they responded.

I explained that my wife would be delighted if they would join us for Sabbath dinner, an invitation they accepted. Today I often find myself thinking back to that long-ago Friday afternoon I spent with Roger in the hospital. It changed his life, but it also changed mine. Not only did it help teach me the power of the Lord's language, but it introduced me to some remarkable people. Roger and his parents all became close family friends. In fact, much later, when my wife and I needed some advice and help with one of our children, it was they who offered a YaD, a hand, to us.

CHAPTER 7

A PLACE OF GRACE

שלחן

SHuL-CHaN

Suggestion: See the alphabet chart and Holy Hebrew! Tools 1, 2, and 6 to get the most out of this chapter.

My bride and I had been married for only a few weeks when we decided the time had come to shop for some furniture. Maybe a mattress on the floor was sufficient for college students, but this rabbi intended to buy his young wife a real bedroom set.

"No," my bride insisted. "If we are serious about building a home, there is another piece of furniture I would like us to buy first."

I was baffled, but only for a few moments before it struck me. Of course! A dining table! A real dining table, not that plastic-coated card table at which we had been sharing our meals since our wedding.

We began scouring the classified advertisements to find a second-hand, large, old-fashioned table. We shared a hearty contempt for the modern ones we saw in the showrooms. They had long, thin, spindly legs and looked fragile, rather like a newborn colt. They were highly polished wood, clearly intended for show; they looked sterile. We wanted a real table, one built to accommodate large groups eating hearty meals.

The two of us also shared an almost mystical conviction that inanimate objects could acquire a kind of spiritual patina that reflects the use to which they are put. A table around which a family had enjoyed many years of warm-hearted meals would surely reveal its history with, well, an almost happy kind of look.

Realtors often relate to this ability of things to reveal their history to sensitive people. They have told me of home-buying couples who would eagerly view a prospective new home. Occasionally, shortly after entering a perfectly delight-ful house, the wife—and it is nearly always the wife—will appear to lose interest. Inexperienced realtors will then try to lure the wife into the kitchen to try to reignite her enthu-siasm. Invariably this strategy fails. More experienced real-tors learn to live with this phenomenon. It is, they explain to me, the woman's intuition telling her that the house "just doesn't feel right," and this objection is quite impossible to overcome.

Yes, I am quite certain that most women and very sensi-tive men can often "feel" the problems and the pain that might have been experienced by earlier occupants of a home. In earlier days we might have spoken of the house feeling "haunted." Conversely, some people can also feel the joy from earlier times radiating from the very walls and windows of a home.

So, my wife and I reasoned, if this was a factor with a home, then why not with a dining table? We wanted to acquire a table with a happy history.

We began each weekend by looking through the classifieds in the local newspaper. One Sunday we spotted an appealing ad and, after a quick phone call, we headed out to an address in Pasadena. As we were ushered into her lovely house by an elderly woman, we saw it—a very large, solid looking table made of great slabs of oak. There was nothing spindly about this table. It was solid and substantive.

The widow showing it to us was leaving the now empty family home and moving to a small apartment. "There's no way the movers will be able to get this table through the front door of my new apartment," she confided.

My bride and I glanced at one another. Yes! We could both feel it! Holding our breaths, we asked the woman how long she had owned the table.

"Why, my late husband's parents gave it to us when we got married just after the war," she said. It turned out that she and her husband had raised seven children in that home. The one family ritual they had observed every evening was the family dinner around this very table. With that bit of information, we could hardly conceal our glee. We had found our table.

Subjects Not Objects

Why do we consider the time a family spends around the dining table more valuable and memorable than the same amount of time gathered around the television? One reason is that we humans find it much more fulfilling to be subjects rather than objects. We feel much more alive and more passionate when we are doing things and we feel anaesthetized by just having things done to us.

Don't you find it more exciting to paint pictures than to merely visit an art gallery? Isn't it more memorable to play a game than to simply watch one? Most of us would rather have a friendly conversation with someone than listen to a lecture, for in conversation we are active participants. As part of the audience at a lecture, we are passive. We are being acted upon, as it were.

Likewise, watching television is a passive experience. The television is acting upon us; we are actually doing very little other than allowing the tube to inform or entertain us. What is more, even if we watch television in a room filled with other people, it remains fundamentally a lonely experience. It is just you and the television. One of the reasons for the popularity of comedy is that the laughter links you with the others watching. It is a reminder that you are not alone.

Unlike watching television, however, enjoying a dinner with family and friends is both an active experience and a bonding experience. You participate, and you know you are not alone.

Place of Grace

The Hebrew word for table is SHuL-CHaN.

$$שׁ \ ל \ ח \ ן$$

N   CH   L   SH

Instead of the more common three-letter root, this particular word contains two two-letter roots and could be read as SHeL-CHeN.

What does SHeL-CHeN mean? It literally means "of CHeN" or "belonging to CHeN." Well, what does CHeN mean and why should my dinner table be its place? When the word CHeN appears in the prayer book or the Bible it is usually translated as "grace."

Grace is one of those words we all use but would be hard pressed to define. Interestingly, before World War II, the Oxford English Dictionary gave the definition of the word 'grace' as the word that the King James Bible chose to represent the Hebrew חֵן. Looking more closely, the Hebrew root of the word CHeN is used in two instances in the Bible. The first of these is when someone in the Bible camps or rests in one place for a while, and the second describes human interaction that generates economic creativity.

Economic Creativity

How do these two apparently unrelated themes of camping out for a while and creative economic interactions merge into one basic idea? Easy! Do you recall the old expression, "A rolling stone gathers no moss?" It means that someone who is always relocating will find it difficult to accumulate any assets. In order to create wealth, transactions must occur. And for economic creativity to take place, the participants must be together long enough to allow those interactions that are a prerequisite for transactions to occur.

For the most part, itinerant people find it difficult to earn a living. To be a sought-after employee, one must stop in one place long enough to acquire a reputation for skill and integrity and to allow word of those qualities to spread. Businesses often tout phrases such as "established 1982" or "in business for over 50 years" as a way to highlight their trustworthiness. Even, or maybe especially, as online transactions grow, we look to do business with companies with a well-known reputation. We want to be sure we are giving our money to a company that will be there down the road if we have a problem rather than with a fly-by-night, take your money and run enterprise.

Ask an airport shoeshine entrepreneur why he polishes travelers' shoes. He might reply, looking at you as if you were rather dull-witted, "I do it in order to put food on my table." Reducing life to its basics, there is really no difference between his reasoning and that of the majority of the world's workers, whether they toil in the boardroom or in the fields. The "table" is the symbolic repository of the results of our economic exertions. In other words, a table really is "of CHeN" or the place of CHeN. A table is where we can see and enjoy the benefit of remaining in one place long enough to build the relationships that allow food to be placed on that table.

So linked is the table to economic creativity and prosperity that the Temple in Jerusalem contained a most important object—a table. Upon this table rested special loaves of bread. An old rabbinic tradition advised anyone desiring an increase in the ability to earn money to worship facing that table. The table was a wellspring of economic abundance. One was praying to God, but facing the loaves of bread in

His House served to reinforce awareness of God's overflowing bounty and remind the worshipper that his business life and spiritual life were interconnected. One's business life needed to be based on God's rules just as one's personal or spiritual life did, and God is as interested in our economic well-being as He is in all other areas of our existence.

Family Stability

The connection of the table to economic creativity and prosperity is one to which I personally relate. A very ancient Jewish tradition informs us that after the Jerusalem Temple was destroyed by the Romans about two millennia ago, the function of the holy altar was taken over by the dinner table in every home. My own ability to return to work and put my shoulder to the wheel is enormously enhanced by the feeling of family unity which follows our sharing a meal. My life is too hectic and the professional demands on me too high to guarantee my joining the family meal around our table each and every evening. However, come what may, each Sabbath we all enjoy a particularly heartwarming Sabbath dinner together. The candlelight reflecting off the bright faces around our table always helps make me more emotionally ready for a week of hard work. Would it be too fanciful to suppose that an entire nation enjoys its greatest economic success if most of its producers enjoy similar family rejuvenation at the table? Recent studies show that the one thing most

> **We eat just as animals eat, but we do so in a uniquely human way.**

successful students have in common with one another is regular family meals. Not access to computers or great wealth, but simply regular, sit-down meals with their families. If so, the dinner table is an appropriate metaphor for family stability and perhaps the most potent tool for achieving it.

Don't Be an Animal

Do you remember your mother forbidding you to rush up to the dinner table and grab some food? Didn't she always insist that you sit at the table until the end of the meal? In other words, she wanted you to "camp" or "rest for a while" at the table. Again we see the table, the SHuL-CHaN, as being the place where we should stop racing and turn every meal into a little oasis in time.

Back when you were a child, you might have expressed youthful indignation at another of your mother's demands. Didn't she want you to wash your hands before coming to the table?

"Aw, Mom, my hands are already clean," was your cry.

"I don't care if they are clean, you still must always wash your hands before coming to the table," she answered. This served to further convince you that most adults were quite mad. This custom of washing hands before a meal is an inheritance from the way that priests would ceremonially wash their hands before approaching the altar. Today we wash our hands before we approach the dinner table. To this very day, the Jewish way of preparing for the dinner table is to wash our hands in the same ceremonial manner as the priests of old. Rather than just holding our hands beneath the faucet, we use a special cup from which we pour water onto each hand. Many Jewish homes today are equipped with beautiful silver or ceramic cups made especially for this purpose.

If your parents were anything like mine, whenever you made some dreadful noise they would respond by requesting that you kindly cease sounding like "an animal." To be told that you were behaving like an animal was a very serious indictment when I was growing up. Not that my family minded animals. In fact, just the opposite was true. We were frequent visitors to zoos and game reserves. It was simply that my parents knew that when people thought they were animals, things fell apart. By remembering that in crucial ways we are quite different from animals, members of a family can be expected to act toward one another with consideration and kindness—conduct mostly alien to the animal world. On the other hand, if enough of us become convinced that we are basically an advanced form of animal, then no reason exists for us not to do exactly as we please, whenever and wherever we please, with whomever we please. People who feel this way are usually tough to get along with.

The dinner table, the SHul-CHaN, can and should be taken very seriously in any home in which family is important. The table serves as a kind of meeting place of the physical and the spiritual—or if you prefer, a meeting place of the animalistic and the Divine. It is where we acknowledge that, yes, we eat just as animals eat, but we do so in a uniquely human way.

Have you ever asked someone to tell you the first word that comes to mind as soon as you say a word?

Psychologists call this little game the "association of ideas" test. Try it out with a few harmless trials. Say "pen" and most people will respond "paper." Say "dog" and you will hear "cat." Now say "table;" most people will immediately say "chair." This is another valuable contribution the dinner table makes to a family. You have to sit at a table in order to most effectively use it. Sitting is a uniquely human posture. When we recline, kneel, crouch, or lie, we are doing something that animals also do. By sitting in a chair, however, we assume a uniquely human attitude.

In this fashion we can again count on the dinner table to help maintain human dignity. Instead of grabbing some nourishment on the run by opening a can and gobbling its contents, we calmly sit down at a table. Though the simple act of eating could be mistaken as merely an animal-like activity, when we sit to eat at a table we are proclaiming our special humanness. To whom are we proclaiming it? Most importantly, to ourselves.

A Place for Enhanced Discussion

It is worth noting that somehow, ideas seem more fertile and more exciting when discussed at the dinner table. Thoughts flow more easily and people seem to listen more attentively during a shared meal than they do at a meeting, for instance. When the ancient Greeks wanted to conduct a serious discussion, they called a symposium. Even someone as serious as Plato would occasionally engage in a symposium. Do you know what the word means? It means a drinking party. Yes, that's right. The very best way to conduct a difficult discussion is around a dinner table arranged with food and drink.

Is it possible that you are more open to my thoughts when
you eat my food? Could this be why business professionals often argue over who will pay for dinner? And could it
be why, even in these egalitarian days, most men on dinner
dates still insist on picking up the restaurant check?

An interesting sidebar of world history illustrates this point.
Many years ago, a brilliant statesman pursued the dream of
a European Economic Community. The father of European
unification, Jean Monet, wanted a building in which meetings between nations could be held. He knew that this
improbable project would take decades to bring to fruition. After all, Europe had been roiled by wars for centuries.
One of those wars lasted a hundred years. Antagonism between France and Germany went back so far that nobody
could even remember when they first fought. Sweden had
contempt for Italy and there were rifts between Spain and
Portugal. The problem was how to get representatives of
these sovereign nations into the same room, let alone forge
an alliance into which each would have to submerge a little
of his precious autonomy.

Monet's subordinates returned with photographs of some
of the largest and most prestigious office towers in Paris. He
gently explained that they had misunderstood him. He did
not want a conspicuous, huge office building in the middle
of the city. He wanted a quiet old mansion somewhere on
the outskirts of town.

"Anything else?" his officials asked.

"Yes," he said, "The one thing my house will need is a great
big dining room—a dining room capable of housing a great

big old dining table." Responding to the startled looks on the
faces of his associates, the statesman explained that any significant steps toward a modern family of nations in Europe
would happen only around a dinner table. People are more
agreeable while they are sharing a meal.

This is, of course, one reason for the business lunch. One
would think that the office would be the best place to
discuss a possible transaction. Yet, experienced business
professionals know that deals work best at meals.This is just
one more example of the magic of the dining table.

A Place to Grow Closer

I may not be capable of advising the world how to achieve
peace, but I do know that the overwhelming majority of
young couples in whose dating life I have been involved
share one important trait. Their acquaintance with one another ripened and their mutual affection grew chiefly during meals they enjoyed as guests in the homes of married
couples. Perhaps the comfortable domesticity of their hosts
penetrated to the very souls of the young men and women
through the food they shared and the table at which they
enjoyed that food.The terrifying prospect of marriage might
have appeared to be a little less frightening and somewhat
more inviting during those times around the dinner table.
So, a word of advice to those stalled in courtships that are
not moving toward the altar as quickly as might be desired:
Forget about those dates spent at a movie. Discard dates that
involve watching sports on television together.They accomplish very little. Instead, try a different approach. Arrange
to be invited, along with the object of your affections, for

a meal at the home of a happily married couple you know. Repeat this treatment periodically.

If you know a young couple with potential, you might consider helping them along the same road that has brought you happiness and fulfillment. Invite them over for dinner. Of course, courting couples should not be the only welcome guests. In the first twenty years of my marriage, I could probably have counted on the fingers of one hand the number of Sabbath meals my family ate with no guests at the table. I would estimate that we have hosted more than 5000 guests at our SHuL-CHaN. Let me clarify. Do not, even for a moment, think that this hospitality is due to saintly, generous, and self-sacrificing motives. You're thinking of the wrong rabbi! Please don't even consider the possibility that we invite friends to join our dinner table in a selfless attempt to alleviate world hunger. No, we invite people to share our family meals because their presence and participation adds to the pleasure of our dining experience. Purchasing a large dining table as young newlyweds was one of the best ideas my beautiful bride ever had.

The look on the face of that charming old lady from whom my bride and I purchased our dining table revealed that she was just as insightful as the European statesman. With a wise smile she promised, "In years to come, that table will be the scene of some of your family's most meaningful and memorable moments just as it was for my family." She was absolutely right!

CHAPTER 8

NATURE OR NURTURE?

הורים

HoRYM

Suggestion: See the alphabet chart and Holy Hebrew! Tools 1, 2, and 3 to get the most out of this chapter.

Not wanting to look a gift horse in the mouth, I was delighted that Charla was applying for work as my secretary. For fear she might change her mind, I engaged her without probing as to why an obviously competent elementary school teacher was willing to come down a notch or two. It quickly became apparent that this was a stroke of good fortune for me.

As we got to know each other a little better over the next few years, Charla's story emerged. A born teacher, she particularly loved teaching the youngest grades. But after a few years she had sadly concluded that within the school system there was little she could do for those in her charge.

What was the problem?

"Rabbi," she said, "into my classroom walked four- and five-year-old children who had never in their lives held a crayon, pencil, or book. They had never had an adult read them a bedtime story. They had spent the entirety of their short lives plopped in front of a TV, neglected by their drug-addicted mothers."

As a teacher responsible for a large class of children, there was simply too little that she could do for them. It broke her heart to watch small lives destroyed almost before they had begun. Charla decided that she could not spend her entire day surrounded by such tragedy; instead, she would volunteer to work with individual children. And so each day after she finished helping me with my work, she headed over to a church run childcare center and tried to be a short-term mother to one child at a time.

Charla's story reminds me of a fascinating fact of life. Many people face unfortunate circumstances in their lives. Some emerge from hopelessness and destruction and build up successful futures, while others become permanently crushed by the same desperate beginnings. What causes the difference between the two groups?

Nature or Nurture

I recall a story of how one girl, after suffering under the vicious communist regime in Cambodia, came to the United States of America. She learned to live, laugh, and feel compassion for others despite the horrors of her childhood. How do we explain this? Why do some people emerge from dysfunctional families to become leaders of their generation, while a sibling may end up repeating the chaos of their parents' destructive lives? How can two siblings respond to adversity in two such different ways? What fills one immigrant with bitterness at rejection and causes him to turn to alcohol and crime, while another in exactly the same circumstances vows to make a success of his life and becomes a successful entrepreneur? American history provides us with a case in point. Think of the Adams family. Two presidents came from that bloodline, but so did alcoholics and wastrels.

Why are these questions so intriguing? I think it is for the same reason that stories of twins separated at birth and later reunited tend to fascinate us. We often discover that they share the most amazing similarities. Perhaps two sisters both married men named Frank and each named their daughter Melissa. Two brothers find that they drink the same unusual beer and both are known in their circle of friends for wearing a hat while everyone else wears baseball caps or goes bareheaded. Twins find that they drive the same car, dress similarly and share food likes and dislikes, although they were brought up in totally different environments. What causes this? When scientists map out a DNA code, where exactly is the gene for Lexus ownership?

What special type of sorrow could raising children and earning a living possibly share?

For parents, these questions are vital. Not because it matters whether my child prefers hamburgers to cottage cheese, but because I yearn to know if my actions and training will impact my son and daughters. Or are they pre-programmed in some mysterious way to be whatever they will be? It is a question about which learned academics and pompous professors argue constantly—the old "nature versus nurture" debate. Am I absolutely vital to my child's development, or did their personalities and characters come into the world with them? When I watched my first child being born, I desperately wanted to know the answer to this question.

No Single Parents

A glance at the Hebrew word for "parents" provides clues with which to solve the mystery. First, we should note that the word is a plural noun. There are many people whom fate thrusts into the unenviable role of single mother or single father. It is important, though, says the Lord's language, to know that there will be extra challenges. Parents, like scissors or pants, only come in a dual reality. There are single mothers and single fathers, but there are no single parents. The Hebrew word doesn't acknowledge that this is a task that any one person can do. A single person can be a very good mother or father, but no single person can parent. That activity demands a man and a woman wedded into a unity and dedicated to the welfare of their children, either natural or adopted.

Archery and Rain

HoRYM, the Hebrew for "parents" (the ym reflects the plural), is related to a number of other Hebrew words. We have the word MoRYM, meaning "teachers." The relationship here seems obvious: Parent and teachers teach us how to live our lives.

But the word for parents, HoRYM, is also related to other words. You can see that HoReH—what the singular of parent would look like if it existed—is very close to the word ToRaH,

God's comprehensive blueprint for our lives. It is also related to another word although the connection is less obvious. This word, YoReH, has two connected meanings which fill in a vital missing piece of the parents puzzle. YoReH can be translated as both an archer and the gentle first rains of the season that allow the newly planted seed to begin to grow.

ם י ר ו ה	–	parents
ה ר ו ה	–	(what the singular would look like)
ה ר ו מ	–	teacher
ה ר ו ת	–	Torah
ה ר ו י	–	archer; a gentle dew

Is the Lord's language perhaps suggesting that in launching a child into life, parents are doing something similar to shooting an arrow? That perhaps our earliest instruction to our children resembles those early rains?

Unlike the English language, in Hebrew we never find one word standing for two completely unrelated things. If I say that I am buying sole so we can have fish for dinner and that I am the sole occupant of a room, you will be wasting your time looking for the common point in the two meanings of the word sole. Not so in Hebrew, where all words sharing root letters are related. So to understand what being a parent means, we need to understand the relationship between parenting and that particular type of rain, as well as its connection to shooting an arrow at a target. That is, the relationship between the word HoRYm and YoreH.

You will recall that early in the Bible God punishes Adam and Eve, and through them all of mankind, for disobeying His word about a tree. Adam is told that from now on he will eat only with ETSaVon, and the same word is used in telling Eve that she will have much ETSaVon in giving birth. (Genesis 3:16-19) What are they being told? A popular mistranslation of that word as "pain" caused some well-intentioned people to decry the use of anesthetic during childbirth, seeing it as a violation of God's will that women should experience pain while giving birth.

Similarly, some translations mistakenly suggest that earning a living is intended to be a painful ordeal. The Hebrew text, however, does not say pain, but rather a very special type of "sorrow." What special type of sorrow could raising children and earning a living possibly share?

No Guarantees

The answer is that neither comes with any guarantee. And this can be very sorrowful. We all know people who put in hours of effort at their jobs, yet fail to see results. In spite of driving themselves relentlessly, the raises and promotions go to others. It does happen. Others work a lifetime only to lose all their assets in a stock market crash or through an act of war. It happens. There is no equation promising that if you put in an eight-hour day, five days a week, and are industrious and responsible, you will never be in need. In exactly the same way, since the days of Adam and Eve, raising children comes with the constant worry that despite all our efforts, things can go wrong. It does happen.

This brings us back to the word HoRYM—parents. Much of

what influences the kind of lives our children will live is beyond our control. Their looks, their intelligence, certain skills and predilections as well as other areas are indeed implanted in them genetically. If they were little racehorses or big breeding bulls, there would be nothing left to add. Their destinies would be set. But they are not animals, they are little humans, and they are our children. They can overcome much of genetic predetermination. If both parents are below average height, that little guy is going to have to work ten times harder to succeed at basketball. It will be a challenge, but not impossible. If, on the other hand, that tone-deaf little girl wants to become an orchestra conductor, she may be well advised to seek an alternative dream. But maybe not. I certainly don't know the limitations of her Divine potential. A little boy built like a refrigerator who wants to become a ballet dancer? Well, who am I to determine his chances? He is a human with infinite capacity built into him. I'd say his chances depend mostly on the grit, determination, and confidence his parents instill in him.

How about those examples of siblings from the same parents who reacted so differently to adversity? Why do some grow one way while others grow differently? Why do some plants grow red flowers while others grow yellow? Well, they were different seeds to begin with.

But there is another far more important reason why different children in the same family grow up so differently. Unforeseen incidents, unexpected opportunities, and unwanted setbacks will occur throughout children's lives and will affect how their lives turn out. But how they react to those events depends mostly on how good a job their parents did. Which brings us to one of the most crucial and difficult challenges facing parents.

Learning the Right Instincts

Parents tend to raise their children in much the same way that an assembly line worker adjusts a bolt on the chassis that rapidly glides by him. That is to say, parents tend to raise each child in their family in much the same way. This is certainly not due to any laziness or indifference. It is just that raising children is such a full-time challenge that when some event occurs that calls for a parental response, that response is usually instinctive. It is a bit like learning karate or judo. Why spend those long days practicing? Why not just take the book home and study the moves? Well, you know the answer. Events happen in rapid succession during combat. When your assailant grabs you by the throat, there is simply no time to quietly reflect upon the response recommended in your little karate study guide. By the time you recollect the appropriate chapter, events will have taken a turn for the worse. Well, raising children is a lot like combat. We become trained to react almost instinctively.

Most parents apply their instinctive responses in the same way to each of their children. That is a bad idea. One of the most difficult and most crucial challenges of parenting is to apply guidance in a way that is appropriate to the particular child in question. One sibling may need more flexibility while another may require swift and certain discipline. How incredibly demanding it is to restrain our instincts and carefully administer exactly the parenting that each particular child really needs. But how rewarding it is when one succeeds at this task. One reason parenting needs both a father and mother is that they can later "post mortem" one another's instinctive responses from earlier in the day, helping one another to gradually acquire the correct instinctive responses for each of their children.

This brings us back to the rains and the arrows. Maybe the rain does fall equally upon each seed, but no archer shoots all his arrows identically. Different arrows have different weights; may have different guiding feathers; may be intended for different targets; and wind conditions will be different for each shot. The wise archer handles each arrow in the unique way its mission demands.

Our role as parents is great. HoRYM serve as both the launching pad and the guide for their offspring, their arrows. Starting in pregnancy (which shares a Hebrew root with HoRYM as well), a mother can either sabotage the precious seed implanted in her or she can nurture it gently and carefully. After the birth of their child, HoRYM—like the archer—can shoot powerfully and straight or, like the mothers of Charla's pupils, leave the arrow to dangle limply from the bow, most likely to fall to the ground.

We did not construct the arrows to our specifications. Nor can we control the winds that might set the arrow off course once it is shot. But it is within our power to do much with what we have been blessed. The fact remains that there is no guarantee. This should encourage us to turn in prayer to God every day. We have no choice but to acknowledge our dependence on Him to protect and guide our children. We can, to the best of our abilities, follow His guidebook and pray that the gentle rain will fall on fertile ground.

CHAPTER 9

TWICE AS MANY SISTERS

אח אחות בן בת
BaT BeN ACHOT ACH

Suggestion: See the alphabet chart and Holy Hebrew! Tools 1, 2, and 3 to get the most out of this chapter.

W hen he was younger, my son Aryeh occasionally—not more than ten times a day—used to complain that he had too many sisters. When a choice for a family video was put to the vote, he routinely lost. Movies based on Jane Austen books garnered his six sisters' votes, while his lone dissenting voice gathered no support. And whenever there was heavy lifting to do, it fell on his shoulders.

To make matters worse, as Aryeh grew more proficient in Hebrew, he had a rude shock. As if six sisters weren't enough, the Hebrew language suggests that he actually has at least twelve. What do I mean?

Hebrew is an almost mathematical system of language, with reliable rules. Unlike English, it seldom baffles the eager student with inexplicable contortions. As in many languages, (though not in English) nouns are treated as either male or female. Male gender nouns usually convert easily and reliably to female gender nouns by acquiring an "ah" sound as a suffix. Some examples might be navi, a prophet;

neviAH, a prophetess; par, a bull; and parAH, a cow. Since the Hebrew word for brother is ach, one would expect the word for sister to be achAH. But it isn't. Rather than adding an "ah" sound, the word for sister is made by adding on the standard *plural* feminine ending, 'OT', giving us the word for sister; ACHOT.

אחות   אח
Sister   Brother

We can conclude from this that based on God's grammatical rules, there is no such creature as one sister! Each one is actually a minimum of two. My son's nightmarish claim was correct; he does have twelve sisters—at least according to the Lord's language.

What possible lesson for my son, indeed for us all, might lurk here?

Figuring Out the Family

Living as part of a vibrant and vital family is joyful—not that it doesn't get frustrating at times. And not that it is without its burdens and limitations. It might be convenient if we were able to participate in family life when we felt like it and live alone when we preferred. But overall, since we cannot change our circumstances by the mood or by the hour, it is better to live as part of a family than in any other way. There can be little doubt that societies enjoy greater stability and prosperity when the prevailing model is the traditional family.

But families are surprisingly complicated organizations. Figuring out the family is a challenge, not just for graduate students of sociology but for each one of us. Among the questions to ponder: Do children owe special respect to parents, as Judeo-Christian tradition demands, or should their main allegiance be to the state, as ordered by Nazi Europe and Stalinist Russia? There are practical consequences to how we answer that question. Sticky issues are involved, such as whether children should be encouraged to inform schools about the lifestyle choices of their parents. There is the possibility that schools may feel justified inquiring whether children live in a cigarette-smoking environment. Educators might feel the need to know whether children are being exposed to creationist worldviews that could clash with the school's position on evolution.

Another question about family is this: Are husbands and wives bound by a holy covenant or is marriage merely a convenient, and possibly demeaning, contract? Should marriage be re-defined to fit in with current cultural fads, perhaps introducing the idea of renewable term limits for marriage, as has been suggested, or should the goal remain a lifetime commitment? Different visions of marriage will determine how society functions and how children are raised to view marriage.

Here is another question we should ask: Do siblings simply have a common set of parents, or is there a unique relationship uniting them? Should brothers and sisters view one another as merely members of the larger society or do they owe one another a greater degree of loyalty than they would a stranger? Is there any difference in the relationship between sons and parents and daughters and parents? How about between male siblings and female siblings?

All of these questions need answers because how we feel about these matters will determine how we conduct ourselves in our family relationships.

For me personally, it is clear that family is a uniquely human form of social cooperation. I consider it unlikely that families evolved accidentally or automatically. A more credible explanation for the existence of the family is that God presented the model as a gift to humanity. Naturally, those who are ideologically committed to a secular, materialistic view of the world will reject any explanation that includes a role for the Creator. They will need to identify an alternative explanation. But for those of us who are intellectually open to the idea, the God-as-a-designer theory enjoys one important benefit: Our Designer was considerate enough to equip His product with an instruction manual. Furthermore, although the manual happens to be written in His language, Hebrew, it is far more comprehensible than some of the instruction manuals that accompany contemporary gadgetry manufactured in the Far East. We do better in life when we follow the manual than when we think we are smarter than it.

Sisters vs. Brothers

The Hebrew word for sister, ACHOT, literally means 'sisters.' (When intending to really say sisters, in the plural, the Lord's language contrives an entirely new word, ACHaYOT). This is what worried my son. According to his correct understanding of this principle, no brother has only one sister. Even if Jack and Jill were the only children of the family, the Hebrew would indicate that Jack actually has two sisters. He would have to introduce Jill by saying, "I'd like you to meet my sisters, Jill."

My son felt placated once I explained that he doesn't *really* have twelve sisters. Instead, he has two separate relationships with each of his sisters: One relationship is with his sister, the single girl; the second relationship is the one he has with his sister after she marries. The relationship between a sister and her brother, or between two sisters, should change after a girl's marriage in a way that the relationship between two brothers should not. This may be politically incorrect, but that doesn't make it untrue.

> **A sister is not merely a female brother. She is a specific and unique creation.**

God created women to bond emotionally more easily and more deeply than men do. This is a tremendous blessing in women's lives, as they amass long-lasting and devoted friendships which bolster and support them. It is good for society as well, as bonds between women build families, neighborhoods and communities. But there is a potential downside. In a desire to be close to many, women can prioritize incorrectly. They can easily neglect to nurture their marriages. They can mistakenly put their parents, their children, their siblings and even their friends before their husbands. Yet, in God's plan, everyone is better off when marriages are strong.

Through his language God is teachings us how human

society works best. While he can count on her loyalty and devotion until her marriage, a brother would be wise to recognize that after his sister's marriage, her priority must become her husband. While unmarried sisters may spend many hours baring their hearts to each other, that degree of closeness needs to be filtered after one or both of them marry. The marriage relationship needs exclusivity not only in sexual terms, but also emotionally. Women should be very careful about betraying their husbands by sharing anecdotes, concerns, troubles or foibles with others. Sisters should remain close as should friends, but I have seen "girlfriend getaways" advertised which promote themselves as an opportunity to behave in ways which can irrevocably harm marriages. The plural language of ACHOT is a warning that married women need to hold back somewhat on their desire to share all.

Sons and Daughters

Let us also glance at the other role of children, namely their role as sons and daughters. Here again, the Hebrew language departs from the expected grammatical convention in surprising and revealing ways. A son is a BeN, which would lead us to expect that a daughter should be called a BeNAH.

To our surprise, a daughter is referred to by a new word, a BaT (pronounced to rhyme with "hot").

בת   בן

Daughter   Son

This suggests that the relationship between sons and daughters is quite different from that between, say, a filly and a colt. In other words, the grammatical departure indicates to us that a daughter is not merely a female son and a son is not merely a male daughter. Each is a specific and unique creation.

We tend to think of placing little value on daughters as a relic of a patriarchal past. Yet still today, in many societies, daughters are devalued. It has long been known that you could visit small villages in India and discover midwives who would accept the equivalent of a few dollars to murder female children directly after birth. Under China's one child policy, it is almost exclusively girl infants which have been abandoned. While all civilized people express horror at this disdain for human life, paradoxically, as society becomes more egalitarian, this anti-female bias does not automatically go away. It turns out that India's sophisticated city dwellers feel much the same way about daughters. In cities such as Bombay, the government had to intervene because the country's richest and brightest were showing the same contempt for girls, using prenatal testing and abortion to ensure male progeny. The Indian proverb: "Raising a daughter is like watering someone else's field," seems to express a common feeling. Societies in which sons enjoy prominence and daughters are devalued are often tribal cultures. A son absorbs his wife into his family and her original family links are methodically obliterated. That society then becomes a collection of clans and tribes. It is only natural that struggles and conflicts erupt between these tribal families.

But we need to look beyond India and China and examine ourselves as well.

Secularism's Contempt for Daughters

Don't for a moment think that *our* richest and brightest necessarily feel any differently. I was quite shocked when a gynecologist in one of America's most sophisticated centers told me that he, too, saw a disproportionate number of female fetuses being aborted. In fact, he was so shocked that it led him to stop doing abortions.

It seems that only the eternal wisdom of God, rather than the ephemeral ideas of man, is able to equally value both sons and daughters. If every human being is created in the image of God, then all life is sacred. But while both sons and daughters are precious, they are not the same. If a daughter is nothing but a female son then she might indeed be "worth less" to her parents.

The Lord's language puts a stop to this precipitous line of reasoning. We need to acknowledge that what a daughter does for a family is quite different from what a son does; but her role is every bit as necessary. God made sons *and* daughters rather than bisexual beings so that each could contribute something unique to the world.

Societies in which men and women are encouraged to shun marriage and seek only self-fulfillment rather than couple-fulfillment, end up being tougher on women than on men as well. Despite decades of feminism we are bombarded with studies showing that women are less happy today than they used to be. Women on college campuses, the bastion of secularism, haven't gotten the joy, respect and fulfillment that they were promised when told that they had the right to the same sexual desires and freedom as men.

However, with a Designer-model family structure, women enjoy an authentically elevated status rather than the empty rhetoric of feminism. By retaining spiritual links to her own family origins as well as bonding to her husband and his family, daughters join two families together rather than submerging their own identity into their husbands' "tribes." Women cement the social network of society into a seamless system that is not a primitive and blood-dependent cauldron of tension. In a Biblical society men who do not marry do not get to hop from one woman to another, casting each aside at will. Society promotes and encourages the marriage relationship where a woman's innate desire for love and affection can be fulfilled. Not surprisingly, in God's model, daughters and all women are safer—and so is society.

Two Separate Relationships

Even parents must interact with their sons and daughters quite differently after they marry. The Hebrew word for son, BeN, is related to the concept of building, BoNeH—while the word for daughter BaT, is related to BaYiT, or home. When he marries, a son's obligations to his new family "build" on top of those he already has to his parents and siblings. When a man marries, he is not leaving his family for another; he is adding a new person, his bride, into his own family. However, as I explained a little earlier, he is to do so in a way that does not overwhelm his bride's personality. On the other hand, when a daughter marries, she is now chiefly committed to building her new "home." Since the structure of that home is more in her hands than in her husband's, she needs to combine the disparate elements of both of their childhood homes (assuming both come from healthy families) into the new creation. While her natural instincts would lead her to only copy the home she knows—her own family—she must extend herself to give greater weight to her husband's customs.

I recently observed how a wise friend of mine, a great American, put these ideas into practice. He is an American of faith who served as a cabinet secretary to one of America's finest presidents; he has also built up a successful business. Once, while visiting him in his comfortable Park Avenue apartment, I commented how nice it must be for him to have his sons and sons-in-law working with him in his business. He quickly corrected me. Only his sons worked with him, not his sons-in-law.

Why not his sons-in-law? I wondered. My friend's answer revealed to me both the wisdom of the president who appointed him and the wisdom that president planned to gain by including this man in his administration. "While I am certain my sons-in-law would follow my directives as surely as do my sons," he said, "their wives—my daughters— would respect them just a bit less for being their father's employees."

This told me how clearly my friend understood the strange dynamics of daughters. His daughters, like other girls, need to transfer their emotional allegiance from their father to their husbands. This they could do only if they could respect their husbands as they did their father. Watching their father hurl directives at their husbands, in what was probably not always the most sensitive and patient tone of voice, could only make their task as wives more difficult.

He was hoping that several of his sons-in-law would join their own fathers in their successful family enterprises. Alternatively, once his sons-in-law established themselves successfully so that it would be clear to all that they would be doing him a favor by entering his business, they could join him. This, he was quite certain, would be far better for his daughters' marriages.

Transfer of Emotional Allegiance

When a woman marries, her relationship with her own family undergoes real change in a way that is not the same for men. Perhaps the widespread tradition of a girl taking the name of her new family reflects the fundamental truth that upon marriage, a woman breaks some subtle bond with her own family. While she certainly should retain very strong spiritual bonds with her own family, there ought to be a healthy transfer of some emotional allegiance. This can be hard for both her and her own original family. It is likely to be a difficult transition for any young wife and it demands considerable sensitivity on the part of her husband. Done correctly, it leads to happy marriages as well as to retaining wonderfully joyful relationships with her parents and siblings.

As a father, this transfer of allegiance poses a real challenge for me as well as for the wise and gentle men my daughters marry. It is necessary for me to help, rather than hinder, each daughter as she begins the process of transferring her emotional allegiance from me to the new man in her lives. It is necessary for me to begin to see them as new people, just as my son will have to get used to having completely new sisters. Their husbands also need to understand that marrying a woman who enjoyed a very close relationship with her father is a great blessing. The emotional intensity of their earlier relationship with their father can be kept aflame in my daughters, but it must become redirected from me and toward their husbands.

Accomplishing this transfer takes most of the first year of marriage. It also demands a sensitivity and maturity not always found in young men. But to marry such special young ladies, they have to be pretty special themselves.

CHAPTER 10

GOING UP OR GOING DOWN?

דור

DoR

Suggestion: See the alphabet chart and Holy Hebrew! Tools 1 and 2 to get the most out of this chapter.

In modern America, the idea of apprenticeship has fallen on hard times. We seem to be obsessed with education as if spending time in the classroom studying is more important than observing and working under talented individuals who are successful in our field of interest. Personally, whether the area under question is law, medicine, parenting, teaching or carpentry, I have little faith in anyone whose knowledge comes only from books and lectures, or even disproportionately from those sources.

I feel for a young friend of mine who works at a magazine. The publication's editors are more or less evenly divided between senior and junior editors. My friend tells me that the senior editors reminisce about how when they were juniors themselves, their senior colleagues would take them under their wings imparting to them the secrets of the trade. An older staffer would sit down with a younger one and carefully show him what he had done right and wrong. As a result, a warm personal relationship often developed between the two.

Nowadays, says my friend, this custom has gone by the wayside as older and younger members of the editing staff go about their business independently. Intergenerational mentoring is a thing of the past.

Sadly, my friend's experience is typical. Whether in the workplace or the family, the importance of ensuring continuity from generation to generation lies behind the Hebrew word that means generation: DoR.

In Hebrew thought, a DoR does not mean a specific number of years, like twenty or twenty-five, but rather a measure of continuity on which all else depends. It is a spiritual, not a biological, measurement. A child, his parents and grandparents add up to three generations only if we can identify something beyond DNA that has passed down from grandparent to parent to child.

We can identify generations in non-familial contexts as well. Science, for instance, has developed wonderful innovations that make our lives easier and more productive only because information uncovered by one generation was carefully preserved and passed on to the following generations. That is why so many prominent scientists acknowledge their predecessors with phrases like, "I wouldn't have succeeded had I not climbed up onto the shoulders of Newton."

A potential Einstein who appears on the scene as a young child, but from whom all knowledge of past discoveries in theoretical physics has been withheld, must start from scratch in his scientific inquiries. Under such conditions, he will never become the Einstein familiar to us as the greatest scientific genius of this past century. In fact, he'll be lucky if he reinvents the wheel. In one person's lifetime it is simply not possible to progress from the wheel to nuclear power without building on earlier discoveries.

You're Either Growing or Shrinking

In fact, in the absence of such "DoR-to-DoR" continuity we are confronted with something much more worrisome than a lack of progress: We actually regress. This is a very important general principle and the magic of Hebrew alerts us to the prospect. We have to realize that we are either growing or shrinking. Stagnation is simply not a human option.

> **We have to realize that we are either growing or shrinking. Stagnation is simply not a human option.**

I remember one member of my synagogue who owned a small printing business. He proudly informed us that he deliberately avoided growing his business since he enjoyed his laid-back California lifestyle. Violating my rule of never offering unsolicited advice, I warned him of this message we learn from the Hebrew word DoR: You grow or you shrink—the only option not available is to stay the way you are. As things often happen, just at that time computers proliferated and desktop publishing began to take off. To remain competitive, most ambitious printers adapted and expanded their services. My congregant, however, firmly stuck to his guns, determined to keep his business at its comfortable size. As you can well imagine, it did not take long for his small company to become obsolete and irrelevant.

The rule also applies to personal development: We either move forward or backward. It also applies to relationships, including to the most important one of all: marriage. We either nurture or grow our marriages regardless of how long we've been married, or they are deteriorating.

Here is how we extract this vital rule from the Hebrew language.

DoR is spelled dalet-(vav)-reish. (The word is spelled both with and without the vav in Scripture.)

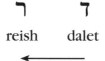

reish   dalet

One of the amazing features of Hebrew is that when you reverse the spelling of a Hebrew word, important insights tend to emerge. In this case, DoR spelled backward is ReyD— reish-dalet.

dalet   reish

ReyD, means "to decline." The operative principle here is that when you reverse a word's spelling you get either its opposite, or its negation—the state that occurs when the condition signified by the first word is absent. When continuity (DoR) is absent, what results is decline (ReyD).

My magazine-editing friend confirmed for me what I already knew from reading his magazine over the years: It isn't as outstanding a publication as it was years ago. Oh, it's a perfectly fine magazine; but ReyD, decline, has definitely set in.

Each generation must be able to draw on the accumulated wisdom and experience of the previous generation. The giant international business-consulting firm, Accenture, knows this. They maintain a vast central repository of information and experience, which has been gathered over the years by the thousands of consultants who have made up the company. No wisdom acquired by any of their associates is ever lost. They understand the principle of DoR, building each generation upon the shoulders of the previous one.

Cultural Continuity Is Vital

This is one reason I worry about America. I fear not only for businesses which will suffer from stagnation if senior management fails to educate and initiate younger employees into the culture and traditions of the firm, but I fear for American society as a whole. Do you recall long ago when our educational institutions regarded themselves as acting *in loco parentis*? They viewed their jobs in terms of acting as parental agents. Today our public schools and universities proudly denounce the past and "reconstruct" it. They act as if their mission is to drive a wedge instead of a bridge between each generation.

If you want your offspring to be your children instead of merely your biological progeny, the responsibility rests entirely upon you to ensure that this happens. This means such things as spending time with your children instead of

allowing television to deaden family interaction. It means using time with children for meaningful conversation rather
than merely tossing a ball around. I do not denigrate the time
parents spend playing games with their children; play is valuable, but only as one component of an entire DoR program.
Investing time in conversation is crucial. Discuss values, discuss ideas, and discuss dreams. In this way you will help your
children stand upon your shoulders for his or her own decisions and achievements.

In the value system of the Hebrew Bible, the responsibility of nurturing cultural continuity falls primarily on males.
This is not a question of "ought"—in other words, I'm not
saying men "ought" to be responsible for teaching values to
youngsters. Instead, we are dealing with a question of "is."
The Bible gives us timeless descriptions of how things *are*—
what can work and what can't—not fussy prescriptions
for how they *ought* to be. It is similar to the way Sir Isaac
Newton described a force known as gravity. He did not *proscribe* gravity, he *described* it. An example of a *proscriptive*
law is the speed limit on our nation's highways. If you violate
that speed limit, you may get caught or you may get away
with it. However, if you attempt to violate Newton's law of
gravity by stepping out of the twentieth floor window of
a skyscraper, it is not a question of whether you will get
caught. You will drop like a stone and the sudden stop at the
end of the fall could be problematic. Don't blame Sir Isaac
Newton. He did not *proscribe* that rule. But he did *describe*
how it works.

The Bible likewise describes rules built into the world by
the Creator. Playing by the rules generally leads to a more

fulfilling (not to mention safer) life than shaking a defiant fist at God. In our case, it is simply a fact that if males fail to provide continuity from DoR to DoR, generation to generation, probably no one will. Alarmingly high rates of single-motherhood alert us to a society in which children have mothers but no fathers. We have already begun to taste of the ReyD-related chaos that this inevitably engenders.

Much that we count on in our lives depends upon continuity of training and knowledge. The benefits of thinking in DoR terms accrue not only to society but also to the individual. It goes without saying that my journalist friend would have been better off as a writer and editor if he had been able to secure a mentor. Less obvious is the observation that older professionals will take more satisfaction from their work when they can pass along their accumulated experience to a younger colleague. Being able to do so is a supremely joyful activity for a human. This is one reason we parents should feel grateful for our children. They provide the opportunity to pass on what we know.

Humanity seems to possess an enduring, ineradicable desire for immortality. When dictators erect statues to themselves or name cities after themselves, they are trying to irrevocably mark their spot in the universe. When individuals write their memoirs or give donations for scholarships which will continue in their name, they are trying to ensure that they somehow remain a part of the world, even after their death.

Most religions speak of life-after-death. But there are two kinds of life-after-death. In one, the individual carries on as a disembodied spirit in a heavenly environment, which we mortals can hardly begin to imagine. In the other type of immortality, even after my death I can carry on my work, my dreams and visions right here on earth. How? By having played a role in training those who survive me. They become stand-ins for me. Through them, I can live forever.

But how does one go about successfully teaching the young? How do we influence anyone over whom we have some authority, whether they are our children, students or employees? The dual concept of DoR/ReyD offers a lesson.

Structure and Flexibility

The key letters these words have in common are reish, which in Hebrew script is written ר, and dalet, which is written ד. Notice the similarity in shape.

ר   ד

reish   dalet

In Hebrew, even the appearance of a letter is worth noticing. In Jewish learning, these two letters, whenever used in contrasting words, immediately bring to mind another pair of words that also start respectively with dalet and reish. Din (first letter: dalet), is often translated as "law" or "structure"; and Rachamim (first letter: reish), as "mercy" or "flexibility." In the spelling of our word DoR, the juxtaposition of dalet/din and reish/rachamim, in that order, yields a lesson in pedagogy: the science of teaching.

A good teacher begins with din—structure. Only when structure is established in his relationship with his students does he proceed to rachamim. To reverse the order is a grave mistake. As a newly arrived rabbi to Southern California during the 1970s, I accepted a position teaching mathematics and Talmud at a Jewish yeshiva high school for boys in Los Angeles. I asked the principal of the school, who had offered to walk me into my class on the first day of school, to let me introduce myself. (Unless General Douglas MacArthur, Winston Churchill, or some other awesomely authoritative personality is introducing you, it is sometimes best to introduce yourself. Doing otherwise can make you look smaller to those you are meeting.)

When I peeked through a window from the hallway, I saw what might have been labeled *Abandon all hope ye who enter here.* A virtual riot was going on. Boys were climbing over one another, shouting and shoving. Even those who weren't engaged in unruly physical behavior seemed unprepared for the study of mathematics. On one side of the room a boy who looked as if he had recently escaped from a penitentiary was eating a sandwich. On the other side, another boy resembling a professional wrestler was peering out the window at a passersby, while behind him a Frankenstein look-alike gazed dreamily off into space.

Taking a deep breath, I strode in and set down my briefcase. They ignored me. I stared grimly at the mob. My resolute stare was wasted—no one noticed. I turned my expression into a horrible scowl. It was as if I was invisible.

This was not an auspicious beginning.

I could see that this situation required a quick application of the "first-din [law/structure]-then-rachamim [mercy/flexibility] principle." Now let me assure you that I am actually a fairly nice sort of guy, generally kind to little children and furry animals. So what I did next wasn't easy for me. Just necessary.

I walked resolutely out of the classroom, leaving the door ajar behind me so the boys could see what I was about to do. Just outside was a rickety bench, the old-fashioned kind with multi-colored slats to sit on. I had noticed earlier that in the middle of this bench, one slat had broken in two and was hanging down to the ground. I grabbed one-half of the slat—a good four feet in length—and rrrripped it from the bench. I then strode back determinedly into the classroom.

I now had the hoodlums' attention. Approaching the desk of one boy who was engaged in arm wrestling the pugilist behind him, I lifted the slat high above my head, took careful aim, and brought the wood down on his desk. *Slap!* As I intended, the slat struck the desk inches from the boy's hand. He looked up at me in horror and—yes—fear.

"Damn!" I exclaimed in an angry yell. "I missed! That has NEVER happened before."

At that moment not a boy in the room doubted that I was positively, dangerously insane. I growled, "This stick has a name. It is called Henry, and Henry isn't happy, and neither am I! If any of you tell your parents or the rosh yeshiva [school principal] what has just happened, or what's about to happen in the next forty-five minutes, this stick will hurt you very badly. Now listen to me…"

And I began to lay out the rules by which my class would operate. No boy would ever speak unless I recognized him. No boy would do anything in class except follow my instructions, concentrate, and breathe. Any violation would be met with swift and very painful punishment. I was fairly certain that I would be fired that afternoon. But somehow, nobody reported the details of my debut.

The school year went very smoothly after that. I never had to bring out Henry again. Those boys and I developed a real fondness for each other, and we were all sorry when second semester drew to a close. We had a fine time, but we also learned mathematics. After I initiated a learning experience with a little bit of din—that tough, structured approach—I could then proceed in due course to the rachamim—the softer, gentler, more enjoyable side of teaching.

Of course, what I am offering here is an account of something I was fortunate to pull off. In the past thirty years society has taken a marked turn toward humorlessness, so you would be well advised not to go threatening people with a stick—even if you, like me, have no intention whatsoever of actually using it. But my point is that if we start out with rachamim, softness and flexibility, the project of teaching young minds is often quite futile. Had I walked into the classroom and tried to sweetly reason with that mob on that first day, the rest of the year would have been an entire waste of time. Those boys never could have been induced to take me seriously.

The same principle may be applied in other areas of life. During the fifteen years that I was the rabbi of a synagogue on the boardwalk of Venice, California, I presided over some 150 weddings. My approach in dealing with newly en-

gaged couples was consistent. Oh, they were often in love
—making dove eyes at each other, sighing, grinning goofily.
In each case I endeavored to pour a bucket of cold Din on
their heads, and Jewish religious practices made this easy.
Marriage rites in my faith community are extremely legal-
istic, and include the reading aloud (in Aramaic) of an ancient text (the ketubah), whose terms every Jewish male
who wishes to get married must accept. In very unromantic
terms it spells all his duties and obligations to his wife.

But this is just as it must be. First Din—structure—and then
and only then comes Rachamim—flexibility. A marriage that
begins with legalities—discussing the difficult issues, wrestling with deep questions that force the couple to articulate
their worldviews—matures into a seasoned love that will
last a lifetime. But a marriage that begins only with the emo-
tionalism of love often ends in legalities. I'm glad to say that
of those 150 marriages I shepherded to fruition, only a scant
few have ended in divorce. Future DoRot (the plural of DoR)
will reap the benefits.

PART THREE

COMMUNITY AND WORK

Chapters 11–16

Be sure to check out pages 337–342
to discover helpful resources on this topic

CHAPTER 11

COMMUNITY RULES

עדה צבר קהל

KaHaL TSiBuR EiDaH

Suggestion: See the alphabet chart and Holy Hebrew! Tools
1, 2, 5, 6 and 7 to get the most out of this chapter.

The jetliner began its takeoff roll down the runway at Philadelphia International Airport early that sunny Friday morning. Comfortably ensconced in my window seat I smiled at the thought of being back home and reunited with my family for *Shabbat*, which would begin at sunset that evening. All of a sudden there was an earsplitting bang and, as the hair on the back of my neck stood up, I saw flames erupt from under the wing and large black pieces of metal go flying out of the engine. In a split instant I recalled my own pilot training and prayed that we were not too far down the runway to abort the takeoff. As passengers shrieked we were flung forward as the airliner braked hard. We came to a standstill, and still shaking I uttered a prayer of gratitude. We were safe and soon found ourselves back in the terminal.

After a few hours we were invited to board another aircraft to resume our journey to Seattle. I did some mental calculations and doubted that we could arrive before sunset which would mean that my faith prevented me from getting on that flight. The gate agent kindly invited me to talk to one of the pilots. He graciously assured me that they planned on 'pressing the pedal to the metal' and promised me a Seattle arrival prior to sunset. I took him at his word but didn't care to go into the explanation that getting to SeaTac airport just before sunset wouldn't allow me enough time to drive the twenty miles to my home.

Being eager to see my family again and spend the blessed Sabbath with them, I called home and discussed the problem with my wife. Do I board the flight and risk spending twenty-five hours on a bench at Seattle airport or do I spend a lonely Shabbat in Philadelphia? As usual, my wife had the solution. "Take the flight," she said, "and I'll take the kids and all our Shabbat meals and we'll take a couple of rooms at an airport hotel. When you arrive, just walk to the hotel and we'll spend Shabbat together there."

Sure enough, we landed just before the sun set into Puget Sound. I thanked the cockpit crew profusely and asked the cabin attendant if she would be able to arrange for my carry-on bag to be stored safely until I could come and retrieve it the following night after the Sabbath ended. She kindly acquiesced so, leaving the plane, I started my walk to the airport hotel where I was joyfully reunited with my wife and seven children. We sang the Sabbath prayers together that evening with special meaning and enjoyed one of our most memorable family Sabbaths ever.

That's right. We Jews do not drive or use any form of transport during the Shabbat. Is this merely an archaic religious regulation that needlessly makes life more difficult? Hardly. You see, one of the serendipitous consequences of this rule is that we tend to locate our homes within easy walking distance of our synagogues. Thus, whether you find yourself in Berlin, Baltimore, Brussels, or Boston, when you have found a synagogue, you have also found a community. On Saturday morning you will spot Jews hurrying along the streets converging on the synagogue for Sabbath worship. And following the services, you may well find yourself invited to join one of the families for lunch, and conveniently, the walk will usually be a mile or less. This is a community.

Why Should We Be Friends?

Think about it. Wouldn't it be true to say that all your best achievements and all your highest moments of enjoyment and fulfillment came about because of your connection with at least one other human being? Every success we experience occurs because of at least one other human being. It might be a friend, a family member, a work associate, a mentor, a teacher, or even an employer. Being connected is the essence of our existence. Being connected with God and yes, also being connected with His other children. Though busy and bustling lives might make us doubt it, the truth is that solitary confinement is not a reward—it is torture. Nobody ever lost his mind because of being surrounded by too many people. However, being utterly isolated from others can be terribly destructive.

Conversely, finding ways to make new friends, even only new acquaintances, is one of the most positive things anyone can do to bring about improvements in the quality of life. Almost any lack one feels in life can be addressed by getting to know more people and making the effort to connect and interact. If you are feeling a little down and depressed, get out and meet people. If you are seeking your life mate, get out and meet people. If you are trying to increase your financial endeavors, get out and meet people. In other words, become part of different communities or form a community. This is an essential lesson of Hebrew. Whether a culture has many words for a concept or none reveals a great deal about that culture. Hebrew contains a variety of words for community, stressing its importance. Let's look at three of them.

Actively Gathering for a Purpose

One of these words, TSiBuR, helps teach us that forming a community or becoming part of one, like anything else of real value in life, takes effort. It doesn't just happen. One cannot passively yearn for community and connection because the only result of that will be to languish in loneliness. One has to get up and act. Like many important words in Hebrew, TSiBuR can be read both forwards and backwards. Because the second letter of the Hebrew alphabet can be pronounced as both a B and a V, we read TSiBuR in reverse as RaVaTS. But here is the best part of Hebrew's magic. When one reverses a word in Hebrew, this new word often means the opposite of the word with which we started. (Though this does not happen in any other language, by way of example, it would be as if BIG means large and GIB meant small.)

ר   ב   צ

R   B   TS

צ   ב   ר

TS   V   R

In Hebrew, the word RaVaTS means to lie down. From some contexts in Scripture we can see that RaVaTS means lying down awaiting someone or something. There is a passive component of not acting until some event occurs. Our word, TSiBuR, doesn't at first seem to be an antonym for lying down. In fact, it literally means to collect or gather. If we explore a little more deeply, however, we see a nuance of gathering is being revealed. There are many different ways for people to gather. We can gather together with others in a bus queue or actuaries might gather us together to form a statistical grouping. Neither of these groupings forms a TSiBuR.

TSiBuR implies the opposite of lying down; proactively doing something. TSiBuR connotes actively gathering people together for a purpose. It is a word of action and vitality. It rejects the notion that you can be a beneficiary of community without doing your part to generate and vitalize that community. In order to gain the most benefit from community, you have to get up and play a role in contributing to that community.

Whether it is your church or synagogue, a school PTA, a civic organization like Rotary International or your own neighborhood community, in order to derive all the available benefit, each individual needs to find ways to contribute and advance that purpose.

Intergenerational Community

We must ask what else forms a community. Would we enjoy a community made up of people exactly like us? Just think how boring it would be to spend time with your own clone.

When you start telling the funniest joke you know, your clone interrupts you to remind you that she already knows the punch line. Or let's imagine you need to solve a problem and decide that brainstorming with a friend would be useful. The only person available right now is your good-looking clone. How helpful could it possibly be to brainstorm with another you? Not very. So clearly, hanging out with people exactly like you, even assuming they exist, has very limited utility and wouldn't even be much fun.

One cannot passively yearn for community and connection because the only result of that will be to languish in loneliness.

On the other hand, being in a group of people with whom you have absolutely nothing in common wouldn't work either. No common language means limited ability to communicate. Okay, let's stipulate a shared language. However, if there is no shared value system any attempt to, shall we say, prioritize the group's activities, would be futile. No shared life experiences means that you have little upon which to commence communication.

So both diversity and uniformity seem to be important. But what should be the makeup of that diversity and uniformity? Should a community be made up of people who share a lot or who share as little as possible? Fortunately an additional Hebrew word for community helps us navigate this dilemma.

This word is KaHaL which serves as the noun for "a

gathering." But a KaHaL is a special kind of gathering; in a word, it is a "community."

Look at the Hebrew letters which form the word KaHaL: kuf-hay-lamed.

ל   ה   ק

L   H   K

30   5   100

If we apply the rule that letters equal numbers, we find the following: The first letter, kuf has a numerical value of 100, the middle letter hay has a value of 5 and the final letter lamed equals 30. We are being told something important here about what constitutes a community.

A verse in the Mishnah's tractate Pirke Avot ("Chapters of the Fathers"), explains the significance of the numbers 5, 13, 15, 18, 20, 30, 40, 50, 60, 70, 80, 90 and 100. Each represents a human age. You may wish to look up the whole rabbinic exposition yourself (Pirke Avot 5:25), but for simplicity's sake we will limit our attention to the numbers kuf, hay, and lamed with the values of 100, 5 and 30.

One hundred? That number represents the elderly. Completely rejecting the idea that older people should be shunted to the side, Hebrew suggests that a community needs old people. Then one needs children, represented by the age of five. And finally one needs people who have achieved "full strength," as the Mishnah puts in—a condition which occurs around age thirty.

Each Detail Matters

As I hope I've made clear by now, no detail in the structure of Hebrew came about by chance. It wasn't left to the accidents and exigencies of the millennia to determine, for instance, the spelling of words. Thus not only the identity, but the order of the letters in KaHaL teaches us something. Why is 100 followed by 5, which is then followed by 30? Our instinct would be to list the numbers from biggest to smallest or vice versa.

To make sense of this you must be aware of another principle of ancient Jewish wisdom. In the Bible and in other ancient Jewish texts, when we find a cluster of three things —numbers, people, inanimate objects—there is typically a correspondence to *past*, *present*, and *future*. But the order in which these appear changes depending on the context. In our case the order is *past*, *future* and *present*. The elderly are our link to the past; youth are our portal to the future and the age thirty represents those years when we are strongest and most able to work. Another verse in Pirke Avot (3:1) gives an example of a similar order. The second-century AD rabbi Akavia ben Mahalalel is quoted as saying that if we wish to have a successful life, we must consider three things: "Know whence you came, whither you go, and before Whom you will give justification and reckoning." In other words, you must know your origins, your past. You must also know your ultimate, future destination: the life that follows after death. Knowing those two truths will direct your behavior in the present. Your deeds are all being recorded by the Creator so that when past and future meet—that is, when you die— you can take credit, or be held responsible, for what you did when you were alive.

This principle of threes isn't so obscure or esoteric as it might seem. You knew it already. Anytime you get on an airplane and fall into a conversation with your seatmate, the talking tends to follow the same pattern. First we ask our new acquaintance where he is from. Then, typically we inquire about where he's headed. Later we'll get around to asking him his occupation, which is a vital clue to a person's present identity.

What, then, makes up a community? It begins with the elderly. From them everyone else receives the wisdom that gives the KaHaL its identity. For a true KaHaL has a spiritual existence independent of its members. The members are just flesh and bone, but the community transcends matter. Think of a well-run corporation, which is just a kind of KaHaL adapted for modern business purposes. Whatever product the corporation makes, it can continue doing so for decades, even centuries, though the members of the corporation will gradually die out and be replaced by other members.

That's because the new members learn from their seniors, who learned from their seniors and so on back to the origins of the group. This intergenerational continuity is especially important if the KaHaL's purpose is very complex. No one person at Microsoft would know how to sit down and write the software for Windows. No one person at NASA knows how to put a human being on the moon. Only the KaHaL as a collectivity can do so, and for this it is crucial that they receive their gathered expertise from the people who went before them in the extraordinarily complicated enterprise of developing the science of computer code-writing or of moon rocketry.

That is the kuf element. The hay represents the young. Without them, we are in danger of landing up in what is called a "retirement community." One finds such places in Florida, in Southern California, in Arizona, wherever the weather is warm. This is ironic because in those which strictly limit the hours when younger people can visit, the atmosphere can tend to be, well, kind of chilly.

Not because the residents are elderly, and hence closer to end of their lives than to the beginning. I have met plenty of old people who are full of life. However, these vibrant elderly are never the sort of old people who spend all their time exclusively gathered together with other old people.

The idea of "retirement" in itself is perverse. When no longer challenged by work, the mind and body begin to really deteriorate. But even if you stop doing the work which has been your focus in the past, you need to keep growing and contributing. If you possibly can do so, it might be an idea not to confine yourself to those well-intentioned community programs intended to "enrich" the lives of senior citizens. I mean those classes, tours and social groups intended for seniors alone.

Are you elderly? Do you want to keep your brain sharp, and learn some interesting stuff in your spare time? Great! Now compare the atmosphere in a "senior enrichment" class down at the Senior Center, to the far livelier one in a classroom at your local community college. In the college class one finds young people right out of high school along with middle-aged folks working to complete a degree, all side by side with ladies and gentlemen in their 70s, 80s, and 90s who want to learn for the sake of learning. That's how it should be.

The senior citizens in the college class are keeping their brains alive and fully oxygenated. The seniors who keep company exclusively with other seniors are slowly suffocating themselves. Indeed, after a few minutes of conversation, you can generally tell whether a particular old person interacts much with younger folks on a daily basis: he's more on the ball and fun to talk to.

It is not true that the elderly have much to learn from the young (beyond computer and other technical skills): that is a misinformed tenet of the youth culture that has wrought such havoc. But the old do require the presence of the young if the former wish to remain vigorous in mind and body.

But obviously a community can't be sustained by the very young and very old by themselves. The hard work, the heavy lifting and loading, must be done by those at the peak of their strength. And what is that work?

Community Glue

Put on your hard hat: here are two more rules related to word-construction in the Lord's Language. First, although Hebrew words are built on three-letter roots, in most cases the first and third letters of the root are most important. Often we can drop the middle letter and arrive at the basic meaning of the word we are analyzing.

An example might be the two-letter "super-root" nun-lamed, NL—easy to remember because it coincides (not by accident!) with the familiar English word "null," which mean "nothing," or "zero." Hebrew roots that consist of the letters nun, followed by some other letter followed by lamed have in them the concept of null-ness: they carry the connotation of "low," "small," "falling," "bottoming out." Thus NaMaL means "ant," the lowest of creatures. NaZaL means "to drip," where a liquid falls to the bottom of something. NaCHaL means "valley," a low geographical feature. And so on.

In our case, if we take away the middle letter of KaHaL, we are left with KL, kuf-lamed, which can be prounced KoL, meaning "voice."

As Jewish tradition has emphasized for more than 3,000 years, learning is ideally done by oral communication, through the voice. The voice is how we interact both with God through prayer, and with people through conversation. While conversing, words acquire added meaning through tone and nuance. One difference between a thought-out and well-written letter and a Twitter post or quickly dashed off email, is that the letter is closer to speech. A written letter is basically writing out what one would say out loud. Social media posts are more likely to express thoughts which might well bypass our mouths. This is why we are more likely to have miscommunication as electronic relationships replace face-to-face ones.

This emphasis is conveyed by the word KaBaLah, kuf-bet-lamed, which designates the secret mystical tradition in Judaism. If you drop the middle root letter, bet, you are left with the same first and last letters as KaHaL, kuf-lamed or kol, "voice." For millennia, Jewish sages communicated the secrets of KaBaLah by oral discourse, not in writing. When anything was written down, as in the classic mystical work the Zohar, the tradition was compressed into cryptic sayings of the rabbis—saying which remained opaque unless explained orally by a teacher who had received the oral explanation from his teacher who received it from his teacher.

In the case of our two-letter root kuf-lamed, we now should pay attention to the middle letter, the Hay. In Hebrew, where each letter name has a specific meaning the letter Hay is associated with God's name and adds a spiritual and eternal element to a word.

We can extract two messages from here. A community differs from a social group built around a common interest such as a tennis club. If one year you belong to the tennis club and the next year you join a swimming team, it will not impact your life very much. If your children prefer soccer to either of your chosen sports, that is fine as well. But a community with an authentic essence is different than a club. It matters greatly if such a community disappears after one or two generations. If it tries to carry on in the absence of a spiritual core preferably conveyed through oral learning, it is a doomed community.

While I was privileged to lead the synagogue I founded, the congregation of Pacific Jewish Center in Los Angeles, we had a strict rule. There were no dues or other membership fees. People contributed what they wished. But anyone wishing to join the congregation had to be enrolled in a shiur, a class in which the rabbi and the students discussed the meaning of ancient texts like the Torah and the Talmud. Though students and rabbi all came from a remarkably diverse set of backgrounds—financially, ethnically, socially, you name it— we were unified in the most wonderful way by our shared passion for learning God's word. This unity made all our differences fade to insignificance.

The difference which remained very significant for the long term was the one entailed by the range of ages: older, younger, and very young. That difference was one we celebrated and relished.

But here the Hebrew word-concept KaHaL is really just telling us something we know already if we gaze at the society around us and know what to look for. You've probably noticed a strange hunger, not least among the most affluent of us, for anything old. (Or rather, anything that is old. Old people are not highly prized.) Thus you have rich young people in big cities whose taste in clothes, household items, and real estate are conditioned by retro chic. Whatever looks old is hip.

I'll tell you what's going on here. There is an intuitive hunger in the human soul for certain very ancient ideas, especially the most ancient idea of all: God. In a world where teachers of old ideas are becoming increasingly rare, the hunger remains, but there is no one to feed it. The hungry soul doesn't even know exactly what it's hungering for. It only senses that whatever that is, it must be old. Hence the appeal of retro chic.

Community Witness

It is time to look at another word for community, which adds yet another dimension to our understanding. This word, EiDaH, has at its root the word EiD, which in itself has two meanings. An EiD is a witness, such as one who might appear in court but the word also refers to the eternal element of time. The Garden of EiDeN's name stems from this root. Just as you go to a floral garden to see flowers or a zoological garden to see animals, in the Garden of EiDeN Adam saw time extending forward throughout history.

A community needs a purpose for which it is assembling. When we associate with a community, we are in effect standing together as witnesses for that which is important to us. A community has a power which an individual does not. A group of people who join together and give testimony to eternal principles is a powerful force. Successful families and businesses have and express core values which bind them together. A community needs the same glue. It is not an amalgamation of people who share a zip code or who shop at the same supermarket.

By accessing these three different Hebrew words for community, we can proactively build a group where each member, of all ages, contributes towards providing mutual support and protecting and transmitting the standards which benefit us all.

CHAPTER 12

THE KINDNESS DILEMMA

חסד

CHeSeD

Suggestion: See the alphabet chart and Holy Hebrew! Tools 1 and 2 to get the most out of this chapter.

There was a popular bumper sticker a few years ago that read, "Do a random act of kindness today." Obviously no one but Attila the Hun would oppose that idea. We all want to be thought of as kind people. We all would like to raise our children to be kind, and we want others to act with kindness towards us.

However, attempting to be kind is an enormous problem. If I tell my child to be prompt, the meaning is clear. I wish her to show up on time for appointments and to finish all chores and assignments at the agreed upon time. If I want to be thought of as a cheerful person, I must stop complaining incessantly and begin greeting people with a smile on my lips. Attributes such as promptness and cheerfulness are easily defined.

But what exactly does being kind mean? Does it mean always yielding to the demands and requests of others? Should people trying to become kind and compassionate avoid accepting positions of responsibility in which they may have to discipline others? How much of one's income should be donated in order to fulfill the requirements of kindness and compassion? This is the problem with kindness. It sounds nice in principle but is incredibly hard to define.

Years ago a pediatric nurse who attended my synagogue told me about a young mother who brought her infant in for the baby's first immunizations. As the doctor picked up the syringe, the mother began sobbing, grabbed her baby, and fled the room saying, "It's going to be too painful." While some parents are wary of immunizations because of potential side effects, this mother was not making a reasoned and thoughtful decision. She was reacting emotionally and, in her view, with compassion. My guess is that she thought of herself as an extremely kind person, perhaps one who avoided stepping on ants and never passed a beggar without dropping a coin in his lap. Yet, as any parent who is aware of the crippling effect of some dangerous childhood diseases could tell you, she may actually have been acting with great cruelty. She was allowing her own emotions to override her child's real needs.

Attempting to be kind is an enormous problem.

In the same way a teacher who is too kind to fail a lazy student may be setting that child up for a life of failure. A judge who lets a first time adolescent offender off too easily runs the risk of the youth interpreting that kindness as license to become even more brazen and ruthless in the future.

Dispensing money indiscriminately to people can have the opposite of the intended effect. All too often, the apparently kind action of giving someone money backfires and ends up in waste or harm. Years ago, Oprah Winfrey generously donated vast sums of money toward a housing project for poor Americans. She finally conceded defeat and withdrew her support of the project when the housing was destroyed by those it was intended to benefit.

Genuine Kindness is Always Linked to God

So how are we to know if we are truly being kind? The Hebrew word for an act of profound kindness is CHeSeD.

ד ס ח

D S CH

Interestingly, God Himself commits both the first and last acts of CheSeD chronicled in the Bible. He tailors suits of clothing for Adam and Eve, considering their fig leaves to be inadequate for their self-respect and happiness. In Jewish tradition, helping people clothe themselves in a dignified fashion is considered to be an even greater act of kindness,—CHeSeD—than giving them food. This is because the latter alleviates only a physical discomfort while clothing protects both a person's body and soul.

Doing an act of kindness for someone, while expecting no repayment, is seen as a special type of CHeSeD. At the close of the book of Deuteronomy, God buried Moses. Burying someone is an act of kindness that the recipient of the benefit will never be able to repay. Thus, God's own book, the Torah, opens and closes with the Creator modeling true kindness, or CHeSeD.

One distinction that is worth making is that we need to separate CHeSeD from charity. Charity is an obligation to give to those who have less than we do. CHeSeD can be bestowed on those who have way more than we do, who are our superiors in many ways and who do not fit the requirements for charity recipients. In many ways, CHeSeD is a description of how we deal with others and should absolutely be a criterion for the way we treat our family even more so than more distant relationships.

The important message for us is that God is intrinsically involved in kindness. Here we have the faintest hint of a solution to our dilemma. Somehow genuine kindness must be linked to God. Why should this be? After all, He certainly possesses vital attributes other than kindness, such as being omnipresent or all-powerful. The message being sent to us is that kindness, as an independent attribute, doesn't really work.

Individuals who don't believe in God may indeed be kind, and certainly many are, but a society cannot survive unless there is an unchangeable, immutable definition of right and wrong. Civilization as we know it can't last if, during one generation murdering old folk or unborn children is wrong, but twenty years later euthanasia and abortion are preached as the kindest way to deal with lives that have a less than perfect "quality of life." Attempts at secular or atheistically based kindness are doomed in the long term by the absence of any defining framework.

Parents and teachers need to know that their role is to guide
and mold those in their care in God's ways. By definition, if
they do their jobs well, they will be treating their charges
kindly. Earlier generations were more aware of this unbreakable link between God and goodness and how the former
firmly defined the latter. Those who now forget that link are
unintentionally leading us back toward a primitive barba-
rism, all the while proclaiming a great commitment to 'kindness' and 'compassion.'

As parents, community leaders and professionals, we should
always remain vigilant against the tyranny of kindness and
compassion without God. Without Him, those words mean,
as Alice in Wonderland would understand, exactly what we
want them to mean, neither more nor less.

The Language of Good

Let us see how even linguistically, kindness is linked to the
Lord. The English language, among others, reveals the connection between God and kindness. As Indo-European languages gradually evolved out of Hebrew, one of the challenges was how to deal with Hebrew's guttural "CH" sound.
That letter chet, the eighth of the Hebrew alphabet, is used
to open the word "CHanuka," for instance. Many Americans
pronounce the name of that holiday as if it were written Ha-
nuka. Yet the letter chet is actually intended to be a guttural,
back of the throat, growl-like sound.

Several European languages such as Dutch and German
retained that guttural sound for their letter G. This explains
certain strange English spellings. For example, there is no
logical reason why the written form of the number that

follows seven should not be written 'ate.' The 'gh' in the middle of the word 'eight' is only there because of the word's original link to Hebrew's eighth letter, chet, or as it might have been transliterated in an earlier time, ghet.

The Greek alphabet starts off with alfa, beta, gamma because it is based upon the Hebrew alphabet, whose first three letters are aleph, bet, and gimmel. Or, if you prefer, A, B, G. Only later did society lop off the tail of the 'G' to make a 'softer' sound, namely the 'C' as in tic, which we use in English. Thus with C being an heir of the G, we can see that CH or GH are essentially the same sound in the early phases of European language development.

This means that if we transliterate the Hebrew word for kindness, CHeSeD, into English, instead of using the two letters 'C' and 'H' together to represent the first syllable—the single Hebrew letter chet—we could use GH, which in English at the beginning of a word is pronounced 'G' as in ghetto. This lets us transliterate CheSed as G—S—D. You can see that we are getting quite close to G-O-D. It is a bit like a detective story or an archeological dig.

Let's look more closely at the middle letter of the trio, 'S'. Glance at the sequence of letters below in the Hebrew alphabet starting from the eleventh letter, Kaf. We find the sequence to be Kaf, Lamed, Mem, Nun, and Samech. If we write the sounds of each letter it looks like this: K, L, M, N, S. Notice how the English alphabet grew directly from these seeds: K, L, M, and N.

Only the letter "O" seems to trip us up. How did Samech, with its 'S' sound evolve into 'O'? If we can resolve this problem, it will be clear to us just how the Hebrew word expressing the ultimate in kindness became the very word we use for the Creator, the origin of all our understanding of kindness—God.

Examine the Hebrew letter Samech, the left-most letter above the 'S'. It looks like an 'O', doesn't it? You see a nice round circle. So the look fits, but the sound doesn't match. Interestingly enough, each letter in the Hebrew alphabet has an intrinsic connection to the first time it appears at the start of a word in the Bible. The first use of the letter Samech at all in the Bible is as the initial letter of the word, meaning 'encircle' in Genesis 2:11. Although every other letter in the Hebrew alphabet occurs by the sixteenth verse of the Bible, this letter alone lingers unused for some forty verses after which it finally makes its significant appearance in the very word that expresses its shape. Coincidence? Of course not.

Greek originally evolved out of the Semitic languages, most notably Hebrew. The Greek letter which was pronounced as a long 'O' sound (as in home), was the letter Omega. If we replace the 'O' with an 'S' we can make out the Hebrew letter Samech. (The consonants in Omega once we switch the O for an S look like this: SoMeGa, or SoMeCHa.) One can readily imagine a round letter that resembles a human mouth saying 'oh' evolving into the sound one gets by doing exactly that. Whether that happened in the Greek period or during some other time in history is not important.

If our hypothesis of the Hebrew letter 'S' and English 'O'

switcheroo is in fact correct, surely we would expect to find other instances of words that contain an 'S' in Hebrew but an 'O' in English. Right? By way of reassuring the skeptical reader, here are other indications that the original Hebrew letter 'S' gradually became an 'O' in popular usage.

We have any number of such words. Many people are familiar with the Passover observance of the SeDeR, that celebratory meal reliving the Exodus from Egypt. Ask anyone familiar with basic Hebrew, what the word SeDeR means, and he will tell you that it means OrDeR, which is why the meal is conducted according to the printed agenda called a Hagada depicting the 'order' of the meal.

Did you notice that transposition again of "O" for "S"? The 'S' in Hebrew's 'SeDeR' became the 'O' in Engish's 'OrDeR'. Terrific!

There are many other examples of the Hebrew 'S' sound becoming an English 'O' sound. For instance, the English word 'OMeN' derives from the Hebrew word for an omen or a sign, which is 'SiMaN'. Since vowel sounds in Hebrew are subsidiary and changeable, we can see that the three root letters of OMeN resemble the original Hebrew word SiMaN.

The main point is that our word for the Almighty, the word G-O-D, clearly and appropriately originated in the Hebrew G-S-D word for ultimate kindness.

The Oxford English Dictionary correctly identifies the meaning of the word 'Goodbye' as 'God be with you'. Thus we see that the English word 'Good' derives directly from the source of all good, which is God. You can see where I am going here. There is a compelling linguistic argument that originally humans understood that God and Kindness were not two separate ideas. There is also a logical argument to be made that all attempts to define goodness or kindness without a framework of reference are doomed. They were not even two separate words.

For as long as they were understood as a sort of merged reality, each dependent upon the other for its meaning, mankind was better off. However, once a culture commences to define kindness with a political frame of reference instead of a religious one, it runs into the danger of stepping on to the slippery slope that ultimately converts kindness to cruelty and tyranny.

CHAPTER 13

FEUD FOR THOUGHT

חלק

CHeLeK

*Suggestion: See the alphabet chart and Holy Hebrew! Tools
1 and 2 to get the most out of this chapter.*

The following scenario will be familiar to any parent.

Johnny and Sally are squabbling over the single remaining orange nestled innocently in the fruit basket. Both tykes are ready to do battle rather than yield to the other. This incessant sibling rivalry is threatening to drive Mom mad! What she really wants to do is seize the orange and hurl it across the yard safely out of the reach of either child. Fortunately, she's enough in control of herself to recognize that such a reaction would be just as childish as the misbehavior of the two pint-sized adversaries presently glaring at one another. With exaggerated calm, Mom starts talking through gritted teeth.

"Why do you want the orange, Johnny? What do you want to do with it?" Johnny reacts with indignation. He has been playing ball in the hot sun. He is thirsty. He intends to use Mom's new electric squeezer (which fascinates him) to extract some refreshing orange juice.

Sally erupts in fury. "No, he can't do that. I want the orange!"

"And what are you going to do with the orange, Sally?" inquires a mother beginning to regain her composure. Well, guess what? Sally is baking her first-ever from-scratch cake. No more cake mixtures for her; she is old enough to follow a recipe. And this recipe calls for grated orange rind!

With a sigh of relief, Mom launches a lesson in cooperation. "It always pays to talk things through with people before starting a fight," she explains. Just a short conversation has revealed that both children can obtain their objectives from the single orange: Johnny can have his orange juice and Sally can have her grated orange rind.

Most of us can think of many more things we want and desire than we have the ability to obtain.

This little tale is more relevant to daily life than we might imagine.

It is in the nature of people to squabble. Most of us can think of many more things we want and desire than we have the ability to obtain. Happy living sometimes involves restraining those rather vague wants and desires from turning into appetites and obsessions. If someone else takes hold of something we not only want, but perhaps even consider to be "our right," we have the makings of a squabble. There are thousands of ways in which well-intentioned people can disagree with one another over property. This is human nature.

Otherwise, why would so much of the Torah consist of rules
for settling property disagreements?

Civilized Dispute Settlement

This is why every civilized society possesses a legal system
to settle such disagreements in a civilized fashion. We do not
aim for a society with no disagreements; that would be unrealistic. Spending time trying to build such a utopia would
also deflect our attention from what we really could accomplish; which is a fair and just system for settling inevitable
disputes.

In olden times and in remote lands, savages would club
one another to death. These days we more often resort to
lawsuits. "See you in court," has become today's relatively
civilized version of the Wild West's showdown. With more
lawyers in Los Angeles than in all of Japan, we have become
over-litigious, but that is still better than the law of the jungle
which prevails in many other countries to this day.

Part of growing up is getting to the point where we understand that we seldom get everything we want. Sometimes
we just wisely accept that fact and devote our energies
to productive enterprises. Other times we decide that an
argument is necessary. However not every argument
requires one party to win and the other to lose. While we
may not always get everything we want, in many instances
we can achieve our main objective while allowing the other
party to do the same. This can be done without resorting to
courtrooms or even to an adversarial disagreement.

Today, in increasing numbers, litigants resort to a process

called mediation, in which a mediator plays the role of Mom. The mediator helps them locate areas of agreement and assists in the process of helping both sides win. If the process fails, they can then resort to an adversarial courtroom encounter.

The Hebrew verb meaning "to argue" reflects this reality. It is based on the word CHeLeK, which literally means a portion or component.

ק ל ח

a portion, a component

ת ק ל ח מ

a quarrel

This implies that when one person is arguing with another, quite naturally, he expresses the one component or element of the debate that most closely advocates his own position. Any responsible judge knows that he should not reach a decision until he has listened to both sides. As involved participants or bystanders, we too have to remember that what we are hearing is only part of the entire story. This seems almost self-evident; however, it is really counter-intuitive. We may know better, but our intuitive reaction to a disagreement, when it involves us or someone close to us, is to assume that our own viewpoint is right and the other is wrong. Almost inevitably, our own position sounds more reasonable and logical. Anyone failing to fall into line with our outlook is, in our view, an obtuse fool.

In almost every disagreement in which we find ourselves, it is worthwhile remembering these two principles: (1) each side is utterly persuaded of the justice of his cause, and (2) each side is utterly persuaded that if he does not win, he will lose. In many cases, we would gain much by at least considering the possibility that these two assumptions are wrong. We should at least suspect that the two positions may be in fact be complementary and that all we have to do is find the key to the puzzle.

Merging Incompatible Views

The puzzle, of course, is how to merge two apparently incompatible views into one synthesized entity. Fortunately an exercise exists which helps mediate disputes.

You see, before we can effectively mediate external conflicts, we have to improve our abilities to cope with internal contradictions. We all instinctively yearn for clarity and simplicity in our lives. We tend to prefer things in black and white. For instance, the phrase "You can't both be right," springs easily to our lips, but the real world is quite different. To avoid and resolve conflict, it is indeed essential to be able to hold contradictory ideas comfortably in our minds.

I had to teach this lesson to a member of my synagogue when he called to tell me that his father had just died. This is nearly always one of the most traumatic ordeals any man will endure. In his particular case it was additionally complicated by the fact that he was the sole heir to his late father's stupendous wealth. When we met an hour later, my friend was in anguish. He had been tormenting himself, trying to overwhelm his being with what he considered an appropriate sensation of grief. However, he also was struggling with an unwelcome urge to break into hysterical laughter at the thought of never having to worry about money again. He was confused and miserable at the guilt he felt about not being able to concentrate exclusively on sadness.

Once I had explained that God intended humans to be able to function with two contradictory thoughts and feelings simultaneously, my friend felt much better. It was for this reason, I told him, that the Bible informs us what sort of cargo was being transported by the Arab traders who bought Joseph from his brothers. Who cares that they were carrying fragrant spices? A young boy had been seized from the bosom of his family and would never see his beloved father again. He was a captive of a caravan of traders. The lesson is that even under these anxious conditions, Joseph enjoyed being surrounded by the aromatic perfumes that accompanied him on his journey to anticipated slavery.

Only God Can Perform Two Actions at a Time

While we must certainly develop our abilities to function comfortably while thinking contradictory thoughts, humans are restricted to only one action at a time. It was fine for my congregant to think and feel both joy and sadness at the same time. However, during the funeral and the subsequent week of mourning he was to confine his actions to those appropriate to mourning.

Ancient Jewish wisdom turns to the Bible to demonstrate another facet of this principle. The Bible presents two separate versions of the fourth commandment, which concerns the Sabbath day. In Exodus 20:8 we read, "*Remember* the Sabbath day to keep it holy." Later, in the last of the Five Books of Moses where the Ten Commandments are repeated, the fourth commandment reads, "*Guard* the Sabbath Day to keep it holy" (Deuteronomy 5:12). Well, which was it? Did God say "Remember" or did He say "Guard"? Surely it had to be one or the other, right?

There is an academic school of Biblical criticism that I utterly reject as frivolous, dishonest and anti-intellectual. Nonetheless, this school of thought has long insisted that a succession of different humans authored the Torah. They talk of a series of documents identified by letters, such as the "J" document, or the "E" document. This so-called Documentary Hypothesis mostly serves to reveal the academics' lack of familiarity with the Hebrew language and ancient Jewish wisdom. Furthermore, these academics describe how some rather incompetent editor redacted or assembled all these old accounts into the one book we today call the Bible. There are many reasons why I know they are mistaken. One reason is that they cite these two slightly different versions of the Ten Commandments, one in Exodus and one in Deuteronomy, as evidence for the existence of several disconnected Biblical accounts. For one thing, the presumed primeval editor, for whose existence no evidence can be found, must have been a little slow on the uptake to not have noticed the difference between 'remember' and 'guard.' On the other hand, if he did notice the variation in accounts, was not his job to edit the different accounts into one integrated volume? Why didn't he simply determine whether to use 'remember' or 'guard' and thus settle the matter for all time? At the very least, having decided apparently to leave both words in place in spite of the conflict, he should have left us a note explaining his reasoning.

He neither resolved nor explained the conflict because he never existed. The two conflicting words, 'remember' and 'guard,' were in the Fourth Commandment from that original day at Mount Sinai. The ancient Israelites would never have tampered with the holy text, and they had no desire to, since their oral tradition fully and satisfactorily explained the purpose for these two versions. This oral tradition teaches that God, in a way that obviously only He could, indeed spoke both alternative words simultaneously. For human ears naturally, the Five Books of Moses portrays the miracle as two separate words: 'remember' in Exodus and 'guard' in Deuteronomy. Only God can act in two contradictory ways simultaneously; we humans have been granted half the gift. We are privileged to at least be able to think of two conflicting things simultaneously. Fully understanding this will greatly assist our ability to deal with conflict.

God's instruction to the ancient Israelites was that they should simultaneously *guard* and *remember* the Sabbath day. They were to guard it by scrupulously avoiding those activities that would diminish the day, such as using it for performing the same work as is done during the rest of the week. They were to simultaneously *remember* it by meticulously engaging in those activities that honor the day, such as eating celebratory family meals. To this very day, heirs to that tradition, once each seven days, observe the Sabbath both in the things we actively do and in the things we refrain from doing. In other words, 'remember' tells us part of the story while 'guard' provides another portion.

We mere humans can obviously not speak two words simultaneously. But we are given the uniquely human talent of being able to reconcile two seemingly conflicting ideas. By thinking of a disagreement as a maCH-Lo-Ket, a part of the whole story, rather than as an argument writ in stone, we are often able to live in harmony together, rather than seeing those who disagree with us as implacable foes.

Win/Win

Understanding this principle of maCH-Lo-Ket is even more important when dealing with personal relationships rather than distant ones. It is nice to get along with my neighbor or fellow citizen, but it is imperative to do so with my spouse. A tremendously difficult but vital adjustment for a married couple to make is to learn how to disagree. The husband and wife must come to the dual recognition that issues must be addressed rather than swept under the rug and that in marital conflicts both parties win or both parties lose. The action the couple chooses to take may well be the one that only one spouse wanted, but that action cannot be forced on the other person. Realizing the great effort that should be expended to understand the motivation and reasoning of one's spouse, and that each side's CHeLeK of the conflict needs serious attention is most likely to result in both members of the marriage 'buying in' to the final decision. Frequently the two viewpoints can be merged satisfactorily if husband and wife see each other as on the same team rather than as adversaries.

Sally and Johnny from the beginning of our chapter may not know how important they are to each other until they grow older, but those of us past the juvenile stage can protect our important relationships by utilizing the message of CHeLeK.

CHAPTER 14

THE FAITH FACTOR

אָמֵן

AMeN

Suggestion: See the alphabet chart and Holy Hebrew! Tools 1, 2 and 3 to get the most out of this chapter.

My father used to indulge my boyish love of the circus by taking me to the "Big Top" every time it visited our town. It wasn't until I became a father myself that it dawned on me: The real reason dad regularly took me to the circus was that he loved the sawdust ring in the giant tent even more than I did.

The favorite part of our expedition was always the after-show visit to the animal housing area. There we would wander past the elephants and their trainers. The lions and tigers would growl menacingly as we walked by. Our favorite animal was the horse that knew arithmetic. Perhaps my own futile attempts to master arithmetic at school lay behind my fascination with this creature. Just imagine—a horse that apparently could do sums of the sort that taxed my own academic abilities!

Once there, the trainer could usually be prevailed upon to show off his horse's mathematical talents a few more times. With his arm nonchalantly draped over the beautiful beast's neck, he would pose a question that would set my head spinning. To me it appeared that the horse was taking a moment or two to figure out the answer. Then the horse would begin tapping his foot...four, five, six times. Yes, that was the correct answer to the problem—six. And so it went time after time. The trainer asked an arithmetic question, and this amazing horse tapped out the solution.

The trainer always gave his horse a lump of sugar after each correct answer. I recall musing about how different school life could be, were candy awarded each time we students cited the correct answer to an arithmetical question. I remained vaguely perturbed by those lumps of sugar. I also recall wondering why the man was called the "trainer" and not the "teacher."

I eventually found out that the horse knew no more arithmetic than I did. He had been trained (not taught) to tap his foot each time his trainer (not teacher) touched his ear. Each time he obeyed and tapped the required number, he was rewarded with a sugar cube. This gave him incentive to continue translating ear taps into foot taps. In reality, he was only trying to obtain another sugar cube. Horses, like other animals, must be rewarded immediately if they are to repeat the trick.

Deferred Gratification

People, on the other hand, can drive themselves to achieve even if their reward is deferred. The more sophisticated we become, the longer the gap between effort and reward we are able to endure. After baby-sitting for neighborhood families, my nine-year-old and twelve-year-old daughters are happiest if they come home clutching their spoils. After school each day, my sixteen-year-old daughter works at a senior residential facility. She receives her paycheck every two weeks. But I have noticed that she can become pretty impatient as the end of the pay period dawdles slowly closer—especially if there is a fashion sale at the local mall. Some of us insist upon being paid by the hour while others are reasonably content to work on a large transaction for a year or more before the payoff.

While the time gap may vary, in whatever way we earn a living we generally have to deliver before we reap the rewards. The farmer who plants and irrigates his crop might work for months before his harvest is sold at market. Then again, it might not sell at all. The craftsman who carefully constructs a bookcase will be paid only once the customer can take delivery. That, of course, depends on whether the customer approves of the product. The shoe store proprietor must courteously respond to the fashion aspirations of the fastidious buyer after which, if he is lucky, he may make a sale. We intuitively grasp that only failure awaits the person who demands guaranteed payment before delivering anything of quality, be it a product or a service. We recognize that anyone wishing to participate in the economy has to be willing to work first and then hope for reward. Nothing is assured, and every enterprise contains risk. It is almost as if built into the very system that sustains us is the need for... what better word than *faith*?

Through His language, God notified us of His program in advance. A participant in the economy, perhaps a craftsman or a businessman, is known as an UMaN, spelled aleph, mem, nun.

א מ ן
←

The same three letters pronounced differently form a word we use frequently in worship—AMeN. A person who is faithful is known as a ne-EMaN, and by responding to a prayer with "amen" we include ourselves among those who have faith. (Remember, the variance in the vowel sounds are all of secondary importance and don't affect the spelling)

Through this connection of business and faith, Hebrew informs us that faith is the one essential tool necessary to function effectively in economic interaction with our fellow humans. That is what is known as the risk element. This is an inviolable rule: If a particular investment carries zero risk, it demands zero faith and will return zero profit. From the viewpoint of the customer, few will guarantee payment for something they have not yet seen.

Faith and faith

Perhaps we ought to try to define faith. First, let us distinguish between Faith and faith. Not every usage of the word faith is within a religious context. The word faith itself simply means the ability to see something presently still invisible as clearly as if it were already there. You might display ordinary faith in a city bus schedule by being at the bus stop on time. The farmer has faith that if he plants and cares for his crop, it will grow and he will be able to harvest and sell it. Without that faith, he would never even venture out to his fields. The craftsman has faith in his ability to construct an appealing product. The shoe store proprietor has faith that if he courteously demonstrates his new line of footwear to as many customers as possible, he will eventually sell out his stock. And anyone who invests in a stock, a bond, a mutual fund, or in any other kind of investment does so because his research and due diligence give him faith that the investment will pay off.

Does faith mean that every farmer will always successfully sell his crop or that every investment will succeed? No, of course not. However it does mean that without faith, no farmer would plant anything and no investor would ever risk his carefully accumulated capital.

The good Lord appears to have arranged matters so that faith, the ability to clearly see what is still invisible, is rewarded. Why would He do this? Possibly in order to reward Faith in Him. Religious Faith refers to the ability of the faithful to see God clearly.

Exercise Strengthens the Faith Muscle

You see, all of our muscles are strengthened by exercise. What is more, any muscle strengthened by one particular exercise can be used for all kinds of other valuable exertions, most of which look nothing like the original exercise that developed the strength in the first place. For instance, I might work out with weights in the gym twice a week. One weekend my wife might ask me to help her rearrange the furniture. Watching this, my youngest child might ask, "Dad may be able to lift barbells, but who says he can lift chairs and tables?" The answer is that if I can lift weights of one shape, I am likely able to lift weights of any shape.

Similarly, our faith muscle is best exercised by regular expressions of Faith in God. I am not saying that no other means of strengthening the faith muscle exist; I am just saying that a relationship with God is probably the easiest and most effective way to strengthen our ability to see that which is not yet visible. Once our faith muscle has been strengthened in this fashion, it is much easier for us to use it in other areas, such as participating in the economy. One would therefore expect that any society in which Faith in God plays a major role would be a society that is conspicuously successful economically.

Could this perhaps be the reason why no atheistic regime has ever succeeded in generating an indigenous capital market? Having no Faith in God usually results, eventually, in no faith toward His creatures or their efforts. Could the AMeN principle also have something to do with the disproportionate success that Jews have always enjoyed in business? This principle may also explain how the United States has emerged as the greatest wealth-creating country in world history. It is, of course, also the country with the highest proportion of Faithful in the entire industrialized world. Needless to say, both Judaism and Christianity place more emphasis on Faith than many other religions and thus benefit distinctively from the strengthening of the national faith muscle. The Bangladeshi peasant may possess some gold, but it is hidden in his mattress. It takes great faith, a practiced faith muscle, to hand that gold and all the time and effort it represents, to a bank or an investment vehicle. With this scene multiplied by millions of peasants, we can see how a country can be impacted by faith or the lack of it. Without that faith, gold remains in the mattress and Bangladesh remains mired in poverty.

It used to be said that poor countries exist because of exploitation by colonial powers. It gradually became clear that colonies ended up costing money rather than producing it. Literature of the period shows that England during her imperial period mostly colonized other parts of the world in order to spread Christianity. Her involvement in Africa, Asia, and even America ended up costing the mother country great sums. So if imperialism did not cause some countries to be poor, what did?

> **If a particular investment carries zero risk, it demands zero faith and will return zero profit.**

The next theory was that creating wealth required both capital and information. In other words, to become rich, countries needed money to build factories and the know-how to build them. During the late twentieth century, international boundaries began falling until money pursued investment opportunity to every corner of the world. The Internet's spreading popularity meant that information also knew no boundaries. Well, with money available everywhere from Australia to Zimbabwe, and with information freely available to anyone with a computer, the question remains— why are some countries still poor?

The answer is surely AMeN. The creation of wealth requires some start-up money and the knowledge of what to do with that money. We do not need the Lord's language to tell us that. What we have not fully appreciated is that while those two prerequisites are certainly necessary, they are not sufficient by themselves. The creation of wealth depends on capital and information, PLUS a widespread system of faith. Everyone in economic interaction needs faith that their labor is likely to be ultimately rewarded. They need faith that the system under which they live will endure and that it will help them protect and preserve the rewards of their efforts. They also need faith that their fellow citizens will deal with them in what we appropriately call "good faith." Without that faith, all effort would cease, credit would never be extended, and the entire enterprise would gradually run down like an old-fashioned clock that nobody wound.

Faith On the Money

I often enjoy posing a question to acquaintances in Europe and Asia who have never yet visited the United States: *There is a phrase we Americans post conspicuously, "In God We Trust." Where do we post this credo?* Not surprisingly, most people guess that we place this phrase on the walls of churches and synagogues. They are astonished to hear that it is to be found upon our currency. I am not. The phrase is not needed upon the walls of churches and synagogues, for worshippers in attendance already know that. We need to be reminded on a daily basis that our very currency and the comfort it brings depends chiefly on Faith.

From the dawn of our national history we have always understood the connection between our Faith and our prosperity. This makes us a most unusual country and perhaps explains why our dollar symbol is made up of our national name—a letter S superimposed upon a letter U. The lower curve of the U coincides with the lower curve of the S, leaving us with a letter S beneath two vertical parallel lines, the original down strokes of the letter U.

AMeN, being both the noun "faith" as well as the verb "believe"—as in "I believe"—helps us understand this most crucial of lessons regarding economic comfort. A believer might utter "I believe" in the context of worship, while an investor might use exactly the same phrase to explain his choice of investment. It also teaches us the practical impor-tance of first delivering and then getting paid. The Lord's language reveals His blueprint. He obviously wants us to first concentrate on doing something for other people, and only thereafter to worry about what they can do for us.

What an incredible education to offer our children, and what a great lesson for us all to absorb. The world is set up to reward us to the extent that we focus on finding ways to do things for other people. If we focus only on what others can do for us, we fail.

Can you think of something material you would like? Who can't? But here is a much harder question: Can you think of something you could do for other people? Not so easy, is it? But when you thoughtfully answer that second question, you will have just written the first chapter of your business plan. Whether you plan a big public company or a small home business, the very first question to ask is, "What can I do that would really make other people happy?"

Isn't it obvious that God designed this system? How helpful

of Him to give us the secret by making one word in His language mean both "faith" and "a participant in the economy."

CHAPTER 15

ADDING TO OUR WEALTH

עשר

ASHiR-ESeR

*Suggestion: See the alphabet chart and Holy Hebrew! Tools
1, 2, 3, and 5 to get the most out of this chapter.*

If you start out with five apples and you give one of them
to me, how many do you have left? Most likely you recall that arithmetic problem or a similar one from your early
school days.

The problem taught you the simple reality that the more
you give away the less remains for you. This is obviously true,
yet we are struck by a mysterious paradox: How is it possible for the wealthiest nation in the world, America, to also
be the nation most infatuated with giving money away?

This is not only true on an individual level, but it is also the
case nationally. For instance, Rotary, an international private
organization of ordinary business professionals, raises an
enormous amount of money through its American chapters. Through their donations of money and expertise, this
amazing group almost eradicated the dread disease of polio
from India. Have you noticed that whenever calamity strikes
anywhere in the world, it is almost always American (or

Israeli) relief teams that arrive first? Invariably, America's charitable and faith-based organizations send generous assistance wherever needed.

Seldom do similar levels of assistance arrive from other countries. Many argue that since America is such a wealthy country, this is merely our responsibility. I think that the correct interpretation is precisely the reverse: We became wealthy because we were inculcated with a culture of charity in the cradle of our national infancy. Expressions of Biblical morality, including a commitment to charity, are enshrined in the founding documents of the United States of America.

America is one of the few countries in the world in which charitable contributions are tax deductible. Some people incorrectly assume that Americans are charitable because of that tax rule. Again, the truth is precisely the reverse: That tax rule is in place to conform to the wishes of American citizens who wish to act charitably and do not wish to be doubly taxed. Large numbers of Americans donate sums that are greater than the levels that would benefit their tax status. The truth is that Americans are in love with the act of giving money away to those who are in need.

Try to count the number of non-profit institutions in America that thrive on the free-will offerings of their supporters. We have countless churches, schools, universities, hospitals, welfare organizations, and other non-for-profits that cannot be found in other countries. We here in the United States seem to be imbued with the desire to give charity, and for many of us that means at least a tenth of our money.

How Did This Come About?

America's founding fathers were quite familiar with the Lord's language. They knew that in Hebrew one word frequently serves to convey what appear to be two very distinct English ideas. When that happens, we are to realize that what seemed to us to be two separate ideas are not quite so unconnected. In our case, the root of both the word *rich* —ASHiR and the root word *ten* or *tenth*—EseR—looks like this:

In Hebrew, one letter, the shin, can sound like either s or sh. A dot is used to distinguish between those two sounds, but they are the same letter. Words that use this letter can be pronounced either way with no significant change in deeper meaning. Thus we see that the idea of wealth is linguistically linked to "ten" or "a tenth." Both those concepts are expressed by one and the same word.

The Paradox

Hence we gain one of the great breakthrough ideas of civilization—the idea of tithing, or giving away one tenth of one's money to others. By linking wealth to the concept of tithing, the Lord's language teaches us a wonderfully counterintuitive lesson. In some strange way, giving away a tenth of our money actually adds to our wealth.

The area of professional sales shines a light on this strange idea. Most sales professionals choose to be paid a commission instead of a straight salary. That way, the harder and more successfully they work, the more they will earn. Sales professionals are remarkable people. They trust their competence and their training and are willing to put themselves on the line. In essence, they say to a potential employer, "You should hire me because you have nothing to lose. You will pay me only after I have made money for you. I will only take a percentage of what I bring in." They are among the most important people who keep the wheels of our economy turning, and their magic is the commission system of payment.

The Lord's language encourages us to view our own means of earning a living as a sort of "commission" arrangement with God. But He offers an incredible payback plan—a 90 percent commission! Instead of keeping only a small percent of every dollar I produce, as happens when I work for most bosses, my Heavenly Boss allows me to keep 90 percent of every dollar. The remaining 10 percent, however, must be passed on to the Boss by giving it to His designated assignees: the poor and the needy. That is an authentically American way of viewing our charitable activities. We deserve no medals for giving away 10 percent of our money. It did not belong to us in the first place. We are just passing it through to its rightful owners.

The Hebrew language identifies this process of donating away 10 percent, or tithing, by the same root word we use to indicate "wealthy." In other words, paradoxically, this process of taking away from what you have does not leave you with less, but causes you to amass more! Amazing! How can diminishing what we have, by giving it away, produce more for us? To understand this phenomenon, talk to any generous philanthropist, or even just carefully examine your own charitable history. You will discover the same startling story. People repeatedly prosper after starting to maintain a regular tithing program.

Television viewers may be familiar with a large and magnificent church in Southern California. Many years ago, prior to the church's construction, its pastor encountered the owner of a small business on an airplane flight. They introduced themselves and chatted. As the flight progressed, the businessman became entranced with the pastor's vision of a great new church. He finally indicated to the pastor that he would like to assist in some way. The pastor suggested a large sum that was way out of the league of this rather modest gentleman. As the businessman told me the story, he related how something inside him made him agree to pledge the extraordinary sum over the next year or two. Returning home, he told his wife of his very major commitment. Instead of feeling crushed by a burden that was entirely disproportionate to the family's budget, both he and his wife felt elated. They agreed that they would pay their pledge in the form of a strict tithe on all their business income. That way, he said, fulfilling the pledge became God's problem rather than his. He felt quite liberated by his tithing commitment—a commitment which continues to this day.

Today that businessman is a famous investor and a pioneer in several cutting-edge technical companies. He attributes his wealth and economic success entirely to his tithing commitment. Like so many other Americans, this man learned a true Biblical lesson. Giving a tithe from your time and assets will lead to more, not less, wealth.

Deduction Means Gain

How can this illogical principle be true? This is the kind of mathematics that almost got me thrown out of grade school! But it does work, and here is how. First, some background.

One of our basic problems as human beings is how to wrest a living from a sometimes reluctant world, using the least possible effort. That simple question lies behind most economic activity. Whether you think of a subsistence farmer on a small plot of land somewhere in Africa or three thousand early-shift workers streaming through the gate of a petroleum refinery in Texas, it doesn't make a difference. They are all doing the same thing: attempting to ensure food in their tummies and a roof over their heads in the most painless way available to them. You and I do pretty much the same thing.

> **My Heavenly Boss allows me to keep 90 percent of every dollar.**

Anyone supporting himself by subsistence farming doesn't have too many alternatives. It is not a desirable way of earning a living. You work seven days a week, 365 days a year. Your productivity is just keeping ahead of your most basic needs—if you are lucky. How would you escape subsistence farming? The only way is the Lapin "Three Cs" method: connect, communicate, and collaborate which I expand upon in my audio CD sets *Prosperity Power: Connect for Success* and *Boost Your Income.*

There is a well-known fourth 'C' that grew out of the first

three. It is the modern corporation, one of the keys to western prosperity. A corporation is a place in which many individuals connect with one another, communicate with one another, and collaborate with one another. In so doing, they help one another earn a living in ways far more pleasant than solitary subsistence farming.

Interaction with others is the first, and perhaps the most important, step in creating a personal revenue stream. Without meaning to sound too metaphysical, we need to establish great big "money pipes" between us and the world out there. I am using pipes as a metaphor for the actual lines of communication that are so critical for our economic success. Of course, it is a mistake to establish links with only those people whom we think might become direct instigators of our hoped-for revenue stream. We should try to expand our connectivity with everyone, not just potential employers or customers. We need to learn to truly appreciate other people rather than thinking of making connections in order to use other people. Yet it does end of benefiting us. One way this happens is when people talk to other people. The word spreads. We call this process networking.

Start the Flow

Remember those "pipes" I spoke of above? They represent our attempts to reach out into the world from which we hope to earn a living. Now you may have no way to persuade someone to build a pipe to you and start pumping money through it into your bank account. However, you do have the ability to build such a pipe yourself—and you can start pumping money through it.

"Wrong direction!" you might yell at me. No, I can assure you, the direction of the flow doesn't matter. You see, once you have built the pipe and started using it by sending money through it, the direction is immaterial. The key is to open up pipelines between you and the world around you. Once those pipelines exist, it is far easier for money to flow your way, too.

To translate the metaphor: Start tithing. Give at least 10 percent of your income to worthy causes. No sooner will you begin pumping money out than you will start to see money flowing in your direction, too.

Think about it. Leaving aside the concept of Heavenly direct intervention, it is almost impossible to become charitable without meeting lots of people. In addition to the direct recipients of your largesse, there are those who staff the charitable organization. Don't forget all the other donors you will meet. When it is time for these people to purchase a commodity or service of the type you offer, they will think of you. When it is time to hire staff, you will be in their consciousness. If they have come to know you, to like you and to trust you, business will likely ensue.

I am not for a moment suggesting that the only reason to perform acts of charity is to benefit your bank balance. Neither am I suggesting that those wonderful fellow citizens of ours who involve themselves in charitable organizations are doing so for ulterior motives. I am simply explaining the principle behind why the Lord's language uses the same word for charitable giving and wealth, and explaining one mechanism by which that principle may apply.

One thing is for sure. Americans have been blessed by their adherence to the strange mathematical model that decrees that if you have ten apples and give one to someone who has fewer than you, tomorrow you will have fifteen apples. Have you been missing that blessing? Begin today to give generously and whole-heartedly, and then watch what happens.

CHAPTER 16

FEEL THE COMPULSION!

עבדה

AVoDaH

*Suggestion: See the alphabet chart and Holy Hebrew! Tools
1 and 2 to get the most out of this chapter.*

Once upon a time, a pair of nineteenth-century railroad
laborers, Bill and Jeb, were laying track in the desolate
wilderness of the American West. This is about the hardest
work you can imagine, and the two were old-timers. They'd
been laying track for decades. One day a surprise visit was
made to the work site by no less a dignitary than the president of the railroad himself. While inspecting the work that
was going on, the great and august man came upon our pair
of dusty laborers. His eyes lit up.

"Well, hello Jeb!" he said. "You old scoundrel!"

Jeb looked bashful at first, but then the railroad president
threw his arms around the exhausted laborer. He asked
about Jeb's wife and family, shook his hand warmly, then
finally moved along to complete the inspection.

Jeb's coworker, Bill, was amazed. "When did you ever know
him?"

Jeb explained that thirty years earlier the two of them had

worked together laying track. Needless to say, through the intervening years the other man had enjoyed greater career success than had poor old Jeb.

"So," asked Bill, "what company were the two of you working for back then?"

"Well," Jeb replied, "he was working for the railroad."

"What do you mean he was working for the railroad? What about you? What were you working for?"

"Oh," said Jeb, looking a bit wistful, "I was working for fifty cents a day."

Some of us work just for the money. For others, work is a great opportunity.

The Lord's language has a word that means work: AVoDaH. This word also means "service"—in the dual context of customer service and of a worship service.

The three letters that make up the root of the word are ayin-bet-dalet

ד　ב　ע

dalet bet ayin

The letter ayin takes the sound of the vowel with which it is matched while bet can sound like a "b" or a "v". Now the meaning of some Hebrew words, including AVoDah, can best be grasped when we analyze the basic structure of the word. Instead of just accepting it as an ordinary three-letter root, we need to probe at a deeper level.

In Hebrew, there are certain pairs of letters which are meaningful when put together. When letters are added between them, the meaning of the newly formed words will relate to the original pairing. If this were so in English, we might find that the word 'AT' is composed of two letters that pair together meaningfully and that the words 'act', 'aft', and 'art' all would be connected, both to each other and to the meaning of the word 'at'. It sounds ludicrous, because in English, it is. But it is one of the ways that the Lord's language conveys a depth of meaning unknown in any other tongue.

In our case, for example, the first and last letters of AVD are the letters ayin and dalet.

ד   ע

dalet ayin

This little word is at the root of our word for work/service, and on its own, pronounced EyD, it means "witness." Some of the other words that are similar to work/service in that they start and end with the letters meaning "witness" are the words for (1) future, ATiD, (2) the root for 'to stand up', AMaD, and (3) the root for "to bind," AKaD.

ד י ת ע   –   ATiD: future

ד מ ע   –   AMaD: standing

ד ק ע   –   AKaD: binding

Confused? Don't be. Ignore the English vowels in all the words and you see that these three words all start and end with the same letters, with one extra letter inserted in the middle. Summing up, we can now say that "witnessing" (EyD) is an activity that somehow forms the common spiritual link between four related themes: (1) "doing service or work" (AVDH), (2) "being in the future" (ATD), (3) "standing up" (AMD), and (4) "binding" (AKD). Let's see how this works.

Witness

What does a witness do? Before a judge, jury, and anyone else present, he gives testimony regarding an experience he has had or facts he knows. He may have witnessed the defendant committing a crime, or he may have witnessed him sitting on a park bench in New York at the precise moment the crime was committed in Los Angeles. He will present testimony about these things. A witness who gets up before the court and spouts irrelevancies or private opinions ("Your Honor, wow, did I see a terrific movie last night!" "Well your Honor, what I believe is…") will quickly be admonished to stick to the facts of the case. From a witness, anything that is merely personal is useless. What is needed from a witness is information that is more important than the witness himself. The reason a witness might be treated as a minor celebrity or placed in some elaborate witness protection program has nothing to do with how charming or witty he may be. He is important only on account of the testimony he will offer. His function, you could say, transcends his own individual importance.

In fact, to stress this importance, a court witness will typically take an oath binding him "to tell the truth, the whole truth, and nothing but the truth" before giving testimony. That "binding" oath makes him a *witness* rather than just a person with an opinion. We emphasize that being a witness "binds" you to testify. If you are reluctant, you can even be officially summoned to the courtroom. Once there, you are again "bound" to tell the truth. Do you recall that one of our four related words was "bind"?

We might say, then, that "witnessing" includes: (1) an element of transcendence, that is, to say something that takes you out of and beyond yourself, and (2) an element of binding or compelling the witness. You will now see that all four words spun off from the two-letter root for "witness," or EyD, are marked by precisely these two qualities.

The Future

Thinking of the "future" (ATiD) forces and compels us to transcend the present and recognize that in a blink of the eye the present will become the past. The present does nothing other than seize the future and instantly turn it into the past. When we focus on the future it forces us to try to make each moment of the present worthwhile. Thinking of the future compels us to prepare for future necessities, even if we must do things that are not what we would most like to do in the present moment. In fact, this three-letter root ATiD can also mean "to prepare thoroughly."

Stand Up

"Standing up" (AMaD) forces the body from its resting, supine state to an alert state of readiness. The symbolic meaning of a person's body when it stands also alludes to transcendence. When somebody "stands up" for something he believes, that something tends to be a belief about realities that transcend him for which he may even be willing to fight and die, such as beliefs in one's God or in one's country. A person doesn't "stand up" for a mere taste or preferences—say, for chocolate over vanilla. This is why we stand whenever we do things that are really important, things that have to do with our central beliefs and values. For instance, citizens stand while singing their country's national anthem. We might stand for a moment of silence in memory of departed heroes.

Bind

The verb "to bind" (AKD) will cause many of us to recall the story of the "binding" (AKeDah) of Isaac, son of Abraham and Sarah. In the Book of Genesis, Abraham receives from God a command to bind Isaac on an altar, which he interprets to mean that he should slaughter the young man as a sacrifice. The command was ultimately clarified, but not before Abraham had indeed bound his son with ropes for the most transcendent reason of all: because God said He wished him to do so.

Simply tying something up for no greater purpose than to keep it in one place would not be described in Hebrew by the word AKD but by another root altogether: the letters kuf-shin-resh. This is the word we use in describing the task of fastening our shoelaces, for instance. When we are bound, physically or spiritually, compelled and forced by a purpose greater than ourselves, that is an AKeDah.

Toil vs. Work

Each of the words that grow from the word for "witness" carries the implications of something higher than oneself and also of an unbreakable commitment. So it is with our word for service/work—AVoDah. What lesson does this teach us that could be useful as we set off for work each morning? It teaches us the difference between working for a larger vision and working for the money. It really teaches us the essential difference between work and drudgery. Why should we think of the former as wonderfully worthwhile but the latter as soul shattering?

Herein lies the enormous difference between toil and work. A drudge works for his daily bread and that is all. He takes little pride in his effort and enjoys little sense of achievement upon its completion. This could apply to quite a few people in the modern-day workforce, right? What's more, drudgery has little to do with income. You can be a journalist, a dentist, a truck driver, or a schoolteacher and emotionally still be a daily laborer just the same.

In my corporate educational programs, I teach a principle that I call the cathedral concept. It is based on a famous story told of a traveler who encountered a workman fiercely pounding away at a stone with hammer and chisel. When asked what he was doing, the angry man put down his hammer and answered in a frustrated tone, "I am trying to shape this stone, and it is backbreaking work."

The traveler found a second man doing similar work. He appeared to be neither particularly angry nor happy. When asked what he was doing, he paused in his hammering and replied, "I'm shaping a stone for a building."

A third worker was singing happily as he chipped at his stone. "What are you doing?" he was asked.

Without missing a beat of his mallet, the worker responded,

"I am building a cathedral."

The first person felt diminished by his work, almost like a slave. The third man found his work uplifting. They were doing the same task; it was their attitudes that differed. Many people are frustrated by jobs that they perceive as too small for their spirits. They may suffer and tolerate a job, but they yearn for a calling. Grinding away on a daily basis is intolerable, but work can be wonderful.

But how do we convert drudgery into work? Without question, part of the obligation for this conversion falls on the employer. However, as an employee, there is still much one can do to convert one's job into a calling and one's labor into work.

Some of us work just for the money. For others, work is a great opportunity.

The first and most important thing is to take the lesson of AVoDah to heart. Unlike slavery, for example, AVoDah, work, must have two vital elements. First, it must lift one out of oneself; we call this a "transcendent" component. And second, it must also carry a sense of compulsion. In my cathedral concept story, the third worker associated both of these features with his task. He was not just working—he was building something. And he was not building just anything—he was building a cathedral! It was something much more important than his own being. He felt good, as we all might, at being an important part of a project of such magnitude and importance. He also felt driven and compelled to continue regardless of how tired he might have been. He didn't even take advantage of the passing traveler's inquiry to pause in this work.

Certainly, our employers can and should do much to improve our morale and our enthusiasm for our work. But let us assume they won't. It is up to us. What shall we do?

First, identify the ultimate purpose of what you do and find out how it brings benefit to others in society. Don't get bogged down in the mechanics. If you are a journalist, you are doing much more than merely stringing words together. If you are an assembly-line worker, you are doing much more than merely fastening bolts. If you are a truck driver, you are doing far more than merely racking up the miles.

Some of us are blessed with work which we easily see as meaningful. If you are a teacher accustomed to seeing a child's eye light up with understanding or a doctor performing a kidney transplant, you probably don't need to question the value of what you do. But if our work's value isn't readily apparent, we need to search for it. A truck driver is not only transporting needed materials but he is also an important link in keeping a country's commerce flowing. Many countries have faced shortages and even famine not because crops weren't growing, but because they couldn't get to the hungry people. Someone on the assembly line in a factory is vital for producing an item which will make the lives of thousands of people easier and more pleasant. If you absolutely see no value in what you do or what you are a part of—it's time to look for new work, because what you are doing is only toil.

Next, try to start thinking of yourself as absolutely vital to the larger goal of your enterprise. Welcome the pressure this puts you under. Try to do just a little more than the job calls for. Try to achieve a quality of work far above "good enough." Feel the compulsion!

One might even say that there is redemption in the work of someone who regards himself as working for more than his daily bread. Redemption may come in the form of material success. When you work just for the money, money itself tends to elude you. When you work for an idea that you love—usually an idea about the future, not just your own future but the future of other people as well—wealth tends to appear in your hands almost unbidden.

Working for the Boss

But there is spiritual redemption, too. Work can grant us a greater appreciation of what it means to have a Boss. Not just the human boss over in the corner office, but a really important, heavenly Boss. This Boss has extremely high expectations of His employees and watches them constantly. Consider the advice you might give a high-spirited adolescent seeking a summer job. He is going on interviews; he even occasionally gets hired but fails to retain the job for very long. He asks you how to get a job and keep it. You might give him three critical pieces of advice:

1) Show up for work reliably and punctually.

2) Humbly do exactly what you are told.

3) Behave respectfully to your boss, fellow workers, and customers.

None of these rules are terribly complicated, are they? Yet the majority of entry-level workers who get fired lose their positions for violating these rules. We are not talking about advanced vocational training here. We're talking about rules that have more to do with character training. In addition, the qualities we develop within ourselves as we convert drudgery into work are spiritually redemptive qualities. Imagine someone who has never before worked for a human boss. Not only is he ill-equipped to be his own boss, he is even ill equipped to have a real relationship with his Heavenly Boss. It all ties together.

If you can always view yourself as working not only for your mortal employer but also for your Boss in Heaven, the weight lifted from your tired shoulders is too great to be calculated. You will never find yourself working for a mere wage, but with a bigger picture in mind.

You will also be protected from the opposite extreme—that of labeling your work as an all-important career that takes priority over everything else in your life. If you have the proper attitude toward earning a living, everything you do will fill you with the thrill of purpose.

PART FOUR

GROWTH AND SUCCESS

Chapters 17–20

Be sure to check out pages 337–342
to discover helpful resources on this topic

CHAPTER 17

THE ROAD TO HAPPINESS

שמחה

SiM-CHaH

Suggestion: See the alphabet chart and Holy Hebrew! Tools 1, 2 and 6 to get the most out of this chapter.

As a young rabbi, I naively assumed that only destitute people sought refuge in drugs and alcohol. It was not until my friend Michael Medved and I established our synagogue in West Los Angeles that I discovered that there was no shortage of alcoholism and drug abuse among the affluent as well.

How can this be? I wondered. From what did those Californians, living in the lap of luxury, need to escape? I saw them at the University of California in Westwood. I saw them among the successful wheelers and dealers of the entertainment industry, and I saw them on Venice Beach near our synagogue. Why were so many, among the luckiest generation of Americans, walking around during the day in a drug-induced haze and falling asleep every night in intoxicated stupors?

The great psychiatrist Karl Jung pointed out that the old Latin name for alcohol, *spiritus*, hints at the answer to this problem. People depend on chemicals such as alcohol and drugs in order to assuage their suffering not from a material void, but from a spiritual one.

Apparently there is a form of poverty that is even worse than not having enough money in your pocket; it is the poverty of not having enough in your soul. The pain we experience when we lack that deep, internal happiness can be only temporarily anaesthetized by means of chemicals. Unfortunately, the aftermath generally leaves us feeling even more empty and hollow. The next time we need a little more of the chemical, or perhaps a stronger chemical. Pretty soon the periods of time between dosages shrink, and the dosages themselves grow bigger. Eventually we are facing a huge problem in addition to the original pain.

The Non-chemical Solution

There is a better way out of depression, sadness and self-loathing, and it has to do with growth. A sense of achievement is the natural, organic, non-chemical solution to our spiritual void. Forget the tablets, the bottle, or the syringe. Find a way to fill the hollow space in your soul with a sense of progress, and all will be better.

How does all this work? First, we should examine the source of this knowledge, which is SiM-CHaH, the Hebrew word for "happiness." The three root letters SIN, MEM, and CHET mean "happiness." If you glance at your alphabet chart you will see that the letter shin can be pronounced as shin or sin as necessary. It is one letter with two pronunciations.

ח   מ   שׂ

chet mem sin

We have a general principle in Hebrew that the two letters
TSADI and SHIN

ש   צ

shin (sin)   tsadi

enjoy a special relationship. The former, on the right above,
stands for righteousness and represents a saintly individual, while the latter, with its appearance of three tongues of
flame leaping heavenward represents ultimate attainment of
heavenly bliss through closeness with God. The special relationship I alluded to springs from the observation that we
would expect the tsadik, the righteous person, to be seeking the SHIN, or heavenly condition. Thus, when we encounter any word that starts with either of those two letters we
should also study its mate, the word that is otherwise identical but for starting with the other letter. This pair of words
will reveal their inner meaning when we recognize that the
TSADI word leads us to the SHIN word.

In our case SHIN, MEM, CHET means "happiness." The word
that precedes it or leads us to it is TSADI, MEM, CHET, which
means "growth."

That's right. Growth leads to happiness! Our souls simply
reject stagnation. Deep down, we rebel when the feeling
that we are going nowhere subconsciously overwhelms
us. When each day seems to follow upon the next with no
progress that really matters, most humans find our spirits
shutting down.

One obvious solution, then, is to reintroduce an element of meaningful growth back into our daily schedule. That is easier said than done. In fact, it is a real challenge. Perhaps that is why so many go for the other far easier, if sadder solution—suppressing that uncomfortable link between growth and happiness by means of chemicals.

Another piece of wisdom about happiness is revealed by the structure of the word. The three root letters can be arranged as the first letter, followed by the remaining two letters which comprise a short word, like this: SHIN, and then MEM, CHET. The final two letters spell out the Hebrew word MoaCH, meaning "brain." SHIN, as we have already learned, means striving heavenwards. Taken together then, the Hebrew word for happiness carries an additional meaning: Ultimate attainment of heavenly bliss is through your own brain. In other words, except for rare chemical imbalances, being happy is an act of mental will on your part.

What an astounding novelty—my happiness does not depend on anyone else! No other person in the entire world has power over my state of happiness. Happiness is not a state of mind brought about when *others* create an environment that I favor, it is just a decision I make, no more and no less. My happiness need never depend on anyone or anything. What an enormously liberating idea! For the vast majority of people happiness is a choice, and the road to achieving it is marked by growth.

Neither Easy nor Impossible

It would be helpful to note that there are two general rules about the Torah: First, no commandment exists that requires us to do anything that comes naturally. For instance, there is no commandment or *mitzvah* in the Torah that requires God's people to breathe regularly for good health. Breathing comes naturally to us and requires no special commandment.

Second, no commandment is impossible for people to obey. Hard maybe; but not impossible. Thus if you come across any commandment that seems quite easy, even natural, you can be sure that you do not fully understand the instruction. Honoring your parents seems too easy and natural? You probably are not even close to fulfilling what is required.

The second rule assures us that nothing God commands is impossible. For example, in the tenth commandment we are told not to feel a desire for things belonging to other people. My instinct is to respond by saying, "I can't help the way I feel! I will certainly obey the prohibition against stealing other people's possessions, but I cannot prevent myself from coveting them." Wrong! We are quite capable of controlling our thoughts and our feelings. It is not easy, but nobody ever said that the ultimate program for developing human potential would be easy. It is *not* easy, but it *is* possible.

Similarly, the Bible commands us to be happy. My instinctive response might be, "I feel miserable. I cannot help how I feel. Perhaps if you give me the things I want, then I'll be happy." Wrong again! We do have the capacity to obey all commandments without any outside assistance.

If it is possible for humans to obey the commandment to be happy, how is this accomplished? We saw the clue a bit earlier. Unless we want to head down the dangerous path of chemically induced happiness, we will have to depend on personal growth to produce the happiness we pursue. How do we deploy the growth = happiness principle?

One way to do this is to set yourself a daunting challenge. The more difficult the challenge, the more of a sense of accomplishment you will experience and the more happiness will result. Obviously, one has to approach this challenge with wisdom as well so that it is achievable. Overnight success isn't the goal. A clear, laid out path with a plan for dealing with setbacks is more realistic. This challenge might be a physical one such as maintaining an exercise regimen or a rigorous diet. It could also be a moral challenge.

Perhaps you realize you have acquired the unfortunate habit of gossiping about other people. Try setting yourself the task of not talking about a single human being for an entire week. The first step might be picking a time of day when you know you are tempted to gossip and making plans that will help you avoid the temptation. Gradually increase the 'no gossip' time and add techniques to your repertoire that aid you in removing yourself from troublesome conversations. As you achieve each milestone on the path and get closer to your goal, you will inevitably feel a great sense of accomplishment and happiness.

Perhaps you tend to procrastinate. Well then, challenge yourself to attend promptly to your work. Whatever it may be, seek a tough challenge. By embarking on this program and building success upon success, you will find an almost inexhaustible reservoir of happiness to draw from.

Our state of happiness truly is dependent upon feeling a sense of steady growth and progress in our lives. One reason

some women feel a sense of let-down after giving birth is
that, up until that moment, they are constantly participating
in the ultimate miracle of growth. While still pregnant, the
mother-to-be is almost effortlessly engaged in progress and
growth. That is why so many women enjoy being pregnant;
it is hard to think of a more profound contribution that anyone could make. As soon as
her baby is born, however, it
all changes. Now in order to
maintain the same ongoing
growth, Mom endures sleep-
less nights and incessant demands. It is no wonder that
most mothers experience a
blue period at this turn of
events.

> For the vast
> majority of people
> happiness is a choice,
> and the road
> to achieving it
> is marked by growth.

Happiness or Fun?

In our pursuit of happiness, which is certainly a morally legitimate endeavor, we must always be vigilant to distinguish
between happiness and fun. Here is a quick and easy way
to tell the difference: Fun is usually pleasurable at the time
but leaves a slight feeling of emptiness and waste following
the activity. (Think of an entire afternoon spent watching
television, for instance.) Happiness is usually a little more
demanding while you're engaged in the activity or thought,
but it leaves you with a wonderful sense of contentment.

Interestingly, the Lord's language has no word to describe
fun. If you are not surprised to hear that, it means that you
are becoming quite accomplished at spotting the lessons in

Hebrew! Let me explain the appeal of fun and how easily it can be mistaken for happiness. Think of motion as a metaphor for growth. Our bodies can only sense movement if the velocity of our motion changes. With our eyes shut, we are quite incapable of distinguishing between being stationary and moving smoothly and steadily.

Have you ever sat in a railway carriage and been unable to detect whether your own carriage is moving or the adjacent train has started moving? However, we can easily sense any change in our velocity. If our vehicle is picking up speed, even if we are blindfolded we feel ourselves being thrust backward. If the conveyance is rapidly brought to a halt, we feel ourselves flung forward in the direction of motion. Even if we are riding in a car that is sharply turning, we feel the change in velocity caused, in this case, by our change of direction. The general rule is that we are acutely sensitive to any change in the conditions of our motion.

In similar ways, our spiritual beings are exquisitely attuned to any change in growth. If our condition is stationary and stagnant, we feel nothing. If, however, we experience rapid change in our spiritual condition, we feel it very strongly and the sensation is basically pleasant. The problem confronting us is that negative change can masquerade as fun, and in the short term can feel even more pleasurable than the early stages of positive change.

Remodeling

Positive growth can also be compared to a remodeling project. The initial result is horrendous. You find yourself surrounded by excruciating noise, suffocating dust, and bedlam.

Only when it is well under way do the benefits start to unfold. Similarly, the initial response to a physical or spiritual exercise program is frequently an intense desire to stop. But after persevering for a while, the positive emotions and benefits kick in. Growth and achievement that result from struggle, diligence, and sacrifice feel very good to us and make us feel happy down the road.

Unfortunately, the sensation we feel when surrendering to indulgence is immediately enjoyable. For example, gambling can be fun, but it seldom produces happiness. The appeal it exerts comes from the illusion of growth that it offers. You see, while it is easy for us to feel a change in our spiritual condition, it is sometimes difficult to sense right away whether that change is positive or negative. It is only later that we can tell. Just as in a car, we can sense that the car is changing velocity but the only way we can detect whether it is slowing down or speeding up is by checking to see in which direction we are being flung. With our eyes shut and our sense of direction disoriented, we might know the car is changing velocity but we'd never know whether it is speeding or slowing. Not until later and the blindfold is removed would we know what had taken place.

Some activities produce a superficial sense of fun while others produce a sense of deep, inner happiness. The best way to tell the difference ahead of time is to ask ourselves whether the activity will contribute to our growth and development in a worthwhile kind of way. The answer will point unerringly toward genuine and durable happiness. Both poor and rich people can be happy. What matters is not what is in their pockets, but what is in their souls.

CHAPTER 18

THE SINISTER SNOOZE BUTTON

חלם

ChaLoM

*Suggestion: See the alphabet chart and Holy Hebrew! Tools
1 and 2 to get the most out of this chapter.*

Though I host my own talk-radio show, I enjoy listening
to other shows as well. One genre in particular enter-
tains me. Generally airing in the middle of the night, callers
and hosts on these shows seem obsessed with conspiracies
and often identify numerous and varied "threats to civilization." I have heard of green Martians and mysterious black
helicopters, but I have yet to hear about what I think of as
one truly frightening peril.

I believe that one of the greatest, unrecognized threats to
civilization is the feature found on most alarm clocks. I refer
to the snooze button. This devastatingly dangerous device
may even have been anticipated by the ancient rabbis of the
Talmud a millennium and a half ago.

No, I am *not* pulling your leg. The Hebrew word that casts a
laser beam of clarity on this matter is CHaLoM, the Hebrew
word for "dream." The Talmud reports a very curious fact
related to dreams. It observes that if, upon rising in the
morning, a person cannot remember his dreams, he should

be considered wicked. The Talmudic sages aren't pulling your leg, either. They are merely putting their collective finger on a problem that is ancient, but which finds its ultimate modern-day technological crutch in the form of the snooze button you have next to your bed.

Consider what the snooze button allows us to do. Before bedtime, we carefully decide what time to get up in the morning. Then, when technology does its job and the alarm goes off, our first action of the day is to procrastinate. We can even do so numerous times! By the time we actually clamber out of bed, it may be a full hour after we first hit the dreadful snooze button.

The Benefits of Leaping Out of Bed

Why do I refer to the snooze button as "dreadful"? What difference does it make if we leap out of bed or linger beneath the covers? There is a big difference between setting the alarm for six and snoozing in repeated cycles until seven, and setting the alarm for seven, and leaping out of bed on the first ring. One result of not getting up with alacrity is that we can't remember our dreams.

Try it yourself.

The time during which we doze following that first moment of wakefulness is when our dreams fade into mist and disappear from our memory. In order to remember our dreams, we need to keep our finger off the snooze button. And to understand why remembering dreams is essential, we need to look more closely at the Hebrew word for dream, CHaLoM.

There is a Hebrew language principle that spelling certain Hebrew words backwards yields opposing ideas. In this case, we see that CHaLoM spelled backwards becomes MeLaCH, or 'salt.' This leads us on a fascinating journey of understanding.

מ ל ח = ם ל ח
ח ל מ   מ ל ח
salt   dream

Have you ever wondered why we find a saltshaker on most tables, but not a potassium or magnesium shaker? After all, our bodies need many minerals to survive, not merely salt. Fairness alone would demand equal time for, say, calcium. You might respond by telling me that potassium, magnesium, and calcium are amply provided in any normal, balanced diet. And you'd be right. The problem is

We can add purpose and gusto to our lives by jumping out of bed the moment our eyes open.

that more than sufficient salt is also provided in any normal, balanced diet, yet we still place saltshakers on our tables.

Salt is the only mineral we ingest in its pure state. In our normal daily diets we consume iodine, iron, and various nitrates. In fact, our bodies can't function if they don't get enough of these and many others. But all the minerals we require occur naturally in the foods we eat, or are added during processing as in iron-fortified cereals. Salt is the only mineral elevated to a place of honor at our tables—even appearing in specially designed holders.

Amazingly, because the Hebrew words for salt and dream are the reciprocals of one another, understanding salt gives us greater insight into the concept of dreams. We need to ask how a dream might be the opposite of salt. Now I realize that such a crazy-sounding question sounds like something you might hear in a particularly surreal dream, but bear with me.

In the complex scheme of Biblical nomenclature, salt is a symbol. The Torah pictures the world for us as a realm of existence composed of four basic elements: mineral, plant, animal, and *medaber*, or "speaker," meaning human. This is similar to the children's game of "animal, vegetable, mineral," though the Torah resolutely distinguishes between animals and people, thus the fourth category. When the Bible wishes to allude to the mineral kingdom, it chooses the mineral that is more familiar to us than any other—salt.

This explains why salt played a key role on another kind of table: the altar on which animal sacrifices were offered daily in the Temple in Jerusalem. The Book of Leviticus enjoined that most sacrifices were to be offered on the altar accompanied by salt. Though this may sound arcane, it is not at all. Entire books could be written about features of ancient Jewish customs that have found their way into the customs of the Western world, and the salt of sacrifices is a fine example. Each time you pick up the saltshaker on your dining room table, your meal becomes a symbolic representation of the Jerusalem Temple altar.

But this leaves unanswered the question: Why salt? Why was salt integral to sacrifices? Why must it have an echo on our kitchen table? And what does any of this have to do with dreams?

Map of Human Experience

The answer to these mysteries lies in the four-part organizational pattern of mineral, plant, animal and humans. Thousands of years ago, when the priests slaughtered cows and bulls and salted the flesh before offering it to God, they were evoking this pattern. The Temple altar became a miniature map of the whole of the human experience. Every primary ingredient of the world, each of the four main categories, was represented there. Animal, vegetable, human, and mineral: human, in the form of the priests; the animal being sacrificed, the grain accompanying the sacrifice being offered was the plant; and finally the mineral, salt. In our day, when we place salt on our "altar" or dining table, we are replicating that ancient pattern.

The Temple ritual might, on the surface, have resembled nothing more than a comical-looking barbeque, but it was elevated to dizzying heights of holiness. What converted these sacrifices from primitive procedures into national activities that preserved the morality of a people? It was all taking place only for the sake of pleasing God. Of course, it was not God who needed the sacrifices but humans who craved the experience. By bringing representatives of every one of the four aspects of His worldly creation before Him, we acknowledged that everything on earth was a gift from Him, and we undertook to use that gift properly. Similarly today,

our table can become a kind of altar when we dedicate what
goes on at that table to higher, spiritual ends.

There is a world of difference between table conversation
revolving around gossip and discussion that elevates and en-
nobles us. There is no comparison between grabbing a bite
on the run versus sitting down at a table carefully laid with
dishes and cutlery. If only we knew to keep this in mind, our
tables would become the most spiritually important places
in our homes. After all, in order to stay alive, animals also feed
themselves. We, however, can choose to eat as if we were animals, regarding meal time as nothing more than an occasion
for physical survival, or we can take the opportunity when
consuming meat, vegetables, and minerals to do something
much more spiritual and profound. We have the opportunity
to transform feeding into a uniquely human and spiritual
action. This is accomplished by how we dine and what we
talk about during the meal.

Understanding this brings us full circle back to the meaning
of CHaLoM, dream. Just as the dedication of every aspect of
our lives to a higher purpose is the most fundamental meaning of the Hebrew word MeLaCH, so too is this the ultimate
meaning of CHaLoM, dream.

As I mentioned earlier, we should expect to find in the CHa-
LoM and MeLaCH some quality of oppositeness. The two
ideas do indeed allude to infinitely separate aspects of our
experience. On one hand there is salt, a mineral, the most
base and physical of the four components our world. We
even refer to a person who is well grounded and decent as
"the salt of the earth."

At the opposite end of the spectrum we have a dream, a familiar experience that is almost totally ethereal, disconnected from the realm of mundane physical existence. Classifying someone as a dreamer suggests a lack of connection with the real world. The challenge that is captured by the linguistic connection between these two words is to try to dedicate both our CHaLoM and our MeLaCH to a reality that transcends both. We can keep our unique and God-given humanity in mind whether we are engaged in the most basic activities represented by salt or groping toward the intangible and the ethereal represented by dreams.

This may sound daunting, but CHaLoM and MeLaCH tell us that built right into us is a human need to dedicate everything we do to a higher purpose. Our food consumption can supply us with nothing but the nutrition necessary for our physical well-being, or it can be a spiritual activity bonding friends and family to each other and to God. We can see each new morning as another sixteen hours to "get through" until we can escape into sleep again, or we can leap up joyfully, with gusto, and begin living a passionate existence from the very second our eyes open. And one important way to monitor how energetically and quickly we are rising is to see if we can remember a dream we had during the preceding night.

Rise Like a Lion

The very first sentence of the classic code of Jewish law, the *Shulchan Aruch*, advises us to rise early in the morning "like a lion, in the service of God." Being a servant of God is not like being an employee of a human boss or manager. Our bosses expect us to arrive at the office at a certain time, and after eight or nine hours we are expected to stop working and go home. Not so with God. By energetically and promptly rising out of bed, we are acknowledging that our actions throughout the day are dedicated to Him. In this way, whether we can remember our dreams serves as key to understanding what sort of attitude we take toward life. As a thermometer can gauge our physical well-being, our morning rising habits can serve as a gauge of our spiritual well-being.

Let me illustrate with an old story.

A very prosperous, corpulent gentleman once visited a rabbi to discuss something that troubled him very much. How to put it? Well, the man just didn't feel up to snuff. He had considered the possibility of consulting a physician, but he was pretty sure the problem wasn't physical.

His main symptom was a generalized sense of ennui. He felt vaguely dissatisfied with life—though life had brought every material blessing a man could ask for. The rabbi listened closely, stroked his beard, and said "Ah hah. I see. Yes, I do understand what you mean."

"Rabbi," said the man plaintively, "what can I do to make myself feel better?"

Truth is, the man wanted from the rabbi the spiritual equivalent of a pill or a lotion—a quick fix that would solve his problem with a minimum of effort. The wise rabbi intuited this and proposed a remedy.

"I want you to drink a glass full of dew each morning." He explained that this must be fresh morning dew, gathered at dawn each day, drop by drop, from the blades of grass on the swooping, expansive lawn outside the man's mansion. "Remember to gather it at the break of dawn, not later; otherwise the dew you need will have evaporated at the first rays of the sun."

The man went away satisfied. This was exactly the kind of thing he had in mind.

However, despite the glass of dew he drank religiously each day, the man felt no better than before. He went to see the rabbi and complained about the ineffective "cure."

The rabbi listened, and then asked one question: "How is the dew collected?"

"Well," the man replied, slightly puzzled, "it's very simple. Each night I direct eight of my household servants to rise before dawn and flick drops of dew off the grass blades outside my house into test tubes. When each has gathered as much as he can, the drops of dew are poured into a drinking glass. When I get out of bed later that morning, I drink the glass of dew, just as you prescribed. But Rabbi, it's done nothing for me!"

"Ah hah," said the rabbi, "I see. Now I understand why this remedy has been ineffective. I should have specified that every last drop of dew must be gathered not by your servants, but by you!"

Gathering dewdrops or remembering dreams—there are many possible proofs that a person has risen from bed each morning with no dawdling.

When the early transmitters of the Torah say that the

person who doesn't remember his dreams is a naughty person indeed, it is alluding to the fact that he is limiting his day by surrendering to his physical desires. Indulging oneself physically can certainly feel good momentarily, as when one gulps a hamburger from a fast-food restaurant instead of awaiting meal time. The problem is that it produces a corresponding lowering of spiritual vitality.

There is a fundamental lesson here. We can add purpose and gusto to our lives by jumping out of bed the moment our eyes open. It is one of the healthiest, life-affirming things we can do. Rather than being groggy and irritable the rest of the day for the lack of that extra ten minutes in the sack, we feel great. Ignoring the snooze button and dining rather than merely eating—both help us avoid the purposelessness and emptiness that truly are among the greatest threats to civilization.

CHAPTER 19

BECOMING ROYALTY

מֶלֶךְ
מלכ

MeLeCH

Suggestion: See the alphabet chart and Holy Hebrew! Tools 1, 2 and 5 to get the most out of this chapter.

Few experiences in life are as illuminating as a high school reunion. If you have never attended such an event, I strongly urge you to do so at your next opportunity. What's more, should that reunion happen to be scheduled for the same night as the reunion of your college class, skip the college reunion and go to the high school gathering instead.

What you will see is fascinating. No matter what school you attended, there was a certain social hierarchy among the students. Teenagers today establish the same hierarchy. Kids naturally divide into little groups—cliques, castes—which they instinctively know to rank in order from most to least cool. At the top are the jocks and other "beautiful" people: the most athletic boys, the cutest girls. At the bottom of the ladder are "nerds." When I was a boy these individuals flocked to the Chess Club. Now it would be the Computer Club, but the idea and the identity are the same.

Nothing much can be learned from a college reunion because, while you'll find your classmates a little richer, grayer
and fatter, they'll be basically the same people you knew
from university days. There are few major reversals to be observed in identity or social station. By contrast, what you'll
find at your high school reunion is that the social hierarchy
hasn't merely been toppled; it has been stood on its head.
Before, the football-tossers and basketball-throwers were
on top; now it's the bookworms. Today those former nerds
are Internet millionaires; the jocks are seeking jobs at the
companies owned by the nerds.

Campus Monarchs

For a few golden years of adolescence, those jocks were
monarchs of the campus, but their reign was doomed to end
early because they never understood what it means to be a
king. The kings are dead, one might say. Long live the kings.

In the Lord's Language, a king is a MeLeCH. We would do
well to understand the hidden meaning of that word. The
spelling is significant, of course: mem-lamed-kaf.

The ancient rabbis of the Talmud taught that the word
MeLeCH is really an acronym, with each letter standing for
another word. Here are the words that make up the acronym:

- מ (mem) stands for mo-ach, which means "brain"

- ל (lamed) stands for lev, or "heart"

- כ (kaf) ka-ved (For pronunciation, rhyme it with
  'ma' and 'wed'). This is often translated as "liver,"
  but this is a poor rendition. While ka-ved certainly

is related to the body and bodily functions, this word is used to designate the whole range of physical appetites and desires rather than a specific organ. That is, it stands in contrast to one's intellect, or moach, and to one's emotions, which is to say one's heart—or in Hebrew, lev.

And this is the point of MeLeCH, because the order of the letters which form the acronym allude to the relative priority a king must assign to moach, lev and ka-ved. This is vital information not just for the few kings still around, but for you and me. We may not aspire to royalty, but—whether at home, in the community, or at work—we owe it to those around us to aspire to leadership. And that is what this life lesson is all about.

Government of Self

Any king who wants his rule to be long and successful must govern first himself and then his realm—primarily by his intellect and then by his heart, keeping his own appetites low on the priority list. And so it must be for all of us if we want to be successful in life.

Pathetic as they may have seemed at the time, the nerds you knew in high school had their priorities straight. They were all head, all brain. You might even have noticed something vaguely ascetic about them. They didn't pay a whole lot of attention to sensual pleasure. They wore ratty clothes, neglected to take care of their skin, never quite got down the art of shaving or hair care. Now asceticism can be taken to unhealthy extremes, but a little bit of it, especially in one's

schooling years, can have highly beneficial results down
the road. Ask Bill Gates. At the very least, asceticism balances
being unhealthy preoccupied with one's looks.

Those jocks, on the other hand, really enjoyed their high
school years, didn't they? They obeyed the mood of
America's youth culture and set out to taste as many of the
appetitive pleasures of life as they could, from beer to sex.
(Of course, I know there are plenty of tea totaling and sexually abstinent young athletes out there. I am merely employ-
ing the word "jock" as a theoretical model.) They paid ample
attention to their lev and their ka-ved, to the neglect of their
mo-ach. They obeyed the compelling call of their young bodies and fell victim to the siren of emotional seduction. But
the reign of those monarchs ended on graduation day.

Just for fun, let's try an experiment. Let us apply here the
rule that if you spell a Hebrew word from back to front, the
reverse spelling produces another word whose meaning is
the opposite of the word you started out with.

Intriguingly, when MeLeCH is spelled backward we get the
letters kaf-lamed-mem, which is pronounced Ka-LeM and
means "shame" or "embarrassment." In this Hebrew word we
can see its English derivatives: calumny and calamity. (Did
you think I would suggest this experiment if I didn't know
beforehand that the results would be instructive?) If we understand kingship as the ultimate expression of honor that
can be bestowed on a human being, then shame is certainly its opposite. If following our heads instead of our hearts
brings us to aristocracy (in its good sense) and leadership,
then following our hearts (or, perish the thought, our bod-

ies) will inevitably lead to calamity and eventual calumny.

Remember, in Hebrew there are no coincidences. Therefore, since we found that MeLeCH is both a word in its own right and an acronym, we should naturally look for an acronym in the word Ka-LeM. You won't be shocked to learn that the words constituting the acronym are the same words we found in MeLeCH, but in reverse order. You may also have guessed that the lesson to be derived here is the converse of the lesson we observed in MeLeCH.

What is the road to kingship—to success in the life-long struggle to fulfill our highest and best hopes and dreams? It lies in subordinating heart to head and appetite to heart. The road to failure is the same road but taken in the opposite direction. It lies in subordinating head to heart and heart to appetite.

One further quality any leader must display is the ability to rule himself before he can hope to have his authority accepted by others. People with military experience know this instinctively. By running his life according to the dictates of his head rather than his heart or body, the leader demonstrates quite clearly that he is capable of ruling himself. Another way of describing this most necessary of leadership qualities is self-discipline.

This applies not only to would-be kings in the sense that George V was king of England. If any person in any context wants to be a leader, he must think of himself as a king. This doesn't mean he should go around issuing high-handed rulings by fiat. Nobody follows leaders like that. A leader must have a leader as well. This is why, among the laws of kingship found in the Torah, we find the law that a Jewish king must at

all times carry with him a scroll of the Torah. While we may
and should have many trusted advisers in life, we can find no
better counselor than our Creator.

Beams of Light

This idea was carried over into the theories of kingship
developed in Europe over the past two thousand years.
In the European nations, kings were regarded as ruling by
divine right. A king who ruled without such a sanction was
an illegitimate ruler. A king who could legitimately claim
divine sanction declared himself a spiritual heir of Moses
himself.

While the Jewish people have had many kings, most famous-
ly David and Solomon, our first king really was Moses. He
never ruled explicitly under that title, but the Bible under-
stands him as filling a monarchical role. When he descended
from Mt. Sinai, where he had been consulting with God for
forty days, the text informs us that he had karne ohr, "beams
of light," shining from his face. (Michelangelo, basing his
work on an imprecise translation of the Hebrew for the
word "beam," put horns on the his statue of Moses. This is the
origin of the myth that Jews have little spiky horns growing
out of their heads. Most of us do not.)

These beams of light constituted the first crown God ever
bestowed on a monarch, and the kings of Europe emulated
the Mosaic model by designing for themselves crowns from
which spikes of shiny precious metal emerged—karne ohr.
The idea was to artificially emulate the royal pattern, set by
Moses, of beams of light emanating from a monarch's head.
This was seen as a a sign of royalty and nobility—and is

behind our understanding of halos of light around the heads of great figures.

Every Home a Castle

We would be wrong to think that only a man with a crown on his head, or the title "Chief Executive Officer" on his office door, can be a king. When Jewish law sets out the rules of kingship, it offers a model of what it means to be a MeLeCH or king—whether in the boardroom or even around the humblest of family dining room tables.

Fathers, and those men who wish to be fathers someday, should pay special attention here. One ancient Jewish law still practiced in many homes today declares that no one should sit in a parent's chair. If fathers are to receive honor appropriate to their roles as leaders of the family, a good place to start is with their throne or chair. A father's dining room or living room chair is no mere resting place for anyone to use while consuming food or watching TV. It must be his throne exclusively.

Any king who wants his rule to be long and successful must govern first himself and then his realm.

On the 1970's TV show *All in the Family*, Archie Bunker was made a figure of ridicule because he had a chair in the Bunker family's living room that was exclusively his. His modern son-in-law mocked him for insisting on this right. But the idea of a father's special chair is actually very important. The point is not to elevate Dad alone, but to uplift the entire family. In a family where the father is king, his wife by definition is the queen and the children are princes and princesses. The family table becomes the site of royal feasts.

What about Queens?

An additional point gets lost when you discuss kingship in English rather than Hebrew. In the English language, the word 'queen' is not a derivative of the word 'king'. In Hebrew, it most definitely is. The word queen—a MaLKaH— is formed by adding the letter 'hay' onto the end of the word MeLeCH.

מ ל כ ה

H   K/CH   L   M

The 'hay' serves to feminize the root word, but basically, the two words are the same. The lessons we have learned about the MeLeCH apply to the MaLKaH as well. A wise and aristocratic woman makes sure that her intellect and rational thought processes control her emotions rather than her emotions controlling her thoughts.

Many stories have been told about Jewish families who endured periods of great economic and social persecution. The tyrants and their mobs could take away people's money or even their lives, but they could not take away an individual's self-worth. In face of deprivation and humiliation, Jewish families clung to the family as a place where father was king and mother was queen. Especially on the Sabbath, in ghettos across Eastern Europe the family converted their humble hovels into royal palaces by practicing the principles of leadership and aristocracy. Whatever the outer trappings, nobility will shine through when reason and wisdom trump emotions and instincts. To this idea of kingship we can and should all aspire.

CHAPTER 20

CONQUER YOUR FEARS

שנה

SHaNaH

Suggestion: See the alphabet chart and Holy Hebrew! Tools 1 and 2 to get the most out of this chapter.

A friend recently told me that he planned to ask a certain young woman to marry him. He had made up his mind to pop the question, and knew the exact locale—a lovely beach overlooking Lake Washington—where he would offer her a diamond engagement ring, but he was uncertain *when* to do so. After all, this would be one of the most important days of his life, and he wanted the time—the place on the calendar—to be as special as the physical location.

It was approaching the season of Passover (in the spring) and, to his surprise, I recommended that he propose to his beloved just before Passover began, an hour or so before nightfall and the start of the first holiday meal, or *Seder*.

Why that day? Well, time is a slightly weird phenomenon. A young child who quickly acquires a sense of size and weight will still have difficulty estimating time. With a little experience, he knows whether a particular package is likely to be heavy or light. *Those large suitcases being loaded into*

*the car for a family vacation—better let Dad carry them.
But anyone could carry that box of breakfast cereal to the
table.* Time, however, is less intuitive. It seems to take forever
for a long-awaited vacation trip to arrive. Once embarked on,
though, that trip seems to pass by in a flash.

Try this experiment: Ask a child to hold a medium size book
at arm's length while you time her for forty-five seconds.
Then allow your young subject to munch on a favorite candy
for exactly the same period of time before you confiscate it.
Now ask the child which time period was longer. For most
children, the time spent holding the book will seem like an
eternity. And most will incorrectly estimate that you allowed
the candy enjoyment for a far shorter period.

A Life-Train Spiral

Another way in which we misperceive time is the way
we visualize its passage. We tend to think of time as a very
long, straight, railroad track coming from nowhere and
going nowhere. Life resembles a train upon which we
and our loved ones progress. Upon the track are railway stations, representing notable dates like birthdays and
holidays.

The reality is that, while our journey through time may be
compared to a railway voyage, it does *not* take place upon a
long, straight track. Think of your life-train as traveling along
a track laid in an ascending spiral or helix. It takes a year to
travel one complete circle at which time you return to the
original embarkation station. However, this time, the train
has entered the next-higher floor of this multi-level station.
The stations are not conventional, long platforms but large,

multi-story structures.

When my own life-train arrives at the Jewish holiday of *Shavuot*, Pentecost, I am returning to the exact day upon which my ancestors stood at the foot of Mount Sinai and received the Torah from God. The reason I do not run into my ancestors is that they are on one of the lower levels of the station.

Ah, I know what you are thinking: Couldn't I just take the elevator down and meet up with the ancient Israelites? That enticing idea is precisely why there is such a fascination in literature and movies with time travel. We yearn to be able to move backwards and forward in time, but alas, in reality it is not so simple. Nonetheless, the spiral staircase view of time serves us well.

Celebrating our religious, national, and family holidays each year helps keep us linked to our timelines. We commemorate the passing of our parents, and we observe the days upon which great wars ended. Passover, the Fourth of July, and Thanksgiving recur from year to year. Each year as we reach July fourth, it is Independence Day all over again—a different Fourth of July from last year but still, mysteriously, the very same day.

I suggested that my friend propose to his bride-to-be on Passover Eve because in doing so he would be giving her a gift. She would always know that the anniversary of her engagement was doubly memorable for its having occurred on a day which Jewish people around the world already recognize as very special. Each year at Passover, she would receive an additional boost of warmth, delight, hope, and love from remembering the day her husband proposed to her.

Holidays are funny. Just the change of date on the calendar fills our hearts with joy and expectation, or sometimes, for people who are lonely, without the blessing of good friends and loving family, with sadness and despair. The high suicide rate at Christmas time is well known. If we are fortunate enough to associate the revisited stations of our life with progress and achievement, then those milestones on our journey become happy events. Growing children, lasting relationships and successful enterprises are just some of the things that add joy to the train ride.

Something to Show

This may be one of the foundations of the photographic industry. One reason we love collecting photographs of our families is that they prove to us that we have something to show for the journey taken. Tourists do the same thing. After spending considerable sums of money and several weeks indulging in a vacation, we return home hoping to cajole some innocent friends into watching our videos or slides. Why do we feel a need to subject our friends to this torture? It is mostly for our benefit, not theirs. We seek affirmation that all the time and money we spent did not evaporate into nothingness.

> **One of the most loving and evocative questions one can ask during a durable marriage is, "Do you remember the time that we...?"**

This is one of the great hidden benefits in remaining married to one person. Over the years, memories accumulate and affirm that the ride along the tracks was not wasted. One of the most loving and evocative questions one can ask during a durable marriage is, "Do you remember the time that we...?" Our psychic health demands that we constantly try to return to that railway station we visited several circuits ago on that annual railway track. It may be an upper floor but it is still the same railway station, and it feels warm and familiar.

The Hebrew word for 'year', SHaNaH, sheds light on the circular nature of the passing years and teaches us some important lessons in the process. Actually, the Hebrew consonants that spell ShaNaH—shin, nun, hay—hint at other things besides 'year'. The letters of the Hebrew words for year and years can allude to many other concepts as well.

year - שׁ נ ה

years - שׁ נ י ם

Teeth (SHee-Nye-im) - שׁ נ י ם

Two (SH'Nayim) - שׁ נ י ם

The root of the verb 'to repeat' - שׁ נ ה

The root of the verb 'to learn' - שׁ נ ה

Why would the Hebrew word for 'year' also mean 'two' and 'repeat'? As I hinted earlier, a year is indeed linked, first of all, to the idea of repetition. Time only appears to be a long straight railroad track if you think that life is basically meaningless; we're born, second by second we get older, and finally we die. But the truth is, we experience time as a cycle. Comes Christmas or Passover or any anniversary or birthday, and we intuitively feel that we have repeated an experience, returning to a place in time that we had visited on exactly this day last year and for many years in the past, and as we hope to do for years to come. Of course, this year's birthday is not exactly the same as last year's. After all, I am 365 days older; the hair may be a bit grayer; the body a tad less lithe. But in important ways, it is still the same day. So holidays and anniversaries repeat themselves, yet they don't. This is why I describe the passage of time as a spiral.

Okay, that's a nice observation, you're probably saying. *What good does it do me? Where is the life lesson?*

Victory through Repetition

Are you afraid of public speaking? Of flying in an airplane? Of riding in elevators? The Hebrew word-concept, SHaNaH, will come to your rescue.

We learn through repetition. Remember that fear of public speaking? Ask any competent psychologist how you should go about defeating a phobia like that. Probably after some learned and compassionate throat clearing, he'll tell you there's only one effective way: You must repeat the experience that you're afraid of, over and over again. Get up and speak before a group of people—again and again. Afraid of elevators? Go to your neighborhood skyscraper, get in an elevator, and ride it up and down, up and down, till the building manager suspects you of vagrancy and orders you to leave. Airplanes? Same thing. Professional phobia therapists make a nice living by taking people who fear flying on group

tours of the airport. Therapist and patients spend a day
going from plane to plane. They get on board, sit for a moment,
then get off. Next plane, same thing. Eventually, the repeated
experience becomes more familiar, more 'learned'—and less
stressful.

What's going on here? Through repetition we learn to
subject our churning emotions to the calming power of our
intellect—that is, to make our brain rule over our heart. The
more often you perform a certain feared action, the more
you learn that you have nothing to fear.

Repetition is essential to all learning. Just consider that wonderfully useful childhood educational exercise, memorizing
poetry. Unless you happen to be blessed with a photographic memory, the only way to do it is by repetition.

Wisdom Teeth

Recall that SHaNaH, year, is also related to SH'Nayim, two. In
Jewish Talmudic schools, called yeshivas, the ancient, classic pedagogical method is called chavruta learning. One student is paired with another, his colleague in learning, and
together they pore over the text of the Talmud, discussing it
as they go. Not only is this a lot more fun than nodding over
a book by oneself hour after hour, but it also improves the
learning process immeasurably. Thus we see how learning is
linked to 'two-ness,' for two people can learn more easily and
effectively than can one alone. Together, they repeat, repeat,
repeat.

Why would the Hebrew word for year and two also mean
tooth? In the first place, we get wisdom by deriving a lesson

from our teeth. If you want to really learn a subject—or an idea, or a language, whatever—there are two ways to do it. You can repeat it over and over again. In addition, you can chew it (so to speak!) over with a friend.

Furthermore, for our teeth to work properly we need two sets of them, an upper and a lower set. With these, we grind our food till it's soft and small enough to digest. But anyone unfortunate enough to be stuck with only one set of teeth is worse off than if he had none at all. With no teeth, only gums, we can still (if rather slowly!), gum our food, mashing it around till it's more or less digestible. But with just upper teeth, or just lower teeth, we would starve.

Learning works the same way. Two learners together can digest a difficult subject, while one learner by himself has a much tougher time of it.

So from SHaNaH we derive some very interesting lessons indeed: How to overcome our fears and how to multiply our power of learning. Do the lessons work? Try them and see for yourself. In the meantime, it's intriguing to note that this Hebrew word, SHaNaH, possesses yet another indication that buried treasure is contained within.

355 Days in a Year?

Get out your calculator. As I've noted elsewhere, Hebrew is unique among languages. When you convert its letters into numbers and add them up, the sums are peculiarly significant. Don't try this in English! For instance, taking the English word "year" and attempting to add up the numerical values of the letters doesn't get you far. The letter y is letter 25 in the alphabet; e is 5; a is 1; and r is 17. Add them and you get 48, which tells us absolutely nothing about a year. But the ancient science of Hebrew-letter arithmetic, or gematria, informs us that when you add up the letters shin (300), nun (50), and hay (5), you get 355: namely—ah hah!—the number of days in a year.

Wait a minute, Lapin, you say. That should be 365 days in a year!

Yes, you're right if we're talking about a solar year—a year measured by the time it takes the earth to complete exactly one orbit about the sun. But for more than 3,000 years, the Hebrew calendar has been lunar-based, not solar. Each month represents the number of days it takes for the moon to circle the earth: 29 days plus part of the thirtieth day. Twelve such months add up to—you guessed it—a 355-day year.

This lunar year, like the solar year, circles back on itself, bringing with it all the holidays and anniversaries we love. My friend with the engagement ring decided to take my advice and proposed marriage to his beloved on Passover Eve. Each year, for a lifetime to come, amid all the arduous spring cleaning which traditionally goes along with the weeks just before Passover, his bride will recall a day on the shore of Lake Washington. She'll be transported back through the years to that very same day, and she will be able to re-experience the wonderful moment when she said, "I will marry you."

PART FIVE

IDEAS

Chapters 21–23

Be sure to check out pages 337–342
to discover helpful resources on this topic

CHAPTER 21

TRASH OR TREASURE?

ר פ ש

ReFeS

Suggestion: See the alphabet chart and Holy Hebrew! Tools 1, 2 and 5 to get the most out of this chapter.

To this day, I have a hard time throwing a worn-out shirt or even old socks into the trash. Maybe you feel the same way.

Notwithstanding the frayed elbow on the shirt or the hole that's been growing for weeks around my big toe, I just find it hard to toss those items out. I can well afford to buy another shirt and another pair of socks, but I find myself putting them back in the drawer rather than in the garbage. I guess I'm subconsciously remembering how, when I was a kid, my mother also hesitated to throw out old clothes—not because she was cheap or because my family was poor. My mother simply felt that clothing deserved special respect. Maybe your mother was the same way.

My mother preferred giving clothes that had passed their prime, had small indelible stains on them or had merely fallen out of style, to charities. Much as they do today, these organizations would then turn around and, at a nominal cost, sell or sometimes give these donated articles of clothing to poor people. A coat or suit too tattered for us was a highly prized garment among folks less fortunate.

My mother—and yours too, I bet—had the sense that there is something holy about clothing. Food and clothing are two necessities in life. But whereas food gives only physical sustenance, fulfilling a physical need, clothing fulfills both a physical need and a spiritual longing. It keeps us warm and also provides us with dignity. Somewhere in the consciousness of every civilized human being is the awareness that clothing is more than physical.

The very fact that clothing is uniquely human should give us a clue about this. The little French poodle prancing alongside its madam in a little tartan vest that matches the coat on the other end of the leash looks ridiculous. Animals with clothing belong in cartoons. Yet, despite the bravado of those who advocate for nudist colonies, people out in public without clothing are pitiful.

Clothing fulfills both a physical need and a spiritual longing.

After all, the Bible tells us that the first clothing any human being ever wore was created for Adam and Eve by no less distinguished a tailor than God himself. Animals have no need for clothing while, obviously, they do need food. The fact that we humans clothe ourselves no matter what the weather is a tribute to our intuition that we are godly creatures, not animals. This accounts in part for our discomfort in treating clothes as common household garbage.

But Mom also understood something else which fewer and
fewer of today's freshly minted university graduates understand. Maybe old clothing ought not to be trashed, but an
awful lot of other stuff should be! A line you hear all the
time from people educated enough to know better is,
"Everything is relative." But my mother insisted that good
was indeed good and evil was indeed evil. She had very
little confusion about these two concepts. She had no hesita-
tion about throwing out real garbage and throwing out evil
and smelly ideas. I'm reminded of her lesson when I look at
today's garbage industry.

A Sacred Sacrament of Secularism

Dealing with the waste material of our busy lives used to
be a simple utilitarian problem. We expected cities to pick
up our trash and safely dispose of it. That was all. There was
never any reason for reasonable citizens to genuflect at the
altar of garbage. But recently, recycling has become a sacred
sacrament of secularism. Garbage recycling is not being
done because it is the smartest way to deal with garbage;
it is being done for philosophical reasons. I reach this conclusion because draconian recycling rules in many cities require citizens to meticulously and diligently sort their potato
peels and empty cans into different color-coded containers,
each of which must be put out for collection on a different
day. When these policies were implemented, in many places
these carefully collated containers were then emptied into
the same city dump. The cities justified the charade by saying that soon economically viable ways of treating recycled
garbage would emerge. Meanwhile, millions were victims of
a curious doctrine: Waste your time recycling so that city

employees can waste theirs by combining everything you just finished laboriously separating.

Children at school are given the idea that recycling is more than just an efficient and economical way to deal with waste (which it may not be). Instead, they are told that there is something noble about recycling. Once they were taught that visiting sick people in the hospital was the way to do good; nowadays they are taught that the highest form of doing good is recycling. We need to recognize that there is a moral lesson being taught here: Biblical visions of morality are less important than pantheistic ones.

You may think I am being too fanciful, but children are also being taught that almost nothing is garbage. Is this a problem? Yes, it is, because the underlying philosophy also leads to the thought that no *idea* is nonsense and all values and beliefs are equal to one another. Along with the notion that there is no such thing as garbage that should be discarded, we might also be gaining the notion that no *idea* is worth discarding either. Perhaps we are losing our ability to simply and confidently declare, "That is utter and complete nonsense!"

The Hebrew word for "trash"—ReFeS—is instructive on this subject. Let's recall the principle in Hebrew that, unlike in other languages, a word spelled backward does not become a meaningless jumble of letters as it would in English. For instance, "trash" spelled backward is "hsart" and "refuse" spelled backward is "esufer." Neither word means anything whatsoever.

But try this experiment: Reverse the spelling of the Hebrew word for trash. ReFeS is spelled reish-pay-shin. (Pay can be

pronounced either as a "p" sound or as an "f." Shin can be
pronounced either as an "s" or an "sh.")

שׁ פ ר   ר פ שׂ

S   F   R   R   P   S

Spelled backward, ReFeS becomes shin-peh-reish, a root that
can be pronounced in several different ways. From this root
we get, above all, the word SHaPiR, which means "excellent"
or "fine." It is also the origin of the Jewish last name Shapiro.
You will hear in it the English word "super" just as, in ReFeS,
you hear the English word "refuse" (pronounced with a hard
"s" sound, meaning "trash" or "garbage"). The word "rubbish"
comes from the same Hebrew root, easily seen once you
know that in many languages, the letter b tends to morph
into the letter p and vice versa.

Funny, isn't it? In the Lord's language, "trash" spelled in reverse becomes a word that means the exact reverse of "trash."
In other words, Hebrew insists just as firmly as did Mrs. Lapin
that the opposite of super, valuable things or ideas is garbage
and wrong ideas. Some things are absolute after all.

Right, Left, Up and Down

Since I'm an enthusiastic sailor, I'll illustrate this principle
about absolutes with a maritime example. If you are ever on
a boat and the skipper tells you to grab and pull a certain
rope on the port side of the vessel, you'd better make sure
you know port from starboard. Pull the wrong rope on a
boat and you are going to be in big trouble. You and everyone else onboard might need life jackets.

The word port does not mean left or right. It means the side of the boat that's on your left if you are facing the bow. Bow doesn't just mean front. It means the end of the boat that usually is first to slice through the water. If you are facing the bow, the side on your right is called starboard. But if you turn around and face the stern, it is now the side on your left that is called starboard.

You see, on a boat, left and right won't work because they are relative terms. That is why when you look in a mirror, your watch switches from your left wrist to your right. If you have never done this experiment it is worth trying. Face a mirror with your watch on your left wrist. In the mirror it will be reflected on your right side. Notice that the same mirror that moves your watch with such ease, fails to switch your necklace from your neck to your ankles. That is because up and down are fairly reliable directions, whereas left and right are not. If someone, while talking to you on the phone, tells you that she is pointing toward her left, you know very little. In order to know the direction in which she is pointing, you would need to know which way she is facing. Now, had she informed you that she was pointing toward north, you would clearly understand. That is because north and south are absolute directions, as are up and down.

On a boat, we depend on everyone knowing what is going on. Perhaps that is why I so love being aboard a boat. During our family's summer boating trips, all my children effortlessly switch their lefts and rights into ports and starboards. It is not an affectation; they understand that left and right are relative, and Lapins are not crazy about relativity other than in connection with Einsteinian physics. Up and down are useable on a boat since they always mean the same directions regardless of which way you may be facing. But left and right? Never! Only port and starboard have absolute meaning.

Rich or Poor?

Is everything absolute? No, of course not. Funnily enough, one area that is very relative is exactly one which many people consider to be absolute. I refer to these words we use so casually: "poverty" and "wealth." We often speak of "poor people," but who are they? A significantly large number of those designated as poor by governments own their own air-conditioned homes, cars, and more than one color television set. If we talk about 'relative poverty' or designate the lowest X percent of earners as poor, then the term becomes even more meaningless. These 'poor' people could be living extremely well, other than the psychological damage done to them as others tell them that they are disadvantaged.

It is very difficult to define poor when it comes to humans. You see, if an elephant needs a hundred and twenty pounds of hay a day to remain healthy and all he gets is sixty pounds, you could probably label him a "poor elephant." But with people it is much more difficult. Some people choose to work sixty hours a week in order to increase their earnings. For others it is more important to have ample time to go hiking. Should the latter, who have chosen to work only twenty-five hours each week, be labeled poor? Should some of the income of the "rich" group be confiscated and given to the "poor" group, or should we instead recognize that humans make choices? Some people choose to spend all they earn on consumer goods, vacations, and restaurant meals. Others choose to live more frugally and invest their savings. Should the second group be considered rich and be made to help support the first group? These are tough questions; their complexity demonstrates that poor and rich are relative terms that do not really apply to humans.

Each one of us could look over one shoulder and see people who have much more than we do. However, we could just as easily look over the other shoulder and see people who have much less than we have. Whether we ourselves feel rich or poor depends over which shoulder we are peeking. Anyone who thinks that no very wealthy people ever go to bed at night worried about money simply does not understand human nature. Some things like wealth and poverty are very relative, which is why most people are more comfortable living and socializing among others of the same general socio-economic level. If we spend a lot of time among people who have much less than we do, we feel almost sinfully rich. If we spend much time among those with substantially more than we possess, we feel relatively poor. Neither sensation is terribly comfortable.

This is why we have the power to determine whether we feel rich or poor. It is all relative, and therefore, within our power to determine.

The same can be said of experiences. Instead of designating a bad experience as such, we can switch our perspective and try to make the best of it. Just as ReFeS, rubbish, can be viewed from the opposite end and turned into a precious stone, a sapphire (SaFiRe), so can some of the bad hands life deals us be turned around. Some of business and science's greatest achievements have emerged from what at first seemed to be major failures or setbacks. The most painful moments in our lives, the most unpleasant encounters we have with other people or with organizations, can be launching pads for the future.

We must be careful, however, to understand that this is not true for ideas. Every idea does not automatically have value. There really is a great deal of garbage around, and the best thing to do with garbage is dump it. In doing so, we will find that we have more room and energy for that which is truly valuable.

CHAPTER 22

MR. SILVERBERG'S WORD PUZZLE

אמת

EMeT

Suggestion: See the alphabet chart and Holy Hebrew! Tools 1, 2 and 5 to get the most out of this chapter.

I take particular delight in teaching Hebrew to accountants. These dogged number crunchers get an unfair rap in contemporary culture. They are thought to constitute the most supremely dull profession conceived on this green earth, but actually the green stuff they take so much care in counting and recounting provides them with an ideal training program for understanding the Hebrew language. Mind you, it's not the money that does this, but the counting.

When I was a synagogue rabbi, I once had the opportunity to teach a little bit of Hebrew to a wealthy Beverly Hills accountant. We shall call him Mr. Silverberg.

I offered him a challenge. He had never properly learned Hebrew as a child, and considered himself basically illiterate in that tongue. I told him that after I had taught him just a few simple principles, he would be able to figure out the meanings of Hebrew words on his own. Without a dictionary, just by using the mathematical intuitiveness he had gained as an accountant, he could quickly become proficient. I explained that Hebrew is as much a mathematical code as it is a language.

He looked at me dubiously, in the manner of all accountants when their clients are feeding them a line.

"Sure, you can do it," I assured him. "Let's take an example."

"All right," he agreed. "Let's do that."

I explained that I would tell him about the Hebrew word that means "truth" along with a couple of basic rules of Hebrew linguistics, and then he would be able to success-fully predict for me the Hebrew word for the opposite of truth, "falsehood." He agreed to the challenge.

See if you can match his wits.

Position in the Alphabet

In Hebrew, the word that means "truth" is EMeT, spelled aleph-mem-tav.

ת מ א

tav mem aleph

←————

The spelling is important because it provides an insight into the nature of truth. The first thing to notice is the position of these three letters in the Hebrew alphabet.

That alphabets have an order—a proper sequence, as in English where *a* is followed by *b* which is followed by *c* and so on—is not surprising. This aids children when they first set out to memorize the alphabet. Without an order, we would be left with nothing more than a meaningless jumble of letters, very difficult to commit to memory. But why this order in particular? Wouldn't it make more sense to start the alphabet with the letters that we use most often? Then the first letter of the alphabet would be *e* or *s*, not *a*. Or perhaps we should arrange the alphabet so that the vowels come first followed by consonants. Instead, the English alphabet begins with the same sequence, as does the Hebrew alphabet: first *a*, which is similar to the Hebrew aleph; then *b*, which echoes the Hebrew bet.

Just as English has a first letter of the alphabet, and a tenth and twentieth—and these number equivalents never vary—so it is with Hebrew. The difference is that in English and all other tongues, the order of the letters is merely an aid to memorization. The spelling of a word, the numbers that correspond to the letters in the word and their precise order within the word and within the language, is meaningless in languages other than Hebrew. But in the Lord's language, letters and numbers and the way they correspond to each other are rich with meaning, tapping into ocean-deep mystical realities.

This is the first principle I explained to my friend Mr. Silverberg, the Beverly Hills accountant. I then proceeded to enumerate another principle with which by now you are very familiar—that when you reverse the letters of a Hebrew word, the meaning of the word is often thereby reversed.

With these principles in mind, look more closely at the word for truth, EMeT. The first letter is aleph, which happens to be the first letter in the alphabet of a total of twenty-seven letters. The second letter in the word is mem, the fourteenth letter in the alphabet. That is to say, mem falls at the exact midpoint of the alphabet. There are thirteen letters ahead of it and thirteen after it.

The last letter in EMeT is tav. I asked Mr. Silverberg where he thought tav fell in the Hebrew alphabet—given that the first letter is the first in the alphabet, and the middle letter is the middle letter in the alphabet. You can also take a wild guess.

Mr. Silverberg smiled tolerantly at me. He had not become a rich man for nothing. "I would guess that tav is the last letter in the Hebrew alphabet." He was exactly right.

We had not yet got around to predicting the Hebrew word for "falsehood." First I wanted to make clear to him that, just as the numbers in spread sheets are not abstract calculations but instead correspond to real life with all its sorrows and joys—here's the amount we spent on Granny's funeral, here's how much we spent on furnishings for the new baby's bedroom—Hebrew letter/numbers also point in a very concrete way to the world around us. In the present case, the letters that designate the word for "truth" tell us important truths about what truth, EMeT, is in the first place.

Confronted with various and conflicting supposedly true accounts of an event, how do you go about determining what the real EMeT is?

From Beginning to End

I told Mr. Silverberg that while accountants have unique insights into life that other people come by with greater difficulty, so do mothers. Every day our seven children confront my wife Susan with competing "true" accounts. If one child comes crying to her, saying another child hit her (usually it's a girl fighting with a girl; we have only one boy and six daughters), Susan tries to avoid getting in the middle of the quarrel. Sometimes she has no choice but to immerse herself in the contretemps and try to get to the bottom of the story.

When that is necessary, she has the girls tell her the whole story, starting from the very beginning and continuing in sequence, through the middle to the end, leaving nothing out and keeping everything in order.

It usually surfaces that the crying girl who says her sister hit her was not exactly sitting around innocently reading a book when, out of nowhere, up came the other girl and walloped her. More likely the crying girl had first pulled a chair out from under her sister while the latter was preparing to sit down—or some other such hostile act, which was precipitated by some other offense, and so on and on. These sessions of claim and counterclaim can get very complicated. But if Susan persists, insisting that the girls go in order and leave nothing out from first to last, the truth about the affair usually is ascertainable.

In the pursuit of truth, order and sequencing count for a lot.

What happens in the discovery of EMeT, then? It is just this: You begin with the aleph, the very beginning. You proceed in order through the middle, the mem. And you don't stop till you reach the end, the tav.

Leave any of these steps out, and you likely will be left with something less than, or even completely different from, the truth.

Detectives Count

I enjoy detective stories—Agatha Christie, Sherlock Holmes. Maybe you do, too. Imagine cutting out all the pages in an Agatha Christie novel, and putting them together again in an order just slightly different from that intended by the author. If the resulting book were to be re-edited and awkward transitions between sentences or paragraphs smoothed out or slightly rewritten, you could produce a story that made superficial sense. But the "truth" revealed at the end of the book—usually the identity of the murderer—would no longer flow logically from what preceded it. In the pursuit of truth, order and sequencing count for a lot. Even the counting itself—from page one to page two to page three— is crucial.

Another Hebrew root underscores this point: samech-pay-reish, pronounced SeFeR when it means 'book'; miSPaR when it means 'number' or SoFeR when it means 'scribe' or 'counter' (that is, a person who counts).

ר פ ס
R P/F S

A story, especially a true story, of the kind you would find in a book is thus revealed to be profoundly dependent on numbering or counting: If you change the sequence of pages, or the order of events, the story is converted from true to false. English has much the same idea in our verb "to tell." A person tells a story in its proper order, and a teller, as at a bank, is someone who counts money in sequence. In German, the verb "tell" likewise means both "to tell," as in telling a story, and "to count."

Falsehood

"Mr. Silverberg," I said, "I have only one more piece of information about Hebrew for you before you can predict the answer. In Hebrew, certain individual letters are eternally stamped with meaning: Some words and ideas are so powerful that no element of them can be part of the opposite word. Truth, EMeT, is considered to be one of the most important foundations of the world. Now I believe you are ready to tell me what the Hebrew word for "falsehood" is."

(You might want to hum the theme music from a game show, and give it a shot yourself.)

"Well," Mr. Silverberg said, "first of all I'd say that 'falsehood' must be the negation of 'truth.' That might suggest that we reverse the sequence of the letters and begin our hypothetical word with the last letter in the alphabet, tav. But, in our case, the last letter of the word EMeT is eternally stamped with the concept of truth. That letter has no place in the word that means falsehood.

"As a second best," continued Mr. Silverberg, "how about kicking off our word with the second to last letter of the alphabct. What might that be?"

"That letter would be shin," I said, smiling broadly. He'd got it right so far. Shin is indeed the first letter in the word we were looking for.

"Now," he said, leaning toward me, "if order and sequence, starting from the beginning and ending at the end, are the key to truth, then falsehood must consist of stopping somewhere before you've reached the end of the matter under investigation. Very likely it consists of only examining one aspect of a story, not even allowing that there is a broad range of information from which to learn." He asked me what the letters are that immediately precede shin in the Hebrew alphabet.

"They are (in order) kuf and reish," I replied.

Mr. Silverberg reasoned that the Hebrew word for falsehood is composed of the letters shin-reish-kuf: the second-to-last letter in the alphabet, followed by the third-to-last, followed by the fourth-to-last. But he hesitated at this spelling. If proper sequencing is a key to getting at the EMeT, then there is too much sequencing in the proposed root, shin-reish-kuf. The root is in exactly reversed sequential order. That couldn't be.

I have to tell you that at this point I was very impressed. Here was an extraordinarily astute man, wise indeed in the ways of numbers. I resolved to fire my then-current accountant and take on Mr. Silverberg instead to help me with financial matters, if I could afford him. (It turned out that I couldn't!)

"So," I said cautiously, "I sense that you are getting ready to give me your educated guess. How are you going to propose that we spell "falsehood" in Hebrew?"

Mr. Silverberg leaned back in his chair, took a long pull on the cigar he was smoking, and blew the smoke in a gentle draft up to the high ceiling of his study. "Shin-reish-kuf is too 'sequential' to be right," he said slowly, "but on the other hand since shin is very likely the first letter of the word we're seeking, I'm going to place my bet on a spelling that keeps the shin in its place at the head of the word but shuffles reish and kuf, reversing their order. Rabbi Lapin, is the word 'falsehood' in Hebrew spelled shin-kuf-reish?"

reish kuf shin

Well, of course it is. How could it plausibly be otherwise? The root is pronounced "SHeKeR." In human experience, one might say, SheKeR and EMeT are the ultimate opposites. Truth is truth, no matter how you look at it, and falsehood is falsehood.

Not Really Chaos

I never had an opportunity to tell this wonderful and distinguished man an interesting footnote to the question of EMeT and the meaning of truth. When we say that getting at the truth requires that one pursue the matter in question back to the beginning, to its genesis—back in time as far as the chain of events that led to it will go—this itself begs a question:

Once you've started back down that chain, where do you stop?

If one little girl complains to my wife Susan that another little girl insulted her, it may turn out that girl #1 had antagonized girl #2 earlier in the day, leading to the present altercation. But why did she do that? They are both good girls. Perhaps something happened between them a few days earlier. If you wanted to, you could trace a pattern in their relationship, and the relationship between both girls and the rest of the family, between the family and the rest of the world, quite a ways backward in time.

The modern idea proposed by theoretical mathematicians called Chaos Theory is basically a very sophisticated way of saying that nothing in our world started yesterday. Every event is connected to umpteen other events, in an impenetrably complex relationship of cause and effect. A famous illustration of the theory is that of the butterfly flapping its wings in China. Through an indescribably complicated chain of cause and effect, a minuscule change in the atmosphere produces a slightly larger one, which produces a still larger change, and so on—so that the tiny innocent creature could ultimately produce a hurricane in Kansas. Chaos Theory is actually the wrong name for this idea, the essence of which is that in the universe there are no random, chaotic events. Everything is linked to everything else. Nothing is without a cause, or rather causes. There is no such thing as "chaos."

All physicists now agree that the universe is not infinitely old. Before a certain moment in history, there was no universe. After that, there was a universe, and then the chain of events began. If we were infinitely wise and knowledgeable, we could trace any given action in our lives, any thought or feeling or whatever, back to that moment before which there was nothing. Some prefer to call that moment the Big Bang. Others call it Genesis.

The EMeT of the Matter

Tracing events back as far as we can helps us in more practical ways, too. One of the great virtues we can practice in life is gratitude. Sometimes we owe thanks to people who benefited us intentionally. But let us not forget the people who helped us without intending to do so. They deserve our gratitude as well.

The Talmud relates the parable of a man who stepped on a scorpion, which gave him a nasty sting in the foot. The man went down to a river to wash the poison out of his wound. By the riverbank he heard the sound of a little child wailing and coughing. Looking into the rushing current, he saw the child—flapping around helplessly, splashing, gulping, about to drown. The man dived in and saved the child's life.

When the child's father thanked him, the rescuer said, "Don't thank me. Thank the scorpion. If it hadn't stung me I wouldn't have gone down to the river and never would have had the opportunity to save your child."

The scorpion did indeed, however indirectly, save the child's life. That is the EMeT of the matter.

We find the same lesson alluded to in the Bible's book of Exodus. In this story, Moses saves a Jewish man from an Egyptian slave master who is on the verge of beating him to death. Moses slays the Egyptian and, pursued by the authorities, flees into the desert. Soon after, in the land of Midian, he meets some young women drawing water from a well. Local hoodlums have been menacing the girls, and Moses saves them, too. When the girls get home to their father, they tell him about the Midianite ruffians. He asks who rescued them, and they answer that it was a certain *ish Mitzri*, an Egyptian man.

This is very peculiar. Since when did Moses become an Egyptian? The reason Moses had to escape from Egypt was because he saw himself and acted as a Hebrew, not an Egyptian. The Bible, especially read in the original Hebrew, turns out to be full of difficulties like this. Almost every verse is in some way problematic, full of provoking questions. Some say that this is because the humans who wrote or edited the text were incompetent. This seems unlikely to me, but it certainly is one approach to take.

My own view is that the Author set out intentionally to provoke our curiosity. In a chain which reaches back to Mt. Sinai, the Oral Tradition in Judaism has passed down answers to these challenges from one generation to the next.

The answer to the problem of Moses' identity here is that, when the Midianite girls attribute their salvation to an Egyptian, the reference is not really to Moses but to the Egyptian slave master who cruelly beat the Israelite, prompting the compassionate Moses to save him. This resulted in Moses fleeing into the desert, leading to Moses saving the girls from their tormentors. Like the scorpion, the slave master cannot be left out of the equation here. And that too is the EMeT. It is a lesson with very practical and far-reaching implications for all of us as we learn to view episodes and people in our own lives as more complex than they seem at face value.

I never got to tell any of this to Mr. Silverberg. For, as I am sad

to report, we parted ways much too soon. The times I spent
with him, our several sessions of learning about Hebrew and
other related matters, were quite memorable and enjoyable.
But, as I've shown, he was a very smart man, and in the end
he felt that what he'd learned so far was compelling him in
a certain direction, toward certain answers to particular questions, toward an understanding of ultimate Truth,
transcendent EMeT. He realized that if he continued learning, his own sense of honor would compel him to become
an observant Jew. As he said to me the last time we met,
"Rabbi Lapin, I see where all this is leading, and I don't
want to go there." He said so with kindness and, I sensed, a
degree of regret.

Why a person, not least someone possessing such a profound intellect, would hesitate to pursue truth to its final
destination is an extraordinarily tough question, worthy of
a Mr. Silverberg.

CHAPTER 23

HOW DO YOU SPELL FREEDOM?

חפש

ChoFeSH

*Suggestion: See the alphabet chart and Holy Hebrew! Tools
1, 2, 3, 4 and 5 to get the most out of this chapter.*

Did you ever feel so burdened by responsibilities that
the weight of all the "must-do's" in your life seemed to
press down like an elephant on the back of your neck?

Actually, with a lot of folks the pressure tends to settle in
a hot little knot at the base of the spine—the kind of back
pain that can only be relieved by a long hot soak in the bath-
tub—but there's no time for that! You've got to finish that
report for the boss, pick the kids up from school, buy the
groceries, make a dental appointment, call your parents, get
those shoes fixed, drop off the dry cleaning...it just cannot
all be done!

Is it too much to bear? Try the following. Get a nice large
pad of paper and one of those desk calendars, the kind with
a little line for every half-hour interval. Now enter all your
existing appointments in the calendar and write down every
single thing you have to accomplish on the pad of paper. Be
sure to note by when you need to accomplish it, and how
long it will take. Don't leave anything out. Now go through

that list, item by item, and insert each task into an available time slot on your calendar. Are you done? Don't you feel better?

Try it. It really does work.

Logically, it shouldn't. Having filled your calendar with umpteen niggling appointments, duties and tasks, you paradoxically feel more relaxed than before when your calendar was perfectly empty. Anyone looking at your calendar before you began filling it up would think you were the freest person in the world—but in fact you felt crushed. Now you've got every minute packed, and suddenly feel unburdened. Almost...free! How can this be? Why does constraining yourself with a tightly packed schedule make you feel less burdened?

A principle from the Lord's language will begin to clear up the mystery. In most languages other than Hebrew, if you reverse any word, the order of the letters in the resulting new word will bear no relationship to your starting word. Most English words when spelled backward produce mere gobbledygook. This is not so with Hebrew. A three-letter Hebrew root, spelled backward, frequently produces another meaningful word which, in any many cases, is the exact opposite of the original word.

Family, Rights and Duty

What does this have to do with being all stressed out and wanting nothing so passionately as to be liberated from the burden you're under? Well, why not examine the Hebrew word that means "free"? It is ChoFeSH, spelled chet-pay-shin.

(The letter pay can be pronounced, depending on circumstance, either as a "p" or an "f.") Reverse the letters of this three-letter root, and you get shin-pay-chet, which means "obligation to serve." Let's examine this new root.

ח פ שׁ

freedom

שׁ פ ח

obligation to serve

The best place to start is by realizing that a very common word that's formed from this new, reversed root is miSH'PaCHaH, or "family."

מ שׁ פ ח ה

The Hebrew word for "family" is based on a concept that seems to be the exact opposite of freedom and indeed is even spelled with the same letters read backwards. A family is the opposite of freedom? That sounds depressing, I know. But it's not. Allow me to explain.

The same three-letter root that produces the word miSH'PaCHaH, family, also produces SHiF'CHaH, a "(maid) servant."

שׁ פ ח ה

The opposite of freedom, needless to say, is service. This seems to support the idea that family is a negative, constraining institution. But before we come to that conclusion let us continue to examine what freedom really means.

I've known people who, looking forward to a well-earned vacation from work, lean back in a chair, gaze contentedly at the ceiling, and exclaim, "I can't wait to get free of that office. I just wish I didn't have to come back after two weeks!" This is very sad—an unfortunate misunderstanding of what it means to be free. We humans do not thrive when we are free from obligations. The best vacations are when we commit ourselves to a new set of obligations: a hiking holiday, improving relationships with our loved ones or perhaps a vacation spent learning a new skill or hobby. We return from this kind of break energized and rejuvenated, eager to return to our work. However, the person who spends his vacation "vegging out," sleeping till noon and then lolling around the house will return to work at the end of his trip strangely exhausted and dispirited.

A family is a group of people bound together by blood and by love. More critically, it's a group bound by an unbreakable web of mutual obligation to serve one another. The idea of duty is as important in the Hebrew Bible as the idea of a right is in modern America. Unlike English, Hebrew has no word for the concept of right, as used in children's rights, gun-owners' rights, right to privacy, right to life, or the myriad other phrases that reflect our growing obsession with rights and our growing indifference to obligations.

In the language of the Bible there are only obligations and duties. No one has a right to life or a right to privacy. But you and I have a duty to guard one another's life and respect one another's privacy. Similarly, it's a fine thing to love your family, but love on its own can be a bit vague. It is more valuable in a family to emphasize everyone's obligations and to

demand that every member of the family consistently act
on them.

The Meaning of the Sabbath

In the Bible, our weekly mini-vacation is the Sabbath. What
happens then? Is it just a day of rest? Wrong! One might
be forgiven for thinking that the essence of Sabbath rest, as
formulated in the Fourth Commandment, is to spend the
day doing nothing. The Hebrew word for Sabbath, ShaBaT,
comes from a root that means "to stop" or "cease." (It is standard practice to spell Shabbat with two 'B's, but I think that
comes from the two 'B's in the word Sabbath. In the Hebrew,
there is only one letter bet making the 'B' sound). However,
it would be a mistake to suppose that the Sabbath means we
are to do nothing at all.

Each Sabbath, Jews are meant to cease all creative activity.
This is to acknowledge that all creativity ultimately stems
not from me, a human, but from the Creator, who also ceased
His creativity on the Sabbath. Look at the wording of the
fourth commandment: "Six days shall you labor, and do all
your work; but the seventh day is a Sabbath of the LORD
your God; in it you shall not do any work..." (Exodus 20:9–
10). The commandment deals not just with the seventh day
but also with the entire week. This is a key piece of data.

The essence of Sabbath is not to stop and do nothing—
but rather, after spending six days creatively (imitating the
Creator) one should stop that type of activity. The approach
here is holistic. Built into every human being is a kind of
spiritual odometer which needs to be reset to zero each

week. There is no way we would find the creativity of the work week fulfilling if we had no regular period of contrast against which our spiritual odometers can measure it.

> **A person who does no more than sit in a rocking chair, technically cannot observe the Sabbath.**

Think about food. We enjoy dinner much more if we haven't been snacking since lunch. Hunger makes food taste better. No food is more tasteless than matzoh, the dry, thin, unleavened cracker Jews eat during the festival of Passover. Many Jews have the custom of not eating this tummy-torturing matzoh for two weeks before the onset of the holiday, and of not eating abundantly for most of the day before the first festival meal when much matzoh will be consumed. What is the result? By contrast, that first piece of matzoh tastes surprisingly good!

Just so with creative activity. God wants us to imitate Him, to join Him in the work of improving the world through the sweat of our brow. But He knows that if all we do is work, work, and work for seven days a week, not only our creativity itself but also our ability to enjoy creativity will suffer as a result. The reverse is also true: A person who turns sixty-five and retires with plans to do no more than sit in a rocking chair, technically cannot observe the Sabbath. For seven days a week he abstains from creativity, so the seventh day for him becomes just another day of doing nothing.

So doing just plain nothing is not what Sabbath-observance

is all about. Doing nothing is actually depressing and frustrating. Let's take a look at another example: why do many people find art museums tiring? A piece of art, such as a painting, is intended to stir your soul, and the best art does just that. But in a museum, picture after picture is presented to you. Though you walk about the gallery on your own power, your role is basically passive. All you are doing is looking and sometimes listening. Since you are engaged in nothing really creative, you are reduced to an object. And being an object is very boring.

It is more exciting to view only a few pieces, taking the time to analyze, compare and learn about them, rather than force yourself to see each and every piece on display. Invariably, children and adults who visit a museum after learning something about the artist, the times in which he lived, and what to look for in his paintings, will find the experience much more interesting than if they have not done their advance work. In this way the art viewer becomes a participant rather than merely an observer.

The Joy of Preparation

We humans are programmed to find enjoyment and stimulation only when we've worked for it. The truth is, we only appreciate freedom—the freedom of a Sabbath or of a vacation—in the context of the effort that makes it possible. It's actually a mistake to think that a Jewish Sabbath really begins at sundown the previous evening. In reality, a Jewish family commences Sabbath preparation as soon as the previous Sabbath is over. This preparation takes two forms. The first is by being as creative as possible over the first six days of the week. In addition, any delicacy that is found during the week is tucked away to enjoy on the following Sabbath. Special clothing are put aside and the menu is planned and the food is cooked. Sabbath is the seventh day of the week, not the first. Even the days of the week reflect this. In Hebrew the days are named with numbers: the first day, the second day, the third day, etc. If we said the names in full it would be: the first day towards Sabbath, the second day towards Sabbath, etc. The entire week builds towards the final day.

When Jewish women light SHaBaT candles at sundown on Friday, the warm glow of the candles signals the successful completion of all the work they did to make the blessing of Shabbat possible. At the end of the Sabbath, Saturday night, Jews signal the day's completion by holding up a cup of wine. The cup should literally overflow its rim, a symbol of anticipation of the week of overflowing creativity we look forward to, as we launch immediately into preparing for the next Sabbath.

Engraved Freedom

I've had some experience with long-term preparation which makes this idea especially meaningful to me. My family has a tradition of taking boating trips for a month or so each summer. The children are already hearty sailors. Our running joke is that even the younger kids have squeezed more salt water out of their socks than most adults do in a lifetime. They enjoy running the boat and doing the navigation. But fully half the fun is getting ready for the trip.

When you sail across an ocean, failing to prepare can be a big problem. One summer we set out to sail from Los

Angeles to Hawaii. Some goodly distance across the Pacific, I decided to check on the amount of fresh water in stock. Unfortunately, I happened to be more exhausted than I realized and with bleary eyes, I stuck a dipstick into the fresh-water tank and brought it out. To my horror and astonishment, I saw that the tank was empty.

It was my worst nightmare coming true, as we did not expect landfall for several days. I imagined consoling my little children with whatever moisture could be drained from cans of stored fruit and vegetables. "Here, darling, I'm sorry you're thirsty, have some tuna juice." Later, when I was a little more rested, I tried the dipstick again. Thank God! Somehow, through my weariness, I had misread it the first time. In fact, the fresh-water tank was full.

This harrowing experience gave me an appreciation for preparation. Getting ready for a major trip or event is certainly stressful, but the consequences of failing to prepare are ever more so. I can testify that nothing about the trip drew my family closer together than the need to make sure that absolutely everything we needed was ready and onboard before we set sail.

Yet I can also tell you that few activities convey the same sense of freedom as sailing across an ocean. So we begin to see the glimmer of a resolution to the mystery of why CHoFeSH (freedom) is the opposite of MiSHPaCHaH (family)—SHiFCHaH (servant). You see, as we generally use the English language, we fail to adequately distinguish between good freedom and bad freedom. Freedom from all obligations is a terrible form of freedom. It might better be translated as "license."

In Hebrew, the word CHoFeSH has no place in a family. Real freedom, the good kind, is what we experience when we have selected our obligations and are performing them. It is a deep and joyful sense of freedom utterly undiminished by the nagging guilt that often accompanies license. Every school child knows the difference between an evening spent watching television before homework is completed and the same evening once all homework obligations are discharged.

The ancient rabbis of the Talmud hint at the same idea when they direct our attention to another important Hebrew word, CHaRuT, which means both 'engraved' and 'free' alluding to the good kind of freedom. The context here is a discussion of the Ten Commandments, which the Bible tells us were CHaRuT or "engraved" on two stone tablets.

The wise rabbis tell us not to read the root letters with the sounds of CH, R and T, as if the vowel make the word sound like CHaRuT, 'engraved' but rather to read them with the vowel sounds that would turn the word into CHeiRuT, 'freedom.' In other words, these Ten Statements (a more accurate translation of the Hebrew) are not suggestions but ideas we must follow. If we do so, this is what will lead us to true freedom in our individual and societal lives. We are most truly free when our lives are engraved, "written in stone," or "cast in concrete." Paradoxically, the Ten Commandments, because they are "engraved in stone," have the capacity to liberate us and bestow the good kind of freedom upon us. Knowing where the boundaries are really frees us. Children often demonstrate this to us in how more relaxed they seem to be with parents who clearly delineate the boundaries of acceptable behavior, but it is true for adults as well. This may sound strange to our modern ears, but it is really quite clear and rather valuable to know and incorporate into our lives.

Sound crazy? I hope not. Remember how you felt after you wrote out all your tasks on an hour-by-hour desk calendar? You felt a lot freer than you did when your calendar was empty.

Imprisonment

As I've already shared, I served a synagogue on the boardwalk in Venice, California for fifteen years. Venice was, and I believe still is, a rather counter-cultural sort of place. To that beach came young and old in search of freedom—the bad kind of freedom, the kind with no obligations. Those seekers of Shangri-La slept till noon on the park benches, drank beer on the sidewalks, played drums and guitars if they felt like it, and indulged in strange and prohibited substances. No homes, no jobs. Quite free!

Not exactly. These same individuals had no money, no transportation and no stable, lasting relationships—none of the advantages that allow those of us with more settled lives to fully pursue our ambitions and enjoy the Creator's world. Basically, they were stuck there on Venice Beach—a very attractive setting in which to be imprisoned but trapped nevertheless.

Compare the situation of Venice Beach vagrants with that of a typical husband or wife who might have attended my synagogue on that same beach, facing the Pacific Ocean sunsets. A family member is restrained, one might say, by his or her family—obliged, engraved—many facets of life are cast in concrete. Yet he or she is also surrounded by a cocoon of love and support. There is a sheer privilege and exhilaration which derives from being a provider and nurturer. The connections which bind us to others also keep us free from the type of desperation and hopelessness which befall those free-living denizens of Venice Beach. The good kind of freedom, CHeiRuT, comes through service and self-restraint. CHoFeSH, on the other hand has the danger of becoming a negative and the opposite of family and genuine service.

We can practically apply this lesson in areas of our lives well beyond the Sabbath, beyond vacations, even beyond the unfortunate concept of mandatory retirement at age sixty-five. All we have to do is treat each day with all its myriad of tasks as another thrilling opportunity to pursue freedom—the good kind of freedom, of course. I mean the kind of freedom that springs from an obligation undertaken and well done.

How about those of us who occasionally feel a little depressed and bored? Why not take this as an indication that it is time to undertake some new obligations? Perhaps some volunteer service to improve your neighborhood and community. Maybe there is a way in which to make yourself invaluable to some other person or family. As my father, who was also my teacher, used to say, there is only one thing worse than having too much to do - not having enough to do.

Now, start making that list...

PART SIX

SPIRITUAL LIFE

Chapters 24–29

Be sure to check out pages 337–342
to discover helpful resources on this topic

CHAPTER 24

ASCEND TO THE HEIGHTS

פלל

PaLeiL

*Suggestion: See the alphabet chart and Holy Hebrew! Tools
1, 2 and 4 to get the most out of this chapter.*

Some people find that praying comes naturally to them,
but for me this certainly is not true. Praying is not something to which I related instinctively when I was growing
up. In retrospect, I am not embarrassed about this; after all, I
did not grow up naturally able to dive off the high board or
give a speech either. I had to be taught these things as well
as be receptive to learning them, and when I was young it
just didn't happen.

At one point I thought that I understood heartfelt prayer. My
good friend Aubrey was an accomplished mountain climber
who always radiated such joy about his sport that I envied
his passion for sunrises at the summit. "Come with me," he
invited. So I did. It was not too long after beginning our as-
cent that I developed a newfound fervor for prayer. Have you
ever heard people say that there are no atheists in foxholes?
Well, I have news for you. I don't think there are too many
atheists among those who dangle off cliffs from slender ny-
lon ropes either. I desperately proposed a deal to God: *You*

get me through this safely and I will never ever attempt to
climb a mountain again!

Eventually we reached the summit. It was breathtakingly
beautiful, but not as beautiful as the valley below looked to
me after our descent. I lay on my back in the long fragrant
grass gazing up at the peak where we had just been and felt
humiliated by the realization that what I had been doing up
there was not praying, it was simply begging.

Begging depresses the spirit. If your outstretched palm
is ignored, you feel rejected. If a quarter is dropped into
your hand by the pedestrian walking by with averted eyes,
you feel humiliated. So if what I had been doing on the crags
up above the clouds was begging, then what was praying? I
had been taught how to dress and how to drive. I had been
taught how to eat in polite company and how to fly a small
plane. But nobody had ever managed to teach me how to
pray.

Perhaps because praying deeply and meaningfully seemed
second nature to my parents, they weren't able to relate to
my difficulties. I imagine it would have been similarly challenging for the great composer Bach if one of his sons had
been unmoved by the grandeur of music. I felt baffled watching my father swing through his morning prayers with con-
centration. I could say the words but the act did nothing for
me. I felt no sensation other than a vague self-consciousness.
It was like watching someone juggle: I wanted to ask, "How
do you do that?"

It was not until years later, as an adult, that I did ask how
to pray and, not surprisingly, the answer lay in the Hebrew

word for prayer. It had been in front of me all along. The word is PaLeiL or, in actual usage as in "I pray," ani (I) MiTPaLeiL.

פ ל ל

L L P

the root letters of 'pray'

מ ת פ ל ל

MiTPaLeiL: is praying, am praying

Verbs tend to convey meaning with great precision in the Lord's language. Some verbs are what we call "reflexive," meaning that the actions are things you do to yourself; this verb is one of those. These verbs usually start off with the prefix MiT in the present tense. For instance, I dress myself—ani (I) MiTLaBeiSH.

Now why on earth would the verb meaning "I pray" exist only in the reflexive form, as if to say that praying is something I do to myself? I had assumed praying was something we did to God, as it were. How very peculiar.

Reconciling Two Images

We must turn to the meaning of the root of the word. By carefully examining the context in which the word is used biblically, we see that PaLeiL means "to judge" or "to reconcile." Judging and reconciling are really the same idea. Each entails taking two apparently incompatible realities and blending them into a unified outcome. You now have all the information necessary to grasp the meaning of prayer. It means looking at yourself as you see you, and then looking at yourself as God sees you. It means flipping between these two apparently incompatible images of you and attempting to reconcile them with one another. It means, in other words, trying to judge yourself.

But wait! What does this have to do with talking to God? Take it easy—we are not there yet. You didn't think we could dismantle the details of one of humanity's most complex activities in just a paragraph or two, did you? This will take at least another couple of paragraphs, so hang on!

> **It was like watching someone juggle: I wanted to ask, "How do you do that?"**

So far we have deduced that the launching pad for prayer is looking into ourselves and contrasting what we see with what we imagine God sees when He looks into our souls. In other words, we judge ourselves. Does this create a tension? Yes? Excellent, we are making progress. Now flip backward and forward as rapidly as you can between these two seemingly irreconcilable images. Do you remember that old-fashioned children's toy made from a piece of wood that could be whirled around a central handle? On one side of the wooden paddle was the picture of a soldier with his arm raised while the other side depicted the identical soldier with his arm lowered. When you spun the paddle around at just the right speed, what did you see? Instead of two seemingly different and irreconcilable pictures, you saw a soldier waving his arm at you.

Beaming Messages to God

Okay, so you now have this procedure of rapidly flipping between a God's-eye view and a personal-eye view of yourself. This oscillation converts what appeared to be two different views into a sort of three-dimensional matrix. But how can this exercise beam a message directly to God?

Think of how a radio signal is launched into space. You have heard of the term "frequency." For instance, your favorite talk show might be found on the AM band at a frequency of say, 560 kilocycles. This means the station broadcasts a signal that fluctuates backward and forward five hundred and sixty thousand times each second. If you are listening to music on the FM band, you might be tuned to a station that broadcasts a signal that fluctuates 90 million times each second. It doesn't much matter. All that matters is that the only way to make a signal jump off a piece of wire we call the antenna and travel through space is to make that signal oscillate or fluctuate between two apparent opposites. In radio technology we might refer to those two polar opposites as positive and negative.

The resemblance to prayer technology is startling. We must train our minds to fluctuate between two images of ourselves. They are polar opposites. One is how God might see us, while the other is how we see ourselves. Indeed, we could quite reasonably refer to those two images as the positive and the negative views of ourselves. Just as fluctuating between positive and negative causes a radio signal to leap off the wire and beam away into space, fluctuating between these positive and negative images causes a prayer signal, as it were, to leap off our beings and beam away toward God.

Far-fetched? Not at all. Think of how the cowboy cracks his whip to produce that sound small boys find quite irresistible. By flicking his wrist, he sends an oscillation down the whip, a sort of up-down wave shape. Only when the tip of the whip bends back on itself do the oscillations produce a loud report that leaps off the whip and begins the journey to our ears.

Escape the Limitations of Self-Centeredness

According to the ancient rabbis, another key principle of prayer is that when I pray for someone else's need, if I have a similar need, my prayers are answered with greater dispatch. You see, very few beggars beg on behalf of other needy people. They tend to be self-centered. Prayer is one of the wonderful tools a benevolent God has made available for people to communicate with Him and thereby to escape the limitations of their own self-centeredness.

We still have a problem. We may well have explained how we are able to project out some sort of spiritual signal. But how do we superimpose upon that signal the things we wish to talk to God about? The radio analogy can help us still further. I mentioned the AM and FM bands, which you can see on the dial of your radio. They stand for Amplitude Modulation and Frequency Modulation. These are two different technologies for superimposing the words of your favorite talk-show host or your favorite music onto the underlying carrier wave. The basic oscillation or fluctuation allows the signal to jump off the wire antenna. By itself, it contains no intelligible data such as voice or music; it is just a "carrier wave." The intelligible information needs to be superimposed upon the carrier. Well, in prayer the same is true. Once we have succeeded in escaping our self-centered nature and have produced a "prayer signal" that projects outward from ourselves, we must now superimpose what we want to say onto that "carrier wave."

That is what distinguishes prayer from begging. Begging is an act of self-centeredness: I have a need so I am asking you to take care of my need. You are only a facilitator for what I want. Unlike begging, prayer requires us to find a way to emerge from our self-centeredness. The best way to do so is to focus on what we each look like from the outside looking in. By reconciling God's view of us with our own self-image, we judge ourselves more dispassionately. Then—and only then—are we ready to superimpose our own communication with God.

I would like to clarify one more point. There is no meaning to judgment if the system under which I am being judged is capricious. Anytime someone uses terms like good, bad, moral, or immoral, we ought to demand to know according to what system they make those judgments. This is why praying without a very specific concept and knowledge of God is meaningless. We can only pray to a God who has expectations of us. Without those expectations we cannot hope to create a tension between how we view ourselves and how God sees us. And it is precisely the tension between those two polar opposites that makes prayer possible.

You have certainly heard of the fellow who cried that he had prayed to God for a Ferrari but God ignored him. The wise man listening then tapped him on the shoulder. "Excuse me," he politely said, "God did not ignore you, He listened to your prayer and then He said no." History does not record how the European-car enthusiast responded. But there is one thing we do know. Prayer is more than simply tacking a list of requests onto that carrier wave we beam out by flipping between the images. In reality, we are asking God to help us diminish the contrast between the two images so as to become as worthy as possible of the benefits we request.

Clearly there is a painfully large chasm between how I view myself and how God views me. This I know because I fully understand the system by which God judges, and I also know His expectations for me. He may not expect me to be as great as Moses, but He certainly wants Daniel Lapin to achieve whatever greatness Daniel Lapin can possibly achieve. We are further asking for the ability and wisdom to accept a "no" to requests that are far less frivolous than a Ferrari, in full understanding that God knows best. Once I was taught these principles and techniques, I became a little better at praying. I also was better able to understand the effectiveness of prayer.

We even know from famous medical studies, some of which have been conducted by doctors who do not believe in God, that prayer helps in the recovery of the ill. Remarkably, prayer is effective not only when the patient is aware of prayers being said on his behalf; prayer also helps even when the patient is oblivious of anyone praying for his recovery.

Communicating with God through prayer is one of the most exciting adventures imaginable. I no longer feel stupid for having taken so long to learn how to do it. I am only grateful that, unlike so many other skills still hidden from me, prayer has become accessible. We still do not know the full extent of prayer's power, but only those who practice the skill regularly will stand any chance of finding out. I may not climb mountains anymore, but through the magic of prayer, I can ascend great heights just the same. So can you.

CHAPTER 25

OVERCOMING LIMITS

מָקוֹם

MaKOM

*Suggestion: See the alphabet chart and Holy Hebrew! Tools
1, 2 and 5 to get the most out of this chapter.*

Some people blame the crash of the *Hindenburg* for alter-
ing the course of twentieth century travel. They argue
that when the great German airship crashed and burned in
New Jersey in 1939, it not only demolished the Zeppelin
company's prospects, but it also frightened people away
from that mode of flight. If so, this was a pity. Travel on a large
dirigible was so much more comfortable than flying is today.
Instead of being sealed into a narrow aluminum cylinder
and hurtled across the country, airship travelers enjoyed
sleeping cabins, dining rooms, observation windows and
other comfortable amenities during their journeys. I suspect,
however, that the airship was doomed anyway.

For most of the twentieth century, great ocean liners sped
across the Atlantic. In three days or so, they conveyed comfortable and cossected passengers between London and
New York. But the possibility of covering that distance in
six hours on an airplane doomed the ocean liners. In spite
of the memorable cuisine and ornate surroundings that the

trans-Atlantic voyage promised, passengers preferred speed
to comfort when it came to "crossing the pond."

This assures me that it is wrong to blame the *Hindenburg*
crash for terminating the age of airships. Those regal blimps
were goners long before that fateful disaster. In the futile
quest to achieve instantaneous transport, humans would
have eventually rejected the sixteen-hour airship crossing
just as they rejected the three-day ocean liner crossing once
a faster alternative was available.

Just think how few contemporary Americans relish the de-
lights of a train journey across our beautiful land. Now that
it is not more expensive to fly from Los Angeles to Washington, D.C. in an airplane than it is to make the same journey more slowly in a railway carriage, we have abandoned
railway travel in droves. Although the train is spacious and
luxurious, people seem to prefer a crowded, uncomfortable
airplane. How do we explain our feverish quest to save time?
Why do we appear to be consumed by a desperate desire to
get there faster? Why do we not delight more in the journey
than in the arriving?

Being Two Places at Once

Another way of framing those questions is by noticing how
consumed we seem to be with shrinking space or place. We
strive to come as close as possible to being in two places
at almost the same time. It seems to be a stubborn fact of
human existence that we simply cannot be everywhere at
once. That inability to be in more than one place at a time is
quite frustrating when we have to be in the office on a beautiful, sunny day or home with a sick child when a friend is

getting married. When we risk a ticket by speeding through traffic, we are expressing our inner frustration that we simply cannot be in two places simultaneously.

But only being able to be in one place at a time, of course, is not true of God. And this is exactly the Divine quality we describe when little children question us about the Almighty. We tell them that He is everywhere and they struggle to understand how God can be listening to their bedtime prayers while He is simultaneously over at little Jimmy's house hearing his.

Answering these questions is a lot easier when we examine Hebrew's word for "space" or "place," MaKOM.

מ ק ו ם

Things become clearer when we realize that MaKOM is the Hebrew word that not only means space or place, but it is also one of the words used as a name for God. Whenever we need to discuss God with particular emphasis upon His ability to be everywhere at once—His ability to be omnipresent—we can use the word/name MaKOM. It is odd that we seem so driven to emulate God in this particular Divine attribute.

Our Current Love Affair

Transport is not the only way in which we seek to overcome the frustrating human limitation of being in only place at a time. We are in the midst of a love affair with constantly evolving telephones, radio, television, and the Internet.

Do you recall the seductiveness of old walky-talky radios? Or how excited people were about citizens' band transceivers? We are continually enthralled with whatever latest technological advance allows us to more easily and quickly be in touch with others. These technological marvels appeal to us because, on some level, they allow us to escape the frustrating limitation of space. We can communicate with someone far off as if we were in the same room. All these electronic breakthroughs allow us to sprawl in our favorite living room chair while enjoying the feeling that we are not merely somewhere else, but actually everywhere else. We can chat with our daughter in Baltimore while watching some of our fellow citizens chasing a ball in a Dallas stadium.

> **The desire to imitate God is planted in us; how we achieve that goal defines us.**

Social networking lets me communicate with thousands at a time? Sign me up. For humans, feeling godlike is enormously pleasurable.

All this becomes better defined when we realize the implications of having a name for God that means "ultimate place" or "everywhere." We can understand that our desire to be everywhere at once, our desire to escape the limits of our own bodies, is nothing other than our desire to become godlike or at one with God.

Any great book that makes you utterly forget time while it escorts your soul on a soaring adventure of discovery is taking you outside of your body's limits. After reading for a while, you finally return to reality with a start and look

at your watch, incredulous at how much time had passed.
Where were you? It was almost like an "out-of-body-experi-
ence." You found it a satisfying interlude, partially because it
made you less material—godlier. You were operating in the
spiritual and intangible sphere of those thoughts and ideas
that leapt off the page and into your brain. Where were you?
In a sense, you were everywhere. Exactly like God.

Numerical Insight

MaKOM is made up of the four Hebrew letters Mem, Kuf, Vav,
and Mem. From the numerical equivalents on the alphabet
chart, you can see that the word's numerical value is 186.

ם   ו   ק   מ
40   6   100   40

$$40+100+6+40=186$$

Store in your memory the fact that the numerical equivalent
of God's omnipresence or being everywhere is 186. While
you are keeping that in mind, you should add the knowledge
that the basic and most frequently used name of God in the
Bible is made up of these letters—Yud, Hay, Vav, Hay—with
the following numerical equivalents, 10, 5, 6, and 5. What do
these four numbers have to do with 186? Watch!

Stick with me while we review some basic geometry. How
do we convert length measurements such as inches, feet,
yards, or miles into area or space measurements? We square
them, arriving at area measurements such as square inches,
square feet, square yards, and square miles. For instance, let

us imagine that we owned a small, square field. The length measures twelve yards while the breadth also measures twelve yards. The seed package informs us that corn can be planted at a density of, say, ten stalks every square yard. How do we find out how many corn plants we can sow? We need to discover how many square yards we have available. To find that out, we multiply the length of one edge by the breadth, or the length of the other edge. The area or the space available in our field for planting corn would be twelve multiplied by twelve yielding the correct answer of one hundred forty-four square yards.

Imagine now that the numbers 10, 5, 6, and 5 represent the four-letter, linear name for God. What would we do if we wanted to obtain the area or space value of God? Why, we would use the same process we used in the earlier example of the little corn field. To turn a line into area, we square it or multiply it by itself. In this case we take God's "linear name" and multiply it by itself.

$$10 \times 10 \ = \ 100$$
$$5 \times 5 \ = \ 25$$
$$6 \times 6 \ = \ 36$$
$$5 \times 5 \ = \ 25$$

Adding the results all together gives us 186.

$$100 + 25 + 36 + 25 = 186.$$

That, I hope you remember, is the numerical equivalent of God's attribute of omnipresence or being everywhere, the numerical value of His name, MaKoM. In other words, if 10, 5, 6, and 5 represent the straight-line depiction of God, as it were, then the spatial or omnipresent depiction of God must be God squared, or 186—or, of course, MaKOM.

Imitating God

One way to be godlike is to imitate God, and that is precisely what many of us try to do. Even unreligious folk find themselves attracted to the godlike feeling that can come from overcoming human limitations. Every time we strive to push beyond where we previously thought we were stuck, we feel exhilarated. Athletes, business professionals, housewives and everyone else all experience the "high" that comes from pushing just a little harder. This sense of exhilaration we feel is nothing other than our souls exulting in the tiny triumph of becoming just a bit more godlike. We are thrilled to feel just a little less limited and restricted. To some extent, this exhilaration can be experienced in different ways. Some sense it by running a mile in four minutes, others by increasing sales targets or by building a large and successful business. Less thrillingly, you could feel it in a passive way by watching television or listening to the radio. Anything that takes you beyond and outside of yourself will do it.

However, chasing over the globe, constantly buying the latest technological means of communication, escaping the limitations of being human through movies and even too frequently through books, can be wearying. Even building a thriving business, excelling in physical achievement, or attaining high office can leave us feeling temporarily fulfilled but unsatisfied in the longer term.

In contrast, when we imitate God by expanding our souls—

for example, by battling and overcoming a character deficiency—we can feel an even greater "high" than an athlete enjoys after a strenuous and satisfying physical workout. The desire to imitate God is planted in us; how we achieve that goal defines us.

One of the most thrilling ways to emulate God is to overcome a moral challenge. Trying to be a little better than we were yesterday, or struggling to be a little more compassionate, a little more thoughtful and considerate, a little more disciplined than we had been, is just plain fun.

Parents are blessed with the opportunity to grow through interaction with their children each day. Friends can practice growth within their relationships. Work provides most of us with other opportunities to reach beyond our limits. As we take care of daily tasks, we can push ourselves to do so in a more Godly way, exhibiting more kindness, more patience and more restraint.

The trick is to awake to each new morning reveling in the wealth of opportunities the day will provide for us to experience the inner joy of escaping limits. Of course we are going to rush around trying to save time. Of course we will feel dismay at numerous frustrating delays. But through it all, we can remain happy by remembering that frustration with our limitations spring from our powerful, subconscious urge to emulate God by trying to be everywhere and trying to do everything all at once. If we can harness that urge more thoughtfully by using it to expand our awareness and love for God and one another, we will have discovered the joy of truly overcoming our human limits. It may not be possible to fully achieve, but it is really fun to try.

CHAPTER 26

THE SOURCE OF SPIRITUAL ENERGY

ברכה
BRaCHaH

Suggestion: See the alphabet chart and Holy Hebrew! Tools 1, 2, 3, 4 and 5 to get the most out of this chapter.

L et's pretend to be screenwriters.

The scene: *A modern traveler hurtles back in his time machine to a primitive and remote village.*

The action: *The time traveler is captured by fierce-looking warriors* (I could get into this) *who roughly drag him to the hut of a chief well known for his cannibalistic tendencies.* (Do you think that is laying it on a bit too thick?) *Eager to escape his desperate plight, our hero extracts a flask from his pocket and pours what appears to be water around the feared chief's hut. As his tormentors watch the futile antics of their helpless captive, he takes a cigarette lighter from his pocket and ignites the liquid. The hut erupts in flames within minutes and is completely destroyed. Our hero escapes the burning hut while the chief is roasted, and the amazed villagers immediately appoint him their new chief.*

That is as far as I can go with the story for now.

Time travel is a popular plot that we find both in books and movies. From ordinary suburban surroundings, the hero finds himself thrust back to an earlier age. Because of the things he knows and the things he can do, the locals of the day assume he possesses magical powers.

In our story, our intrepid traveler has proven himself to the villagers to be more powerful than their chief. After all, with only a flick of his wrist he destroyed the powerful chief along with his hut. Yet from our vantage point we know that our voyager is actually a rather ordinary sort of fellow with no special powers.

He caused the impressive damage simply by using the highly concentrated energy stored in gasoline. It was not his own power that caused the hut to vanish in flames, but rather his ability to harness the energy that had long ago been captured within the chemical make-up of petroleum. In modern times, that substance is extracted by a petroleum company and made available to customers. Within gasoline is wonderful molecular magic—great quantities of potential energy that had been, originally, the gift of the sun.

Our adventurer possessed no magical powers; he simply unleashed a source of energy. He did not put the energy there in the first place; neither did he even understand the complex chemistry involved. He simply knew the rules of using that energy—light it and it burns.

There are other wonderful sources of energy in our world. We may not understand the complexities of their origins but as long as we know how to use them we can all benefit from them.

I tell this story because it helps us to understand the mysterious power of a blessing; what in Hebrew is called a BRaCHaH.

Doubling

The ancient rabbis insisted that we should never despise a blessing. That would seem to be obvious. I am sure we could all benefit from blessings. But the rabbis had more to say. They added that we should greatly appreciate a blessing regardless of how very ordinary the person offering it may be. Even a fool offering us a blessing is bestowing something of great value.

This would suggest that the power of a blessing has little to do with the qualities of the individual delivering it—the one igniting the gasoline, as it were. It is not only famous sages or holy saints who can bless others to wonderful effect. Sometimes even ordinary folk like you and me can do so, too. This is because if we do it right, when we bless another person—much like our time-traveling hero—we are deploying or triggering an ancient power much greater than ourselves.

Insights into the Hebrew language have been handed down through the millennia by Jewish tradition. Analyzing the Hebrew word BRaCHaH lets us understand what blessing really is. Let us look closely at this word and observe an interesting peculiarity.

The three root letters of BRaCHaH, bet-reish kaf, share a common factor.

כ   ר   ב

20   200   2

kaf reish bet

In *gematria*, the aspect of Biblical teaching which deals with extracting meaning from Hebrew words by calculating their numerical equivalents, these letters are assigned the following values: bet stands for the number 2, reish is 200, and kaf is 20. (In Hebrew, letters function both as letters and as numerals.)

Now these letters which spell the root of the word BRaCHaH happen to be unique, for they are the only letters in the whole Hebrew alphabet whose number equivalent is exactly double the number equivalent of the letter immediately preceding it. The value of bet, 2, is twice that of the preceding letter, aleph, or 1; reish, 200, follows kuf, 100. And kaf, 20, follows yud, or 10 in the sequence of alphabetical letters.

While no scholar of French, English or German would bother to make such an observation about those languages, Hebrew is unique. As I've already observed, the Lord's language is as much a mathematical code as it is a form of conventional linguistic communication. When we recognize that the three letters that compose the basis of the word BRaCHaH are the only letters whose numerical value is exactly double the letters preceding them, we see that a blessing has something to do with *doubling*. For confirmation, take a look at some of the other words formed from the same three-letter root, albeit with the letters appearing in different order. Each one has a meaning that alludes to the 'doubling' or 'twoness' reflected in the letters themselves. Here are some words formed by mixing up and rearranging the letters bet, reish, and kaf.

reish kaf bet

BeCHoR

BeCHoR: This word means "first born," and the first born enjoys one famous distinction. In Biblical law, the first-born boy in a family is entitled to a share of inheritance exactly double that of the other children.

ב ר כ

bet reish kaf

CHeRuV

Cherub, a kind of angel. The most famous cherubs in the Bible are those that surmount the Ark of the Covenant, which resided in the Holy of Holies of the Temple in Jerusalem. There were, of course, *two* of them.

Interestingly, the Talmud relates that these cherubs functioned as a type of spiritual barometer measuring the level of closeness between the Creator and the Jewish people. When the Israelite nation was in close communion with God, the cherubs faced each other across the top of the Ark. In periods of alienation from Him, the cherubs pivoted and faced away from each other. When Jerusalem was conquered and the Temple sacked by the Roman Empire in A.D. 70, triumphant Roman soldiers entered the Temple and carried off the Ark. The ordinary Jews in the streets of the holy city were overcome by depression until they saw the Ark as it was

carried past them: The cherubs, they noticed, not only
faced each other but were locked in the closest possible
embrace. God was, so to speak, lovingly accompanying the
Jews into exile.

ר כ ב

bet kaf reish

RaCHaV

RaCHaV: To ride. Though this word may be a little less obvious, upon reflection we can see that "riding" is a 'doubling'
activity for it can be done only by the interaction of two en-
tities, namely the rider and that which is ridden be it horse,
motorcycle, or any other combination.

And finally, miCH'BaR:

מ כ ב ר

reish bet kaf mem

miCHBaR

Cover. The idea here is much the same as with RaCHaV.
When you "cover" something, there is again a necessary "two-
ness": the covered object and the cover itself. Imagine the
waiter at an elegant restaurant serving with a great flourish
the roast duck you ordered. Out he comes with an outsized
silver dish, held aloft on his right hand, but the bird itself
is invisible till he removes the shining, silvery, dome-shaped
cover surmounting the dish. The cover is as much a part of
the show as the food.

In BRaCHaH we likewise find that a blessing wraps up a requisite 'two-ness'. Every blessing diminishes the self-centeredness that can trap us in the prison of ego and oneness. If a blessing does nothing more than lead us to acknowledge God as the source of all blessing, we have already escaped the pain of seeing ourselves as the only entity of significance. But it usually does far more. It links us in a powerful embrace not only to other people but also to the very world around us. Merely uttering a blessing emphasizes the reality of me and something or someone else. When I express a blessing, I am acknowledging that the "me" is not all there is.

The word BRaCHaH has another grammatical message imbedded in it. BRaCHaH is a feminine word. The last letter of the word, which we have so far ignored in our discussion, expresses this noun's femininity.

ב ר כ <u>ה</u>

In Hebrew, as in Spanish, French, and other Romance languages, nouns are either masculine or feminine. Consequently, verbs and adjectives are modified slightly depending on whether they are being used in conjunction with a masculine or feminine noun. The Frenchman may not understand why he says 'La Benediction' rather than 'Le Benediction,' but the Hebrew aficionado finds a lesson here —because Hebrew is a language without coincidences. Every fact about a word is significant and subject to explanation. So too here. If a blessing is feminine in its linguistic form, we need to know the reason.

The Ability to Reproduce

One of the most inescapable realities of being a woman is the ability to give birth. While some small physical material from the man is needed, it is a woman's body that forms and nurtures a growing baby and from which the baby emerges. There is a natural connection between mother and child. Her body is the one that sustained the growing baby and continues to do so after birth by supplying milk for the infant. It is her hormones that intimately react to each phase of the baby's development and birth. In her ability to reproduce, she shares something in common with every feminine Hebrew word like BRaCHaH.

What do I mean? Well, this idea occurred to me late one night when my car ran out of gas on a lonely road. The infrequent passing driver barely saw me as he sped by. I was alone, and assumed that I'd have to wait till morning to flag down a passing car. As I sat in the driver's seat for a couple of hours, on the verge of dozing off, a car approached from behind and stopped. I saw the headlights go out and watched a trio of somewhat rough-looking characters emerge from the car.

I braced myself when the men tapped on my window, but their faces announced no menacing intent. In fact, they very kindly offered to fill my tank with enough gas to reach the next town. When I asked them how I could possibly repay them for this kindness and began to take out my wallet, they gently refused. "Don't worry about it," said one. "When you get to the next gas station, just buy yourself a gas canister and keep it in your trunk. That way, if you ever come upon some other guy who runs out of gas on a road like this, you can help him like we helped you."

And that was exactly what I did. Whenever those I helped
would ask how they could repay me, I gave the answer I
heard from my three benefactors on that dark, lonely night.
You might say that their blessing to me was reproduced over
and over again. A blessing has the capacity to reproduce and
create new blessings. Will every blessing reproduce? No, of
course not. Not every woman gives birth, either. However, a
woman has the ability to reproduce and so does a blessing.

A blessing links us in a powerful embrace not only to other people but also to the very world around us.

One finds an analogy in
the natural world. Scien-
tists have formulated
what is called the Laws of
Conservation of Matter
and Energy. In the physi-
cal world, matter and en-
ergy can convert into
one another, and they
are eternal. For example,
when you burn a candle, the quantity of wax that melts
doesn't cease to exist; it turns into fumes as well as into energy in the form of light and heat. Blessings are like that too.
They never die. God blessed the seventh day and called it His
Sabbath, a fact that Jews acknowledge by saying a blessing
over a glass of wine each Friday night. God's blessing didn't
simply expire at the conclusion of that first Sabbath. The Sabbath never uses up its share of blessing. The offspring of that
original Divine blessing continue to bless each human who
steps under the shelter of the Sabbath each week.

A BRaCHaH is about continuity. This is why one of the most conspicuous examples of a cyclical blessing is the one religious Jewish parents bestow upon their children each week as the Sabbath commences. Children are the key to our continuity. They confer immortality upon us just as we do for our parents and grandparents. Through our children maintaining the values that shape our lives, we in a sense continue to live here on earth through them. If they reproduce and are blessed with their own children, in whom they inculcate the very same values, then in a sense we never die.

Staying Grounded

We now arrive at the next clue contained in the Hebrew word for blessing: The word for blessing is the same as the word for knee. Insignificantly, the vowels are slightly different, giving us BeReCH; however, the root bet-reish-kaf means both blessing and knee.

If, like me, you've occasionally hurt your knees by running in insufficiently cushioned running shoes, you know how essential a part of the body your knees really are. Without knees, there are basically three things you can't do: You can't reach down to touch the ground. You can't run. And you can't jump. Your knees allow you do all these things; metaphorically speaking, so does a blessing.

Try touching the ground without bending your knees. If you are extraordinarily lithe, it can be done. For most of us, however, touching the ground without knees would require hurling ourselves to the floor and falling flat on our back or face. That's no fun. Fortunately, we can just bend our knees and *kneel*.

Kneeling, of course, happens to be the classic pose most associated with prayer. Many of us who worship will find ourselves on our knees from time to time. For Jews, kneeling is so important that it constitutes a crucial aspect of the Yom Kippur service on the Day of Atonement. In America it is not uncommon, when petitioning God, to fall on one's knees and ask for His blessing—a custom derived from the worship service in the Jerusalem Temple. Our English word "kneel" is derived from the word "knee."

There are two reasons why, in the context of a blessing, one might wish to touch the ground. First, it is proper to physically demonstrate subservience to the Source of all blessings—God. Any person expressing a blessing is merely triggering the blessing whose power originates not with him but with the Creator of our world. It is not a bad idea to demonstrate our awareness of this; getting close to the ground, down on our knees, accomplishes precisely that.

At the same time, saying a blessing, a BRaCHaH, has the virtue of grounding us. It is all too easy, especially for those who are ambitious in their spiritual lives, to sometimes lose sight of life's practicalities. Has my desire for closeness with God caused distance to develop between me and my loved ones? Is my determination to love God with all my heart, soul and strength causing me to act a little less considerately toward the people among whom I live and work? Is my yearning for a spiritual link with Heaven diminishing my joy of living in this wonderful world? As we strive for ever-greater closeness to the Creator, we run the risk of getting

caught up among the clouds and the stars. Blessings help
keep us grounded; they help us keep our feet on the ground.
It is frightfully easy to become so caught up in lofty aims
that we lose sight of our real goals and purposes. Blessings
help us recall that God made the ordinary, physical world as
well as the spiritual one.

I believe it is part of God's plan for us that we should not
only jump high, but also—and more than just occasionally—
get down on the ground, feel the grass, smell the earth, and
thank God for the wonder of Creation. To do this we must
set aside time to appreciate the world of ordinary things—
thunder and lighting, mountains and oceans, even new
clothing or a perfectly yellow banana—just as we set aside
time for prayer, meditation, or other more obviously "spiritual" activities.

Another ability that knees give us is jumping. If our knees
didn't bend, we couldn't jump or reach for the sky. Every
creative, ambitious person is always actively jumping—
stretching his body and soul to reach as high as he can. This
uniquely human desire of ours, to reach for the stars, is itself
a blessing. Uttering frequent blessings is one way to constantly challenge ourselves to reach beyond the limitations
of our own vision. We all remember the old aphorism "look
before you leap." Well, blessings remind us that sometimes
the only way to cross the chasm is by leaping, even if the
landing site is not visible. Yes, sometimes it is necessary to
leap before you look. Knees and blessings, being the same
Hebrew word, remind us of how important it is to be able
to jump.

Finally, knees allow us to run. In fact, they are essential for running. Without them, we'd have a hard time moving at a pace much faster than a goose-stepping walk. Notice the way competitive runners crouch at the starting line before a race. Their knees bend at the ideal angle to launch them into the race. Running sends one simple signal: urgency. When we see someone running, we know that, to him, time is short. Well, that also is a message we should each carry with us. The commodity that is in shortest supply is not money, but time.

My late father, who was also my Torah teacher, harbored an intense dislike for card games. I don't think I ever really understood his feelings until my first visit to a Florida retirement community. There I saw many elderly-yet-vital human beings whiling away their final years on earth…playing cards. To my dad, card games suggested that you had all the time in the world—there was no urgency about you.

In my work as an advisor to business executives, I am sometimes asked to evaluate the condition of a company or office. One of the first things I try to measure is the average level of urgency felt by employees and associates in the enterprise. If too many people are gazing out of windows, ambling down the hallways or otherwise exhibiting no sense of urgency, I know that the company has a problem.

Both running and jumping require us to not only use our knees, but also demand that we should be in touch with the ground. You see, if we were suspended in mid-air we could convulse our leg muscles with all our might but go nowhere. Unless a runner can thrust back against the ground, he will achieve no speed at all. Unless a jumper can launch himself from the firm, unyielding ground, he too will not achieve lift-off. Thus, the fact that the Hebrew word for blessing is also the word for knees helps to tie together the themes of running, jumping and the ground. Only by being in touch with the ground can we adequately reach for heaven and achieve urgency. Only by correctly using the gift of blessing can we maintain the exquisite tension between our need to be reliably rooted to the ground and our yearning for spiritual completion. To put it as simply as possible, there is built into our nature a human need to join Heaven and Earth.

When a wheelbarrow full of uranium fuel is loaded aboard a nuclear submarine, it is enough to provide propulsion, electricity, air, and water for the vessel and its intrepid crew for about a year. Nobody on board possesses that kind of power within himself, but each person possesses the ability to deploy the almost unlimited nuclear power that is hidden in the nuclei of those uranium atoms. By ourselves, we are not very powerful people. But we all possess the ability to deploy the almost unlimited power that God has hidden deep within the heart of a blessing.

CHAPTER 27

OUR TWO LIVES

חיים

CHY-YiM

Suggestion: See the alphabet chart and Holy Hebrew! Tools
1, 2, 4 and 7 to get the most out of this chapter.

If you want to know something about other people's inner
lives, I advise you to eavesdrop. I am certainly not suggesting that you pry into other people's lives, just that you don't
block your ears when others talk at the top of their voices.

Often I can hear another airplane passenger, seated three
rows back, relating his life story. He is managing to make
himself heard above the roar of four large jet engines, and I
pity his victim trapped in the middle seat.

The other day I overheard an older man going on and on
about his health. At great length he was informing another
fellow about the peaks of fitness he had attained. He was a
recent triathlon participant and was expounding on how, in
pursuit of top form for running, swimming, and bicycling, he
had limited his intake of dietary fat. "Now," he said, "I hardly
eat any fat at all!"

I was amused to hear his listener attempt several times to

turn the conversation to other subjects, such as family or a recently published book. However, the speaker remained oblivious to the distress of his audience and doggedly continued listing his vitamin regimen.

The conversation, such as it was, stuck in my mind because this trim athlete is a type of person you meet all the time: the health bore, obsessed with prolonging youthful flexibility beyond all previously held records and determined to tell everyone considerable details about how he is doing so.

Our society has become quite obsessed with physical safety. I am not opposed to seat belts, bicycle helmets or food safety inspections, yet I do think that something in our culture is out of kilter when we focus disproportionately on physical threats like these. We are rightly concerned about dirty air polluting our lungs, but how about dirty lyrics polluting our souls? When we are more concerned with a cell phone tower being built in our neighborhood than the sexual promiscuity of our high school students, I worry that we have a serious blind spot. This fixation on the physical, as demonstrated by the man at the gym as well as by safety fanatics, interests me because it illuminates the peculiarity of the Hebrew word for "life": CHY-YiM. What is unusual about this word is that the YiM at the end signals that it is a plural noun.

Many people wear a necklace with a little pendant at the end consisting of the Hebrew word CHY (rhymes with guy), spelled chet-yud, which means "life" in the singular sense. While this is often transliterated as CHAI in English, the Hebrew spelling is as below.

ח י

But when the Bible speaks of human life, the word used is CHY-YiM, literally "lives." Were an individual to talk in Hebrew about his life, he would grammatically be speaking about his lives. Had the talkative athlete in my gym wanted to say in Hebrew, "I've had a long life," he would have had to say, "I have had long lives."

One of the two trees prohibited to Adam in the Garden of Eden was called the tree of life, or in Hebrew, Etz ha' CHY-YiM. (Tree is Etz and the 'ha' before CHY-YIM functions as the definite article, 'the.') Literally 'tree of the lives.'

Not One Life, but Two

The Lord's language is telling us quite unequivocally that human beings have not just one life, but two. You wouldn't have known it to listen to that chap in the gym, but this is the whole point. We possess not only a biological life, but also a spiritual one. Most health bores I've come across fail to realize this. For them, the physical body is the sum total of human existence. So, naturally, exercising the body that is the vehicle of their only life becomes the supreme value.

In the Bible we find the word CHY, the word for (singular) life, in the story of Adam and Eve. Here the First Lady of human history is called em kol CHY, "mother of all life." From this phrase Adam derived the name he gave to his wife: in Hebrew, CHaVaH.

Now I am striving with all my might not to bore you with the technicalities of Hebrew grammar. But you should know that, in turning CHY into the name of a woman, as he wished to do, Adam would more naturally have given Eve the

Hebrew name CHaYaH. This would be the feminine form of the word CHY. (Transforming a masculine noun, like CHY, into its feminine form is typically accomplished by adding an "ah" sound.) Yet Adam introduced a new "v" sound rather than follow the rules. Why? He needed to do this because CHaYaH was already used during the days of Creation to refer to animal life. Adam's point in naming Eve is that there is a very profound difference between animal and human existence. Adam chose the name CHaVaH, or Eve, to avoid any potential confusion among his descendants.

Animals have only one life, the biological one. Whatever they do is predicated on instinct, not reasoned choice. They certainly have no urge to pray to God or to read an uplifting poem. Indeed, an animal's chief concern is the preservation of its physical self and the production of progeny.

Built into animals is an instinct for self-preservation. As a child growing up in Africa, our family often went on trips to various game preserves. It was amazing to see how careful the wildlife was about protecting their health. Often we would come across elephants drinking from a river, while other elephants rolled around and muddied the waters of the same rivers. No doubt they also relieved themselves there. But the elephants never varied their pattern. Whatever they did in the water was always downstream from where they would drink.

By contrast, people in some countries still pollute their own water supplies while in other societies, proper sanitation has been learned and improved over many centuries. Even now, new technologies are being employed. Unlike humans, animals do not build upon generational experience; instead they instinctively do the same thing generation after generation.

More than the Physical

Unlike animals, we humans often risk and endanger our lives for purposes that have nothing to do with physical survival. Only humans risk everything to climb Mount Everest or skydive. Obviously we humans consider some things more important than mere physical survival. On occasion, certain types of animals—for example, dogs—will sacrifice themselves to save their owners. But, other than in fanciful literature, dogs will not gather together and decide to die for an abstract idea. On the other hand, history is replete with accounts of humans willing to die rather than renounce their faith. We see the same noble commitment to ideal over physical survival when men and women march off to war in order to protect their country.

Only humans risk everything to climb Mount Everest or skydive.

The point that humans care about more than physical survival is even proven when people risk their lives in pursuit of less worthy goals. Humans abuse alcohol and drugs, smoke cigarettes to excess, or challenge a rival in a dangerous activity for the sake of achieving what's called a "high." These goals may be less lofty but they are nonetheless spiritual. I need to stress that "spiritual" is not a synonym for "good" or "holy"; it is merely the opposite of material. Patriotism and selfishness, good and evil are all spiritual concepts that cannot be measured with any scientific instruments. Each of these is a non-material concept. Nothing in the physical realm of our existence explains the human need to feel "high"—elevated, lofty, free of physical constraint. Physical addiction to certain drugs may occur; but the motivation that led the addict to start shooting up or snorting in the first place was spiritual pain, not physical need.

Not for nothing is alcohol sometimes called "spirits"—from the Latin *spiritus*. When we get drunk or high, we are seeking a substitute for some lack in our spiritual lives. The resulting buzz is a counterfeit spirituality. But imitation is the highest form of flattery. Drug addicts are a reminder to us of the powerful need we all have to achieve a spiritual high. One can achieve it the ancient and authentic way, by pursuing God or one can attempt to do so in dangerous and debased ways.

Invariably, people who live their lives with a material orientation are the same people that find themselves attracted to dangerous pursuits. In one way or another, the call of the soul will be answered. It is almost as if a little voice goes off saying, "You think that nothing matters except your physical body? Well, now we'll have you do something really risky, say bungee-jumping, just so the deepest recesses of your soul will know that you don't really mean that. Your action will now demonstrate that you don't really think your physical safety is all that matters." I do not mean this to sound smug, but those who demonstrate their commitment to Godly spiritual health with the same fervor they dedicate to the physical find far less need to climb snow-clad peaks, jump from airplanes, or for that matter, seek escape from the mind-numbing effects of materialism through drugs or alcohol.

Doing the Math

According to the ancient Kabalistic study of gematria, where letters correspond to numbers, the sums of various words convey meaning. Examples of gematria are only valid when they have been handed down through the generations; they would be rather meaningless if they were computer-generated.

If we add up the letters/numbers in CHY-YiM—chet, yud, yud, mem—we get a sum of sixty-eight.

ח   י   י   מ

8   10   10   40

This is exactly the number that forms the word for "wise man," CHaCHaM, whose letters can likewise be added together, producing a figure of...sixty-eight!

ח   כ   מ

8   20   40

In this case, as in others received through tradition, the equivalent value serves to point out a relationship between the two words CHY-YiM and CHaCHaM. In other words, wise people recognize that for humans there are two lives, not just one, and that they need to protect their spiritual as well as their physical lives.

You see, just as there are gyms and pools and running tracks where you can exercise your body, so there are gyms designed to exercise for the soul. They are wherever wisdom, as the Bible defines it, is to be found. This would include houses of worship and religious schools, but also less formal settings such as the homes of wise clergymen and elders from whom we can learn wisdom.

Will just any wisdom do? Sorry, afraid not.

The Blue Lagoon

Try the following thought experiment. Imagine that we were able to replay what I refer to as the *Blue Lagoon* scenario. In this model (named for a very silly Brooke Shields movie) a young boy and girl are placed on a deserted island. They're young, but we leave them plenty of food and shelter to get through their adolescence. The island has plenty of natural resources and no dangerous animals or insects.

Let's assume that we installed clandestine surveillance cameras all over the island, and sat back and watched for, oh, about 4,000 years. What would happen to our pair of Robinson Crusoes? Obviously they would mate, and gradually a human society would appear.

What about God? Remember, the little boy and girl were too young to remember anything about Him from their parents. Will they discover God? Probably not. Like all primitive societies, they will undoubtedly develop superstitions. They will have a vague awareness of a spiritual realm. But there is no reason to think they will develop any consciousness of God. They would need to be truly unique individuals to do so.

Will the island paradise of our thought experiment be a successful society? Will it have real wealth, freedom, or happiness? I don't think so. (Unfortunately there is no way to conduct the experiment for real and find out. Those kill-joys at the Society for the Prevention of Cruelty to Children Trapped on Desert Islands would put a stop to it.) But without knowledge of God, without the recognition that since God created the world we must strive to understand physical creation, our island society will probably remain on a subsistence level.

A fascinating study was commissioned by the Communist Chinese government. The ordinarily prosaic and secular regime convened a group to analyze why China failed to modernize and develop scientific, technological, medical and economic breakthroughs that Europe achieved starting in the 15th century. Eventually, and one can imagine the reluctance of the participants to reveal the outcome of their research, the group concluded that the spread of religion in Europe with the advent of Bible translations, the printing press and Protestantism, was what propelled Europe way ahead of China.

This is an amazing confession for an atheistic regime to make. It reveals the inter-relationship between the two worlds, the need for CHY-YiM, for our material world to be intertwined with a spiritual one.

What is Culture?

Evidence has been emerging for decades now that "culture" supports civilization. I'm talking about real culture—not opera, novels, ethnic cuisine, or a certain style of joke telling, but rather the web of spiritual values that regulates the behavior of the members of that culture. It has become clear that nations blessed with certain kinds of cultures—those closest to ancient Biblical values—do much better at developing and maintaining the sort of institutions that are conducive to a free, tolerant, and wealthy society. The most successful cultures tend to possess, at the core of their web of values, an abiding awareness of God. Not just any god, but the God of the Bible.

The Soviets suffered from no shortage of CHY, life, in the sense of biological life, but they wished to separate it from CHY with its spiritual meaning. Russia is even now struggling to recover from that terrible error.

It should be just as clear that maintaining this dual aspect of CHY-YiM enhances the effectiveness not only of nations but also of individuals. As my father used to quote, "Better a soul without a body, than a body without a soul." When you forget about the soul, the body will be endangered, too.

No one had to explain any of this to Winston Churchill. Now Churchill was a very wise man, but Neville Chamberlain, who preceded him in the role of British Prime Minister, was smarter. At least he was smarter in the ways that can be measured by IQ tests, SAT scores, and the like. He got significantly better grades in school than did Churchill. But Churchill ended up having to fight the Second World War and save Britain as well as the rest of Europe, because of the grievous blunders that Chamberlain made in foreign policy.

Foremost among these was the latter's appeasement of Hitler. Somehow the brilliant Mr. Chamberlain turned out to be entirely blind to Hitler's wiles. If he had not been so, the terror and suffering of World War II might have been averted. But for all his smarts, Chamberlain was a one-dimensional character. He believed in bodies, not souls. Thus he misread the Fuehrer, who was a very spiritual person—negatively so. The truly evil among us tend to be just that. This is part of the key to their power.

I must stress once again that "spirituality" can be good, or it can be evil. A bad person who lacks a spiritual awareness will never do much worse than petty vandalism and low-grade thuggish behavior. However, a bad person with a highly developed spiritual life can easily become a Stalin or a Hitler. Chamberlain was fooled by Hitler's reassurances that he meant no evil toward Czechoslovakia because the Prime Minister assumed that Hitler was, more or less, just like him—a body without a soul. Prime Minister Chamberlain assumed that like an animal, Hitler would never do anything that could jeopardize his own physical survival. Wrong! Bad mistake! Animals are not capable of evil and humans obviously are. We call foxes "clever," but of course they are not. A fox does what a fox does—for instance, raid a henhouse— purely out of instinct. The cunning duplicity of a Hitler was invisible to Chamberlain. Hitler was committed to ideals, not just to physical survival. They were very evil ideals, to be sure, but ideals nonetheless.

Two Lenses for True Perspective

An awareness of CHY-YiM in its full meaning can be compared to looking at a distant horizon using binoculars, as opposed to observing the same scene through a telescope. You see the same objects in your field of vision: trees, a house, and a mountain. But with a telescope the element of depth is missing because you are trying to peer at reality through only one lens. Your vision is therefore fatally handicapped. When you use two lenses you can see truth.

We will all benefit from becoming accustomed to view every aspect of life through not only one, but two lenses. Using both the material lens along with its equally important spiritual counterpart allows us to make accurate judgments and maintain our two lives in full health.

CHAPTER 28

THE CURRENCY OF GRATITUDE

תודה
TODaH

*Suggestion: See the alphabet chart and Holy Hebrew! Tool
1, 2 and 3 to get the most out of this chapter.*

One of my most rewarding moments as a rabbi or teacher came during a lecture I was delivering to a group of young Jewish professionals in Santa Monica, California. As I usually do, I tried to inject a few pyrotechnic effects into what was quite a technical discussion.

My father taught me to design a speech in the form of a musical symphony. There should be a theme and variations on the theme; there needs to be a beginning, middle, and an end. And at unexpected moments, he insisted, much as the composer Hayden did with his Surprise Symphony, there should be a flamboyant outburst of conspicuous virtuosity to help hold the audience's attention.

I can't say that I ever lived up to Dad's oratorical skill, but to this day I never prepare a speech or lecture without at least trying to follow his example as well as his stage directions. As I drew close to the end of that particular presentation I began to pull the pieces together for the wrap-up. I had presented a Biblical puzzle, dissected it, rotated it for examination from different directions, and ruled out most of the apparent answers. Finally came the moment I always enjoy.

With a flourish worthy of any stage magician, I yanked away the black cloth that had concealed the strings connecting all the disparate parts of the evening and there, hanging almost visibly in the air between us, was the brightly glowing answer to the problem that had perplexed us for nearly ninety minutes.

I glanced around the room to see how many people were enraptured by my presentation. I hoped they would appreciate not only what I had taught, but how I had presented it. But most of the attendees were regular students of mine and were quite accustomed to my attempts at showmanship, so my glance was met mostly with knowing smiles. However, one rather shy and retiring sort of fellow, a business school graduate, was hearing me for the first time. My gaze was immediately drawn to his face in the crowd. His jaw was drooping, his mouth open. He had stopped breathing and was gaping at me through wide-open eyes bulging out of his head. Then all the stored up air in his chest came whooshing out of his mouth in one loud, involuntary, monosyllabic exclamation: "Wow!" he yelled.

Horrified at his indiscreet outburst, he turned red and desperately scanned the packed room for an escape route.

"Please don't leave yet," I entreated him. "You can't possibly know how much I appreciate your reaction. I still have to thank you."

He tried to explain himself. "The past hour and a half will assist my business career more than any similar period of time that I spent at Harvard Business School," he firmly declared. "But why did you say that you still have to thank me? It seems to me that it ought to be the other way around."

The Importance of Gratitude

This is what I told him.

The Hebrew word for "giving thanks," TODaH, also means "to admit, confess or acknowledge." The reason is pretty clear. By thanking someone for what they gave me or did for me, I am admitting that I needed their contribution. I am acknowledging that prior to their gift I was incomplete. And yes, I am even confessing that whatever they did for me changed me. This is one reason so many of us find it emotionally difficult to look a benefactor in the eye and utter a sincere "thank you," for something more meaningful than a pair of gloves. Deep down, we recognize that our expression of gratitude is an eloquent confession that our benefactor has just repaired one kind of shortcoming or another in our selves.

Expressing gratitude is considered so important in Judaism that we find the word TODaH is actually the root origin for the word "Jew."

The name of YeHuDaH, Jacob's fourth son, is the name used for the entire Jewish people today. YeHuDaH got his name when his mother, Leah, expressed thanks to God for allowing the majority of the tribes to come through her. Both TODaH, and YeHuDaH come from the same root—yud, dalet, hay—meaning both confession and thanks. As Hebrew

moved through the European languages into English, YeHu-
DaH became Judah, from which the group name in English,
Jews, evolved.

One of the very first words wise mothers teach their infants
is "thanks," or some other baby-appropriate variation. Why
do they do this? Is it because Grandpa or Grandma will be
offended if the apple of their eye fails to properly thank
them for the nice new pink pajamas with a teddy bear on
the tummy? No, of course not. Wise Mom knows that for
his own future happiness, her baby needs to know how to
thank others and to feel comfortable doing so. Adults also
need to know this. We thank, not because the other party
needs our thanks, but because we will be better off for having expressed that gratitude.

Giving and Receiving

While we do need to acknowledge what others do for us, we
humans experience a corroding of our souls if we are only
receivers and not givers.
We feel enlarged by giving
and diminished by only receiving. This is one of the
great tragedies of living on
charity, and why the no-
blest form of charity is to
help the recipient become
independent of our good-
will as quickly as possible.

> **We experience
> a corroding
> of our souls
> if we are only
> receivers
> and not givers.**

Paradoxically, humans dependent upon the largesse of others even become resentful. We often find this in teenagers

whose bodies and young minds are telling them "I am my own person" and yet, frustratingly, they are still dependent upon their parents.

There are two ways to combat this resentfulness and it is important to do so. Resentfulness hobbles a person and keeps him or her from becoming productive and independent. But this danger can be counteracted. The first important principle is to demand gratitude from those who are receiving. This is why a great moral wrong is perpetuated by government usage of the term "entitlement." It may be difficult to ask for and receive charity, but it allows one to feel grateful and accept the obligation to do whatever one can to improve one's situation and become the one giving, not getting. Promoting a feeling of being entitled to the money, time or possessions of others cripples human dignity, trapping the recipient in poverty.

The second way of assisting those in need or young people who are dependent on their parents is to demand that everyone be a giver, no matter how little one has. Teenagers or young adults should be encouraged to earn money in a real job and to give 10% of their earnings to charity. Their fiscal accomplishments will help bring their urges for independence into line with the realities of life. It is also valuable for them to contribute to the family whether by means of chores or even helping with some family expenses. Every member of a family from toddler age needs to see themselves as a contributing member of the family

In national terms, even those receiving money or assistance from the government need to pay taxes or donate time and effort to their country. A country filled with citizens who only receive but don't give is a country heading for downfall.

Since being recipients can diminish us, make us feel resentful toward our benefactors, and even corrode our souls, should we then try to avoid receiving things? Absolutely not! That would not only be ungracious toward those of our friends and relatives who may wish to give to us, but it is also quite impossible. We live in a vast world of human interaction. Being able to buy food or clothes, having electricity and water at the touch of a button in our homes, and living in areas where gangs of marauders don't rampage are all gifts that we receive because we are not independent of others.

Whether we like it or not, we are recipients of the magical gift of life every morning we rise from our beds. Each time we enjoy a wonderful meal or gaze at a spectacular sunset, we are recipients of priceless largesse. Having a daughter's arms flung around one's neck for a goodnight hug, or watching a family of black bears loping along a remote beach in British Columbia is yet another wonderful gift. So many gifts! How do we avoid becoming resentful at being such regular recipients of good?

Pay for Everything

The answer is simple, although perhaps not obvious: We try to pay for everything we receive. Walking out of a store without paying for your merchandise hurts you more than it does the store. The proprietor has certainly lost the money to which he was entitled, but he will gradually recover. You, however, have been irreparably reduced. Each time you use that stolen item, you will be reminded that you are not only a recipient, but a recipient by force. Naturally, over time, this will corrode your soul and fill you with resentment and self-loathing. Smart people try to pay for everything from which they benefit.

In the same way, enjoying that sunset and all of life's other great gifts without paying for them hurts us, too. But how on earth do we pay for those priceless gifts—and to whom do we pay? Well, that's easy. If it is gift from a friend, a relative or a business associate, you obviously cannot take out your wallet and offer to pay for the gift. That would be ungracious and defeat the purpose of the giver. No, you don't need to do anything like that. All you need do is express heartfelt and sincere thanks, either in person or by letter. Gratitude is a currency of human communication. You have now "paid" for the gift you received and are no longer merely a recipient. You are a participant in a transaction of courtesy and friendship. You are an equal participant, and not only have you not been diminished by receiving the gift, but you have grown from the interaction.

That store proprietor would have preferred to receive payment from the shoplifter. That the thief will become irreparably harmed by his folly is not really any consolation for the merchant; he would have liked to be paid. Paying for the product would not only have benefited the customer, but it obviously would also benefit the seller. Similarly, while expressing gratitude chiefly benefits the recipient of the gift, it also adds to the richness of life for the donor. Why is this? Well, have you ever had the unhappy experience of putting all you've got into telling a joke to someone and finding yourself greeted by a blank face? I have. In my case, after my

punch line, my friend resembled a department store manne-
quin. You try to explain the punch line to your utterly non-
responsive friend and he interrupts, "I got it, I got it. It's quite
funny." But his face is still immobile. Well, he got your joke, so
why are you still feeling vaguely dissatisfied?

You felt almost cheated when he did not respond because,
in this case, laughter is the currency of human communication. You reached out to another human with a joke. He did
not respond. He was the moral equivalent of a shoplifter; he
took your merchandise without paying you for it.

Have you noticed how you sometimes force yourself to
laugh at someone's joke that you did not really find funny?
You may just have written off your forced smile as being
polite. However, you were really being much more. You were
participating in the loneliness-banishing rite of human communication and paying someone for his effort of reaching
out to you. It was another way of saying thank you. It was another way of confessing your own need for human contact.

When you give gifts to others, you enjoy their gratitude, too.
Just as a restaurateur would be unhappy if a diner left without paying, so are all of us unhappy when we make an effort to connect with others and they don't react. Part of the
"deal" in these interactions is that the diner is expected to
eat and pay and that the recipient of a communication or gift
is to receive and thank.

When we applaud after a theatrical performance or musical
concert, we are saying thank you. Yes, of course we paid for
the ticket but that only gained us our seat. We now need to
pay for the incredible pleasure we just enjoyed and which

benefited us beyond our expectations. The appropriate way to do this is by clapping our hands and demanding an encore. There is something churlish about just sitting there without applauding. In fact, it is just like shoplifting.

When we tip a waiter after a good meal we are also saying thank you. We are acknowledging that without his efforts, our meal would have been less. It benefits us more to bestow a tip upon someone who delivered exemplary service than it does him. Saying thank you is an enlarging activity because it is an act of giving. Deriving benefit from the waiter's service without thanking him would deprive him of a small amount of money, but would diminish our very personalities.

Thanking God

What if the gift is something for which no other human is responsible? A fresh mountain breeze...the sun shining on raindrops caught in a spider's web like diamonds in a tiara... whom do you thank for these? That's easy, too: God. What if you are an atheist? I guess you are out of luck; I don't have anything else to tell you. Each and every day you receive wondrous and enjoyable benefits for which you have not paid and for which you have no one to thank. Of course, this is going to impact you over time.

Whenever I deliver a speech or a lecture I look around for the appreciation. It is my applause and my tip. It tells me that I really connected with other human beings and made the world a less lonely place for us all.

"When you let loose that yell of appreciation," I told that Harvard Business School graduate, "you gave me the biggest gift. Naturally, I had to thank you. My fear was that you would leave before I had the opportunity to do so, which would have left me sad and diminished. Now, why don't you join some of us for coffee and we can continue the discussion." He did and we became great friends. But he never reacted quite the same to anything I said, ever again.

COMPLETE PEACE

שלו(ו)ם [שלו(ו) מ(ו)*]

Suggestion: See the alphabet chart and Holy Hebrew! Tool 1, 2, 3 and 5 to get the most out of this chapter.

Shortly before he died in 1981, Nobel Prize winning scientist Max Delbruck delivered a lecture at Cal Tech which I was privileged to attend. He spoke engagingly about having encountered the already-famous Albert Einstein in one of the elevators of the Planck Institute in Berlin before World War II.

The audience chuckled as Delbruck described how he almost wished for the elevator cables to snap so he could watch Einstein cope with one of his gravity-themed thought-experiments suddenly turning terrifyingly practical. I found myself not only educated by the lecture, but also entertained. Delbruck peppered his technical analyses with quotations from poetry and allusions to music. Along with the rest of the audience, I was utterly charmed.

---

*Certain Hebrew letters change their shape when they are the final letter of a word. The 'mem' is one such letter.

Returning home, I related the lecture to my wife as best I could and told her of my reaction. Not since I had taken leave of the great teachers at my yeshiva had I encountered anyone who related to almost every aspect of the world as seamlessly as did Max Delbruck. With her style of simple directness that has intimidated me from the day we met, my bride wanted to know why I didn't call Delbruck and arrange a private meeting. Trying to explain to her why this was a terrible idea was quite difficult, so I obtained his phone number and placed the call.

To my astonishment, Dr. Delbruck himself answered the phone. He sounded amused when I described what it was about his speech that enchanted me, and he graciously consented to see Susan and me. Our most undisturbed opportunity to talk, he explained, would be if we accompanied him on his weekly hike over the hills behind Pasadena.

The following Tuesday afternoon, Susan and I met the distinguished scientist at his modest bungalow near the campus of the California Institute of Technology. As we looked around his library he recounted how the previous evening he had hosted a book club at which he had reviewed a recent bestseller. That evening he would be playing the violin for a chamber orchestra recital. We chatted a while longer, then set off at a brisk clip up the rugged terrain. He climbed so swiftly that I began to fear that I would eventually have to carry the elderly man back to town. After an hour had elapsed, I changed my mind; it was quite clear that he would be carrying me.

The afternoon was unforgettable! We discussed history, biology, popular entertainment, chemistry, literature, geology, atomic physics, photography, politics, and genetics. To be perfectly honest, much of the conversation was not so much a discussion as it was Delbruck talking and Susan and me raptly listening.

"Do your students enjoy the same unbridled curiosity about every facet of the world that you do?" I asked him. He expressed deep concern and was uncharacteristically vehement when, with sad eyes, he assured me that nothing could be further from the truth. Most science students today, he contemptuously exclaimed, expressed almost no interest in anything outside their area of specialization, and knew even less. Then, in a prediction that I have come to believe to be increasingly true, he warned that this interdisciplinary illiteracy would eventually threaten American achievement.

Sadly, a few months later, Max Delbruck was gone. But how the memories of that afternoon linger in my mind!

Interdisciplinary Literacy

In the years following that memorable afternoon, it became clear to me that most of the great minds of the past also saw no barriers isolating the many different ways of coming to know our wonderful world. An example is one of my heroes, Winston Churchill. Was he a soldier, journalist, politician, painter, novelist, bricklayer, orator or world leader? Perhaps he was the last only as a result of the seamless unity of the first seven.

What a pleasure it would have been to sit in on a sociable seventeenth century evening with these three friends: poet John Milton, architect Christopher Wren, and scientist

Robert Boyle. Not only did they happily get along with one another, but they were also comfortable and knowledgeable in one another's areas of expertise. Wren designed St Paul's cathedral in London and was also a distinguished astronomer. Milton was a theologian, as was Boyle. The latter not only had a law of physics named for him, Boyle's Law, but he also translated the Bible into many languages in his role as the head of the Society for Propagating the Gospel in New England.

Think of Leonard de Vinci, who was not only a painter and sculptor but also a designer of helicopters! Think of almost any truly great human being and you will find someone who simultaneously developed the many parts of his or her personality rather than focus on only one narrow area to the detriment of the others.

Have you ever heard some cruel critic calling a computer enthusiast a geek or a nerd? The derision you hear in those words might result from this very point. Certain kinds of males seem to find computers all-absorbing. (Very few females seem to fall victim to this particular form of fascination.) These guys' technical obsessions leave them little time or energy for any other pursuits, so they occasionally strike us as psychically misshapen. They are very obviously indifferent to almost anything non-technical while being conspicuously advanced in the one narrow area of digital science.

I suspect that most of us are more comfortable interacting with people with broader interests, which may be why people with intense but narrow interests so often find themselves socially isolated.

Escape from Over-Specialization

There is escape from this dreadful peril of over-specialization, and it is part of the buried treasure found in the Lord's language.

The Hebrew word SHaLoM is the key to welcoming a well-rounded perspective into our lives. It has several meanings and, as always, the treasure lies beneath layers of confusion that conceal how these several meanings really merge into one over-arching principle.

These meanings are
- peace
- complete
- pay
- greetings

Let us start unearthing the treasure by attempting to combine the first two meanings—peace and complete.

Imagine me returning home one evening from work to find an unwashed vagrant camped on my living room rug. He has unrolled a smelly sleeping bag and lit a fire in my fireplace. As I walk in, he insolently eyes me and lazily drawls, "Hi."

"Hi yourself," I might say to him. "You have thirty seconds to get out of this house."

He carefully completes the delicate operation of removing an unappetizing hot dog from the fire before answering. "Stay cool, man. We both want peace, right? I'll keep to my half of the living room, and you can have the other half."

Meanwhile, I am having difficulty trying to decide whether

I should resort to my baseball bat or my twelve-gauge shotgun. Sensing my thoughts, he again assures me that he only wants peace. "Let's sit down together and discuss a peaceful solution to our dilemma," he urges me.

This is a gross misunderstanding of the real meaning of peace. Peace is inseparable from its constituent element— completion or totality. I must be made complete or total before we can even begin discussing peace.

In this instance, that vagrant must leave my house and restore me to the condition in which I was before he intruded into my life. Only then can we discuss peace.

This example also happens to reveal how the third meaning, payment, fits in. If a customer takes a pair of shoes from the department store salesman there is no completion and no peace—just yet. She must first pay for those shoes. That way the store and its salesman are made complete or whole, and then peace can reign. Were she to walk out of the store without paying, there would be little peace. Instead there would be a charge of shoplifting and considerable turbulence for all involved. Peace is far preferable, but can only be attained by all parties achieving totality through payment. Not only does peace depend upon payment for things taken, but it must also be fair— a market-value payment. This is the genius behind the Fifth Amendment to

> **Peace is inseparable from its constituent element —completion or totality.**

our great American constitution. In it we find the words, "nor shall private property be taken for public use without just compensation."

Our wise founders clearly understood that peace depends upon just compensation. In fact, given the familiarity with Hebrew that many of them enjoyed, it is likely that they also understood that "peace" and "payment" are the same word. Obviously, the fourth meaning—a greeting—simply flows from the first three meanings: peace, totality, and payment. When I greet a new arrival or bid farewell to him by uttering the word "SHaLoM," I am expressing the hope that we shall both enjoy the full tranquility that can only come from totality and discharged obligations or payment.

And is only the first jewel from the buried treasure chest.

The larger diamond lies just beneath the next shovelful of sand. Again we must examine the first two meanings for SHaLoM—peace and complete. The idea is that peace or tranquility can only come from completion. Here we find the warning against that perilous specialization of personality that Max Delbruck so elegantly avoided.

The Different Departments of Our Lives

We all have different departments in our lives. There is an economic element; we each need a means of generating a revenue stream from which we can satisfy our material needs and desires. We also have an emotional element, which makes us deeply desire the closeness and esteem of other human beings. We have a serious side, and we also have lighthearted and playful aspects to our personalities.

Some of us have intense intellectual curiosity about how the world works, and some of us also enjoy a passion for sports. There are those who love nothing more than spending time with their children and those who prefer to be active with communal or service organizations. We can be enthusiastic about our hobbies and about our work. These are just some of the areas that make up a vital, passionate, and fulfilling life.

It is easy to see how quickly we can fall into the trap of expending disproportionate time and energy on only a few of these, while ignoring many others. During my years as a congregational rabbi I encountered one type of unhappy couple more than any other: The wife would beg me to urge her husband to spend less time at work and more time with his young family. Meanwhile, in total frustration, the husband-father hoped I could explain to his tearful wife that he was working so hard only to provide her and their children with the things they needed. She wanted more of his time and attention even if it meant having fewer things. She wanted the balance and peace only found in totality, while he found it easier to focus chiefly upon earning a living.

Then there is the young man who has never been particularly good at sports and discovers computers. All of a sudden they are all that exist in his world. His parents wish he would respond to the call of SHaLoM. "You will only attain true happiness and tranquility by developing all areas of your being," they want to tell him. "Get some exercise, meet people—especially girls." The challenge is to resist the seductive appeal of focusing on only one thing.

I long for the days when we saw this principle at work in the field of medicine. I recognize, of course, that medical science has advanced beyond the point where any one practitioner could possibly know all there is to know; I understand the need for specialists. However, I mourn the vanished general practitioner. How I miss the doctor who viewed me as an entire complete person! He could see links between different parts of my body: He suspected that my allergy might be linked to the new glasses I recently obtained. He was aware of that infection under a tooth and of my ingrown toenail. He made the broad connections that are tough for a narrow-area specialist to see. He knew the principle of SHaLoM—completeness and totality—the avenue to peace and tranquility.

Linking the Spiritual and the Material

The three root letters of the word SHaLoM are the shin, the lamed, and the mem—the sounds of sh, l, and m. The first, the shin ש, with its three verticals appearing like tongues of fire reaching for the sky, represents the spiritual. The last, the mem מ, with its womblike shape and its ability to concretize concepts, represents the material. The middle letter, the lamed ל, represents a kind of link between the letter on its right and on its left. It represents learning, assimilation and understanding, which are perfect metaphors for linking two seemingly disparate concepts.

So, at heart, the word SHaLoM is saying to us: Do not dream of unlinking the spiritual and the material. It is sheer folly to pursue spiritual reality by isolating ourselves from the material, and it is equally hopeless to pursue the material while completely disregarding the spiritual.

This is why I believe that the best doctors, economists, and engineers are those who also enjoy spiritual understanding. Likewise, the best rabbis and other spiritual leaders have an understanding of the marketplace and the sciences.

What Are You?

We should try to avoid overdoing specialization in our daily lives. For instance, we would do better to avoid defining ourselves by just our professions. This is far too limiting for a human being. I have often wondered how to answer the question of what I am. Am I a husband, a father, a rabbi, a writer, a boating enthusiast, a breadwinner, a Bible student, or any number of other choices? The answer is yes to all of the above.

The message of SHaLoM is that for each of us who seek to live in peace, tranquility, and inner harmony, we have no choice but to evade the tyranny of specialization and be as much of everything as we can.

Obviously, specialization is sometimes imperative within parts of our lives. In our professional and business lives we often need to delve deeply into a specific area. In our home lives as well we 'specialize' in our own spouse and children. However, we do need to develop ourselves across a broad front. Let us not neglect our roles as parents, but let us also make certain that we don't ignore our roles as spouses and lovers. We must take care of our bodies, and we must also make certain that we constantly exercise our minds and memories. We need to attend to the material realities of our lives, but we should also constantly strive to keep our spiritual flames alight.

Is all of this easy? By no means. It is far more challenging to think of oneself as a whole person than to simply regard oneself as, say, a bond trader, dentist, or janitor. How you contribute to society through your livelihood is definitely an important part of a person's make-up; but it is not the whole picture.

To get a sense of your completeness—who you really are when you are at peace with yourself—I need to know much more than your business. I want to know your deepest beliefs; I want to know what other human beings share your more private moments; and I want to know what sort of ideas excite you and which enrage you. And that is only a start. You are a complete, exciting, limitless individual, and I would like to get to know you in all your complexity and all your completion.

Which is why, when we meet, I shall extend my hand and say, "SHaLoM."

OTHER TEACHINGS
FROM RABBI DANIEL LAPIN

www.RabbiDanielLapin.com

Books

Hardcover Book

Thou Shall Prosper (2nd Edition): Ten Commandments for Making Money

Thou Shall Prosper explains:
- Why Jews throughout the ages flourish economically
- How you can benefit from this Jewish wisdom
- What "being in business" means, whether you are a professional, a CEO or flipping burgers
- Why you should never retire

Softcover Book

Thought Tools: Fifty Timeless Truths to Uplift and Inspire

2008 (Vol. 1), Vol. 2, Vol. 3, Vol. 4

- Reprogram the software of your soul with these popular bite-sized message.
- Each page provides a launching pad for thoughtful conversation and growth
- Travel with Rabbi Lapin through the pages of the Bible, the Jewish year and the Hebrew language

338

Two audio CD set plus
a 16-page study guide

Genesis Journeys:
Clash of Destiny

Decoding the Secrets of Israel and Islam

- What Muslims know about prayer that most people, even those who pray regularly, don't
- The dark side of laughter
- Why recruits in Arab terrorist training camps say "Heil Hitler"
- How to rise above our cultural and genetic legacy

Two audio CD set plus
a 16-page study guide

Genesis Journeys:
Tower of Power

Decoding the Secrets of Babel

- How every Hebrew Biblical name has a meaning that sheds light on the person's true character
- The seductive lure of socialism and how it affects you
- What both Abraham and Pharaoh have to do with the Tower of Babel
- Why companies often fail after constructing huge buildings

Two audio CD set plus
a 16-page study guide

Genesis Journeys:
The Gathering Storm

Decoding the Secrets of Noah

- What parenting technique Noah used that resulted in his children being saved
- Why the dimensions given for the ark are vital for your life
- The hidden meaning of the entire "begat" section of Genesis
- Similarities between our own days and the days preceding the Flood

Continued on next page

Two audio CD set plus
a 16-page study guide

Genesis Journeys:
Madam, I'm Adam

Decoding the Marriage Secrets of Eden

- Why understanding the Hebrew words for man and woman can improve your marriage
- Can "being in the mood" destroy your marriage
- What is the difference between a physically mature male and a Man?
- Who is more responsible when a couple divorces – the husband or the wife?

Biblical Blueprint Audio Series

One Audio CD

Day for Atonement

Heavenly Gift of Spiritual Serenity

Day for Atonement answers these questions:
- Are you handicapped by yesterday's mistakes
- The truth behind astrology and horoscopes
- Why the Bible mentions the Day of Atonement three separate times
- Jonah's lesson for your life

One Audio CD

The Ten Commandments

How Two Tablets Can Transform Your Life and Direct Our Nation

- Why the Ten Commandments must be displayed in public
- How positive human interaction is based on these vital verses
- Why they had to be on two tablets, not just one
- How crucial differences between America and the old Soviet Union are dictated by each country's attitude toward these phrases

Continued on next page

Continued from previous page

One Audio CD

Let Me Go

How to Overcome Life's Challenges and Escape Your Own Egypt

- What three Bible secrets can help everyone escape difficult times
- Did Moses really say, "Let My People Go"
- How to recognize your angels in disguise
- Why the Jews needed to leave Egypt in broad daylight

One Audio CD

Festival of Lights

Transform Your 24/7 Existence Into a 25/8 Life

- Are you handicapped by how you think of time
- What do the numbers 8 and 25 mean in ancient Jewish wisdom
- What lessons of Chanuka are embedded in Scripture

One Audio CD

Perils of Profanity

You Are What You Speak

- How vulgar speech damages your chances for success in both business and personal relationships
- Why Joseph recounted his dreams to his brothers, knowing that they would be angered
- What damage to the soul comes from using or hearing profanity
- Why everyone, even those who don't curse, should be concerned about the prevalence of foul language in our culture

341

Income Abundance Audio/Book Series

One Audio CD

Boost Your Income

Three Spiritual Steps to Success

- Why Jews have flourished economically
- Do you treat money like candles or cake
- Money advice from Joseph and his brothers
- Do you make money or take money
- Should you do what you love or love what you do

Two Audio CDs

Prosperity Power: Connect for Succe$$

Connection with others is vital to your success. This practical CD will motivate you and give you specific pointers on how to increase your Connectivity Quotient.
- The one thing you can do right now to increase your income
- How to change your life if you're not a 'people person'
- Can social networking replace face to face meetings
- Jump-start your creativity

Hardcover Book

Thou Shall Prosper (2nd Edition): Ten Commandments for Making Money

Ten Commandments for Making Money

Thou Shall Prosper explains:
- Why Jews throughout the ages flourish economically
- How you can benefit from this Jewish wisdom
- What "being in business" means, whether you are a professional, a CEO or flipping burgers
- Why you should never retire

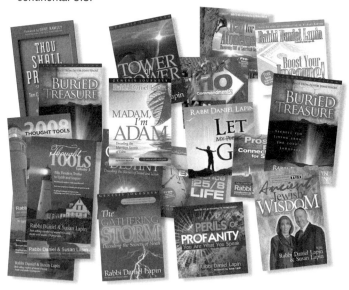

ENDORSEMENTS
FOR RABBI DANIEL LAPIN

"Even those of us who invest our lives in teaching and advising
other people need our own sources of wisdom and advice,
in other words – a rabbi, and Daniel Lapin is my rabbi. His background and scholarship uniquely equip him to help people like
me extract the deep meaning of each Biblical verse to improve
every aspect of my life. And let me tell you, as someone who has
been speaking to large audiences for years this rabbi can really
entertain while he educates – you'll laugh while
you learn. If you want access to a life-transforming Biblical
blueprint for your life, make Daniel Lapin your rabbi – you won't
regret it."

Zig Ziglar, *author and nationally
renowned motivational speaker*
Texas

"Rabbi Daniel Lapin's lectures are entertaining, eloquent, and
elegant. I enjoy the information he provides and the Talmudic
perspective he brings."

Dr. Marvin Olasky, *Editor-in-Chief*
World Magazine
University of Texas Professor

"How is it that this British accented Orthodox Rabbi has gained
the attention and respect of so many leaders from all walks of
life? It doesn't take long to know the answer once you have
heard Rabbi Lapin speak. He possesses the rare combination
of Biblical knowledge, and a compelling intellect coupled with
down to earth wisdom and humor that leaves you truly the
better for having listened."

Rice Broocks, *Senior Pastor*
Bethel World Outreach Center
Nashville, Tennessee

"While many today give lip-service to 'the Judeo-Christian tradition,' I find Rabbi Daniel Lapin to be a true spokesman for it in our time. Like me, he believes that understanding Genesis is the foundation for a correct view of the world. That's why I am pleased to recommend his Genesis Journeys audio program."

Dr. D. James Kennedy, *Ph.D.*
(1930-2007)
Coral Ridge Presbyterian Church

"For over a decade I have been watching my friend Rabbi Daniel Lapin's spell-binding oratory electrify large Christian audiences. His Biblical scholarship, love of America, and command of the English language bring the Bible to life. In a unique way he transforms ancient verses into effective solutions to our modern problems. Rabbi Lapin's insights and depth of knowledge make this a tremendous resource. This brand new audio program can now make America's rabbi part of your life just as he is part of mine."

Jay Alan Sekulow, *Chief Counsel*
American Center for Law and Justice